The Future of
Population Growth

THE FUTURE OF POPULATION GROWTH

ALTERNATIVE PATHS TO EQUILIBRIUM

TOMAS FREJKA

A POPULATION COUNCIL BOOK

A WILEY-INTERSCIENCE PUBLICATION

JOHN WILEY & SONS, New York • London • Sydney • Toronto

Copyright © 1973, by John Wiley & Sons, Inc.

All rights reserved. Published simultaneously in Canada.

No part of this book may be reproduced by any means, nor transmitted, nor translated into a machine language without the written permission of the publisher.

Library of Congress Cataloging in Publication Data

Frejka, Tomas.
  The future of population growth.

  "A Population Council book."
  "A Wiley-Interscience publication."
  Includes biographical references.
  1. Population. 2. Demography. 3. Population forecasting. I. Population Council, New York. II Title.

HB871.F66   301.32   73-1607
ISBN 0-471-27875-0

Printed in the United States of America

10 9 8 7 6 5 4 3 2 1

Foreword

The world's population problem over the next decades is twofold: to cope and to correct. The current trends must be corrected at the same time that their virtually inevitable consequences are coped with. This book suggests the difficulties by indicating the magnitudes and by showing the changes in demographic trends needed to reach a steady state in population numbers.

No one knows the future, demographic or otherwise; thus this book contains projections not predictions. The projections illustrate different paths toward stationary populations, by means of a net reproduction rate of 1, or replacement—which, if sustained, eventually leads to nongrowing populations. The projections, based on explicit assumptions and tested procedures (as of the present state of the art), take off from this query: if various population units, from the world down to individual countries, do reach replacement at different times over the next 70 years, what will be the resultant population characteristics, notably size? The world as a whole, the developed world, the developing world, major areas and regions, many individual countries—how large will each of them be if replacement comes in 1970–75, 1980–85, at the turn of the century, in 2020–25, or not until 2040–45?

v

The answer is anyone's guess, but the demographic consequences of the different dates are not. The numbers documented here dramatize the double task: to accommodate a large increase of the human population and at the same time to reduce birth rates in order to minimize the first task. On the one hand, the job is to provide food and nutrition, health and sanitation, education and jobs and housing, opportunity for individual fulfillment, and an improved quality of life to the large numbers ahead. On the other hand, the need is to reorder social priorities, to modify outmoded institutional structures, to provide effective services, to inform and educate—in short, to change the conditions surrounding human fertility in order to hasten its modernization, in harmony with the emerging conditions of the modern world. Either task alone is great in scope as well as in consequence; together, they must be addressed with great dedication and energy if we are to come through.

For these projections do make clear that a much larger human population almost surely lies ahead before mankind reaches stabilization. Such is the momentum of population growth that even if the replacement level were reached in the developed world by 1980 and in the developing by 2000, the world's population would go to 8 billion. Where will such growth end: 8 billion? 10 billion? 15 billion? More? Whatever the figure, our children, and certainly our grandchildren, will look back at today's world of 3.5 billion as the good old days. For these projections show the inexorable, long-term consequences of short-term trends, and illustrate the large numbers to be added in the twenty-first century, for developed countries as well as developing ones.

Nor are these numbers to be viewed as "dry-as-dust statistics." They are people—being born, living, dying. And just behind them are the large social problems that can only be aggravated by such demographic trends—for example, the need for ecological balance and environmental cleanliness throughout the world, the requirements of social and economic development, the potential international discord residing in long-term demographic differences among geographic areas or between haves and have-nots, the improvement in man's quality of life.

The numbers contained herein are objective assessments, given the underlying assumptions, and in themselves are neither alarmist nor complacent. In this spirit, these projections must be taken into account by all men concerned with the development of social policy and program in the years ahead. They must ask themselves: What needs to be done *now* to meet the probable human flow of the next decades? What needs to be done *now* to dampen that human flow in an acceptable yet effective manner? The questions are high on the world's agenda, for these demographic trends constitute a unique challenge in mankind's history. And whatever happens to them in the next few decades will have a fundamental effect on the realization of human values in the next century, and beyond.

Dr. Frejka has put us in his debt for a rational, realistic view of what human numbers can lie ahead and where the choice points are. It is up to mankind and its leaders to respond, for the coping and the correcting also lie ahead.

BERNARD BERELSON
President
The Population Council

April 1972

Preface

Many people concerned with the economic and social development of nations are at the same time concerned with population growth. This book presents for social and economic planners, national and international civil servants, academicians, politicians, and interested citizens a perspective on population change that intends to help answer the following questions:

1. Should the population of the world or of a specific region or country cease to grow?

2. If so, when is it reasonable to expect that nongrowth could be brought about? Immediately? In two to three decades? In a century?

3. Is the population of a country likely to decrease in number? If so, when?

4. Is it reasonable to assume that a specific population size is attainable by a certain point in time?

5. What are the population growth consequences implied by current demographic features of populations?

In view of the universal significance of these questions we have attempted to make the book directly accessible to a wider range of readers than merely to the academic demographer. To enable all those concerned with matters of population policy—whether in national or international organizations, whether in academic or administrative positions—to make use of the conclusions of this book, demographic relationships underlying population growth are discussed in Chapter 1, in which the necessary demographic terminology is also explained. And in general, the language of the book is intended to be comprehensible to a rather broad audience.

Such an approach seems justified not only because matters of policy importance are being discussed, but also because the substance of the book does not bring any innovations in demographic theory, nor does it explore any new aspects of interrelations between social and economic phenomena on the one hand, and demographic trends on the other. This book, however, uses known demographic theory[1] to reveal various aspects of the demographic paths toward a population equilibrium.

A general idea underlying the research that led to the book is the belief that populations must reach a nongrowing, or stationary, state at some point in the future. Based on this belief *the book utilizes the technique of population projection to identify the demographic trends necessary to reach a nongrowing, stationary state.*

Toward this end we have utilized known demographic theory in a nontraditional way. We do not intend to predict what the future size of various population units will be, but rather, we have selected the future goal (the nongrowing state) and have computed those demographic situations that can bring it about. This method differs from the more familiar use of the population projection as a calculation of the *future* development of populations based on *present assumptions* about various demographic trends (mortality, fertility, migration). The familiar projection is used in estimating short-term population growth for purposes of economic and social analysis and decision making. National governments and international organizations (such as the United Nations) estimate future population developments by alternative projections founded on demographic assumptions.

Our projections are founded on a methodology that first establishes the objective and then identifies the relationship of real demographic factors to it. In effect, our method complements the more traditional projections in that it can be used to illustrate their long-term implications. Also, although not the main purpose, the method can focus on the realistic or unrealistic features of certain demographic trends, thus presenting a general view of the future. The primary purpose of this method is the identification of the demographic situation that could create a desired result.

Other approaches might render the same or similar results more effectively and more efficiently; for example, the use of mathematical formulae could lead to the development of the basic findings of this study. There is, in fact, a procedure recently developed by Nathan Keyfitz[2] that enables calculation of the ultimate size of a population if fertility were to decline to a replacement level immediately. Formal mathematics and formal demography will eventually provide such tools. For the present, however, those that would cover the entire range of our interest in the future are not available. Even if such formulae were already available, in comparison, the present procedure is likely to have not only cons but also pros: it would still be more comprehensible to a wider audience, the major policy implications could probably be better illustrated and become clearer, and several implicit subtleties are revealed.

In 1968, in research[3] exploring the possibilities of achieving a nongrowing population in the United States, I used the described approach for the first time. The evidence presented showed the alternative that the United States' population could stop growing instantly to be most unrealistic. The demographic conditions and consequences—that is, the fertility trends and age-structural changes—were illustrated not only for this particular case but also for several alternative paths to a United States stationary population. After publication, these findings and the approach I applied appeared to influence other research, including official documents and environment-population debates. There was a surprisingly large response to this study in the academic community and beyond, and it seemed to indicate that it might be useful to continue work in this direction. By the time I joined the Population Council in New York, the framework for the present book was almost totally clear. It became intriguing to work through the mechanism of population change in other types of populations, both in the less developed countries and in other advanced countries. The book took shape as an approach to the world population as a whole and to its major components.

During my research at the Population Council, the ideas and methodology of the earlier United States research were also adapted by the International Demographic Statistics Center of the United States Bureau of the Census. It published a study using similar projections for 34 less developed countries.[4] The significant differences between the Census Bureau publication and this volume are the following: (1) This volume explores the implications of moving toward stationarity in the supranational population units; (2) this volume discusses in more detail the interaction of demographic variables; (3) this volume evaluates some concrete objectives of population policies in individual countries; (4) this volume puts traditional population projections into a long-term perspective.

Many of the necessary skills for this project were acquired during the academic year 1966–67 at the Office of Population Research at Princeton University, under the guidance of Ansley J. Coale. I am also most grateful to Professor Coale for the opportunity to discuss the present project with him in its initial stages.

I am also exceedingly grateful to the friends and colleagues who provided advice and criticism on earlier drafts of the book—Bernard Berelson, Thomas K. Burch, Sidney Goldstein, W. Parker Mauldin, Frank W. Notestein, William Seltzer, David L. Sills, Etienne van de Walle, and Eva Frejka—as well as to anonymous reviewers. Milos Macura and Mohamed El-Badry were helpful in providing United Nations data. My sincere thanks also go to Stuart Boynton, who edited the draft and improved it stylistically in many ways.

Finally, I would like to acknowledge the invaluable assistance of the Population Council staff, mainly Irene Falkenstein, who helped me during all stages of the project, especially with the gathering and processing of data, and also Philip Chen and Carol Smith, who assisted in the computer work. Louisa Noé read the manuscript to detect passages where greater clarity was desirable. Eva Obarzanek deserves unlimited praise for the typing of several drafts of the manuscript and for the drawing of the initial figures. Bernice Liblick and Susan Ellien aided me as the book was nearing completion.

TOMAS FREJKA

New York, New York
Spring 1972

NOTES

[1] Among the literature that formed the theoretical basis for the current study the following are of prime importance: Louis I. Dublin and Alfred J. Lotka, "On the True Rate of Natural Increase," *Journal of the American Statistical Association*, Vol. 20 (September 1925), pp. 305–339; Ansley J. Coale, "How the Age Distribution of a Human Population is Determined," *Cold Spring Harbor Symposium on Quantitative Biology*, Vol. 22, pp. 83–88; Ansley J. Coale, "Increases in Expectation of Life and Population Growth," *International Population Conference Vienna 1959* (Vienna: I.U.S.S.P.), pp. 36–41; Ansley J. Coale, "Birth Rates, Death Rates, and Rates of Growth in Human Populations," M. C. Sheps and J. C. Ridley, Eds., *Public Health and Population Change* (Pittsburgh: University of Pittsburgh Press, 1965), pp. 242–265; Ansley J. Coale and Paul Demeny, *Regional Model Life Tables and Stable Populations* (Princeton: Princeton University Press, 1966); Ansley J. Coale and Melvin Zelnik, *New Estimates of Fertility and Population in the United States* (Princeton: Princeton University Press, 1963), pp. 82–89; Alvaro Lopez, *Problems in Stable Population Theory* (Princeton: Office of Population Research, 1961).

[2] Nathan Keyfitz, "On the Momentum of Population Growth," *Demography*, Vol. 8, No. 1, February 1971, pp. 71–80.

[3] Tomas Frejka, "Reflections on the Demographic Conditions Needed to Establish a U.S. Stationary Population Growth," *Population Studies*, Vol. 22, No. 3, November 1968, pp. 379–397.

[4] U.S. Bureau of the Census, *The Two-Child Family and Population Growth: An International View* (Washington, D.C.: U.S. Government Printing Office, 1971).

A Brief Chapter Outline

Chapter 1 discusses features of the mechanism of population growth and describes some important demographic concepts.

Chapter 2 outlines the methods and assumptions of the study.

Chapters 3 and 4 present a selection of the empirical findings in regard to the world population, the less developed regions, and the more developed regions, and in regard to major areas.

Chapter 5 discusses some typical countries within each major area and certain aspects of their possible population prospects.

Chapter 6 tests a number of modifications in the applied assumptions.

Chapter 7 discusses the subject matter with regard to the United States population.

Chapter 8 evaluates some quantified objectives of population policies.

Chapter 9 compares population projections of the United Nations and of individual countries with projections ultimately leading to a stationary population.

Contents

1 Some Basic Demographic Interrelationships

Occasionally there is confusion over demographic concepts. To ensure that the reader understands the basic principles underlying this work, the concepts used in the discussion are defined, described, and interpreted as we go along. The list of concepts discussed is by no means exhaustive, but it should facilitate the understanding of this book. Persons familiar with basic demographic terminology can bypass this section, although they might want to look at the interpretations given to some of the concepts.

The *population* of an area is the total number of all individuals alive at a particular point in time. The population can be classified by sex, which provides information about the *sex distribution* of the population. The population can further be divided into age groups (1-year, 5-year, or broad age groups) and, if each group is expressed as a fraction (for instance, percentage) of the total, information is provided about the relative *age composition* of the population. Figure 1-1, gives examples of the age structure of female populations of Belgium and Costa Rica. These two age structures differ by the proportions of women in the various age groups. To take the most distinct features: Belgium has a high proportion of older persons (say above 65) and Costa Rica has a larger proportion of young population.

During a particular period, such as 1 year, a certain number of births and deaths occur. By subtracting the deaths from the births one learns the size of the natural increase of the population.

To enable comparison in space and time, several types of demographic measures have been created, of which the most commonly used are the *crude birth rate,* the *crude death rate,* and the *crude rate of natural increase.* They are constructed by relating the specified number of events occurring in a year to the total population. For example, in Belgium in 1967 there were over 146,200 live births, and the population in mid-1967 was 9,580,000 inhabitans. The crude birth rate, which is customarily shown per thousand inhabitants, was 15.3 (146,200/9,580,000 × 1000). The crude death rate, computed in the same way, was 12.0 per thousand in 1967. One can arrive at the crude rate of natural increase by subtracting the crude death rate from the crude birth rate; however, in contrast to these two rates, the crude rate of natural increase is customarily shown per hundred inhabitants, that is, in percentages. Therefore, the crude rate of natural increase in Belgium in 1967 was 0.3% per year (15.3 − 12.0 = 3.3 /10 = 0.3). The corresponding figures for Costa Rica were a crude birth rate of 39.0 per thousand, a crude death rate of 7.1 per thousand inhabitants; thus the crude rate of natural increase was 3.2%.

In such a way we gain a fairly good picture about the basic demographic situation in both countries. But our example at the same time shows the need for more detailed information. By comparing the crude birth rates of both countries one would assume that the level of fertility in Costa Rica is over twice that of Belgium. The rate of natural population growth in Costa Rica was 10 times larger than in Belgium. The relations of the crude birth rate and the crude rate of natural increase are in line with common perceptions, but the crude death rate in Costa Rica is only half of the volume of that in Belgium. The latter relationship seemingly does not correspond to what one would expect, namely that the death rate in Costa Rica should be higher than in Belgium.

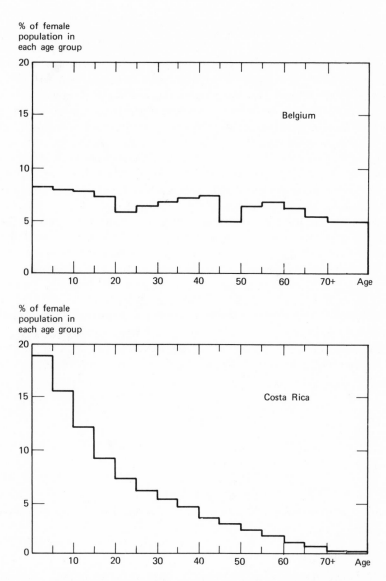

Figure 1-1. Female age distribution, Belgium and Costa Rica, 1965. Sources: Statistical Office of the United Nations, *Demographic Yearbook 1970*, New York, 1971, pp. 304, 305. Ricardo Jiménez Jiménez et al., "Proyección de la Población de Costa Rica por Sexo y Grupos de Edad, 1965–1990," *Revista de Estudios y Estadísticas*, No. 8 (October 1967), p. 43.

1. A DISCUSSION OF MORTALITY

How is it possible that the crude death rate in Belgium was almost twice as high as it was in Costa Rica? If one obtained detailed data about the age of death in both countries and if these data were related to the number of persons of corresponding age, one would get *age-specific death rates*. As a rule, these age-specific mortality rates are somewhat higher in Costa Rica than in Belgium at all ages (see Figure 1-2). Thus the real level of mortality—at individual ages—is higher in Costa Rica than in Belgium. A relatively good, convenient, demographic measure that summarizes the level of mortality of a population is the *expectation of life at birth* ($e_0{}^0$). This measure is derived from complex computations (which we shall not go into here) on the mortality of the various age groups. It can be interpreted as the average length of life of a hypothetical population that is subject to the age-specific mortality rates of the particular period under observation. The female expectation of life at birth computed on the basis of mortality data between 1959 and 1963 in Belgium was 73.5 years; in Costa Rica (1962–64) it was 64.8 years. These data confirm the earlier statement that the level of mortality is higher in Costa Rica than in Belgium (what can at times be confusing is that a shorter expectation of life equals a higher level of mortality).

Although we find that life expectancy is higher in Belgium than in Costa Rica, we are left with the paradox that the different measures of mortality lead to different conclusions about the relative levels of mortality in Costa Rica and Belgium. On the one hand, the level of mortality measured by age-specific mortality rates and by the expectation of life at birth is higher in Costa Rica than in Belgium. On the other, the crude death rate is twice as high in Belgium. This is so because the former measures are computed without regard for the actual age structure of the populations concerned. The crude death rates, however, are dependent on the actual age composition of populations and therefore reflect not only the "real" level of mortality, but also the age structure. Note in Figure 1-2 that age-specific mortality, although always lower in Belgium, is high for infants. Starting with the age group 1 to 4 years of age, age-specific mortality rates are below 10 per thousand population; these rates remain low (i.e., under 10 per thousand) up to age 55 in both countries; only after age 55 do the age-specific mortality rates attain high values. However, the proportion of the population over 55, that is, with high mortality, is 27% of the total in Belgium and only 7% of the population in Costa

Rica (see Figure 1-1). A high proportion of the Belgian population is at ages with relatively high death rates; therefore the overall, that is, the crude, death rate is high.

The crude death rate of the Philippines in the late 1960s was roughly of the same order as in Belgium, around 12 per thousand inhabitants. The female expectation of life at birth in the Philippines was estimated to be almost 20 years shorter than in Belgium. This seeming dilemma is again caused by the fact that low age-specific mortality interacts with an "old" population in Belgium and vice-versa in the Philippines. If one were to make some statements about the possible direction of future trends (say, to the year 2000) of the crude death rates of these two countries, taking into account the above discussion, one would come out with the following impressions: (1) The

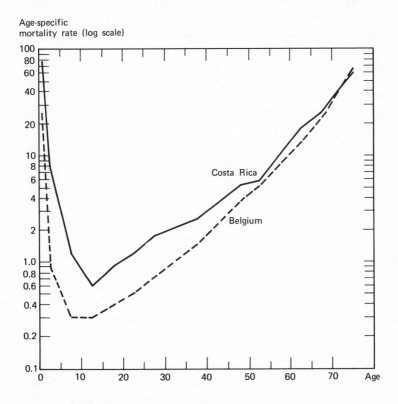

Figure 1-2. Female age-specific mortality rates, Belgium and Costa Rica, 1963. Source: Statistical Office of the United Nations, *Demographic Yearbook 1966*, New York, 1967, pp. 426, 452.

crude death rate in Belgium is not likely to decline, especially if fertility does not change substantially, because the age structure will remain an "old" one and the age-specific mortality rates will not have high chances of further declining. (2) The crude death rate might very well decline in the Philippines, because the mortality level (as expressed by the life expectancy and the age-specific mortality rates) is likely to decline, but the proportion of the old population will not increase meaningfully throughout the remainder of this century.

A third example could be the Ivory Coast, where the crude death rate was much higher than in Belgium; for the 1965–70 period it was estimated at 23 per thousand. Obviously, the mortality level in this country was so high (the female e_0^0 was around 40 years) that it did not counterbalance the differences in the age structure. The "young" age structure of the Ivory Coast interacted with high age-specific mortality rates at all ages (probably infant mortality is very high), resulting in a crude death rate twice as high as in Belgium. One can speculate that in the future the age structure of such a country will remain "young" and the development of the crude death rate will depend on the trend of the mortality level: if mortality declines, it will be reflected in the crude death rate, because the age structure is "conducive" to a low overall mortality rate.

To summarize, the crude death rate is a result of an interaction between the level of mortality and the age structure of the population. The crude death rate does reflect extreme differences in the level of mortality (23 in the Ivory Coast versus 12 in Belgium), in which case the influence of the age structure is not directly visible. In other instances the crude death rate can be misleading, because influences of the age structure override the impact of the levels of mortality. A population with an "old" age structure is likely to have a higher crude death rate than a population with a "young" age structure if the levels of mortality do not differ very much (7 in Costa Rica versus 12 in Belgium). Even with quite different mortality levels, the crude death rate can be misleading if the age structures differ significantly (12 in the Philippines versus 12 in Belgium). However, for countries with similar age structures, differences of the mortality level are adequately reflected in the crude death rate (23 in the Ivory Coast, 12 in the Philippines, 7 in Costa Rica).

Another way of looking at mortality is to speculate about trends that could occur: the crude death rates in countries with relatively old age structures are not likely to decline; even if their now low level of mortality were to decline further, their age structures are likely to become older, especially if fertility remains low in these countries. This is the case of the so-called more developed countries or low fertility countries.

Practically all less developed countries, or high fertility countries have young age structures, but they differ significantly in the level of their mortality. Countries with a low crude death rate will retain this for several decades (e.g., Costa Rica). The crude death rate will increase with the "aging" of these populations.

In all the other high fertility countries the crude death rate orends reflect mortality level trends. The crude death rate will continue to decline if the level of mortality continues to do so. The crude death rate of countries such as the Philippines can decline to a 5 per thousand value within a decade or two. Judging from historical comparisons, one could hypothesize that the crude death rate in countries such as the Ivory Coast is also more likely to decline than to increase. Whatever happens will be an almost clean reflection of mortality level changes, because changes of the age structure are likely to be gradual.

2. A DISCUSSION OF FERTILITY

In the original comparison of Costa Rica and Belgium the crude birth rates are so different (39.0 and 15.3 per thousand population, respectively) that one is quite satisfied with the information provided. One can see that fertility is substantially higher in the former. But let us take a different comparison. The crude birth rates in Greece and Belgium in 1967 were 18.7 and 15.3 per thousand, respectively. The crude birth rate in Greece was over 20% higher than in Belgium. Can one conclude that, on the average, women were having more children in Greece than in Belgium? Can one say that fertility in Greece was higher than in Belgium?

To be able to make judgments of this kind one needs more refined information. Thus several demographic measures of fertility have been constructed: *age-specific fertility rates*, the *total fertility rate* (TFR), and the *gross reproduction rate* (GRR).

Age-specific fertility rates provide information about the level of fertility of women of specified ages, usually on an annual basis (Table 1-1). For instance, the age-specific fertility rate of 0.1514 for the 25–29 age group in Belgium in 1967 was computed by dividing the number of live-born children (42,214) of mothers 25–29 years of age by the total number of women of that age (278,783). These rates are occasionally given per thousand and (taking the data of our example) can then be formulated as 151 children born per thousand women of 25–29 years of age. By comparing the age-specific fertility rates for Belgium and Greece (Table 1-1 and Figure 1-3) one comes to the general conclusion that the values of the age-specific fertility rates in both countries for the same ages are quite similar, and therefore the curves in Figure1-3 are shaped alike. Some differences can be observed: at young ages the Belgian rates are somewhat higher than the Greek ones with the reverse at old ages.

A further step is to construct the *total fertility rate*. The age-specific fertility rates in Table 1-1 are added up and, because they are annual averages for 5-year age groups, they are multiplied by five. Thus for Belgium 1967 the value is 2.40. Interestingly, the TFR for Greece of 1967 is the same.

The TFR can be interpreted as the number of children a hypothetical (average) woman would have if during her lifetime her childbearing behavior were the same as that of the cross section of women at the time of observation. Because the TFR can serve as an adequate approximation of average, actual, completed family size, it is a useful measure of the level of fertility.

The computations of the TFR of Belgium and Greece indicate that

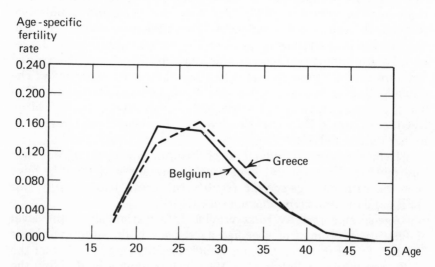

Figure 1–3. Age-specific fertility rates, Belgium and Greece, 1967. Source: See Table 1–1.

Table 1-1   Age-Specific Fertility Rates, Total Fertility
            Rates, Belgium and Greece, 1967

Age Group	Belgium	Greece
15-19	.0336	.0276
20-24	.1564	.1323
25-29	.1514	.1623
30-34	.0856	.1016
35-39	.0417	.0451
40-44	.0112	.0102
45-49	.0010	.0014
TOTAL	.4809	.4805
	x 5	x 5
TOTAL FERTILITY RATE	2.4045	2.4025

Source: Statistical Office of the United Nations.
           Demographic Yearbook 1969. New York, 1970,
           pp. 299, 390, 391.

the fertility levels of both countries are almost identical, yet the crude birth rates differ by 20% (15.3 in Belgium versus 18.7 in Greece).

A comparison of the age structures of the female populations provides an explanation of this apparent dilemma. Let us establish all the necessary facts: the total populations (the denominator in the crude birth rate) of Belgium and Greece were 9.6 and 8.7 million inhabitants, respectively (i.e., the total population was larger in Belgium than in Greece); the fertility level of women in both countries was equal; yet the total number of children born in Belgium was smaller than in Greece (146,000 versus 163,000). This was so because there was a larger proportion of women at all the main childbearing ages in Greece than in Belgium (see Table 1-2 and Figure 1-4); for instance 8% of all the women in Greece were in the age group 25–29 years compared with 6% of the women in Belgium. As a result, even in absolute numbers there were more potential mothers in Greece (321,000) than in Belgium (279,000) in this age group as well as in other reproductive age groups.

A closer look at the interaction of the fertility level and the age structure in Belgium and Greece illustrates the fact that in populations with a similar level of fertility, the age structure (a small or large proportion of women in the childbearing ages) can be the root of differences in the crude birth rate. This would be true in high fertility countries also, but accurate statistical data to demonstrate the phenomenon are not available.

The crude birth rate can be influenced not only by the age structure of a population and by what we have called the level of fertility (as expressed by the TFR), but also by *age patterns of fertility*, that is, by the distribution of fertility in the childbearing ages.[1] For example, the 1967 TFR in Costa Rica was 5.98, and fertility was distributed among the age groups as illustrated by the age-specific fertility rates (Table 1-3). If we hold the TFR constant (5.98) but distribute fertility among the ages the way it was distributed in Belgium (relatively more children would be born to mothers of younger ages), the number of births would increase from 62,000 to over 65,000, thus the crude birth rate would rise from 39 to 41 per thousand population. If the fertility distribution changes in the other direction and relatively more children are born to mothers of older

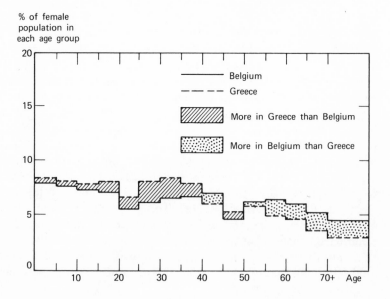

Figure 1–4. Age composition of female population, Belgium and Greece, 1965. Source: See Table 1–2.

ages, the crude birth rate would be lower, even though the TFR would be the same value in all three cases. Such changes can result from changes in marriage or employment patterns of women.

These examples demonstrate that the TFR is useful but also has some limitations. It does not provide any information about the distribution of fertility among age groups, which can influence the value of the crude birth rate and thus the growth rate of a population.

Also, it is a somewhat imperfect measure of a real situation because it covers the fertility behavior of women of all childbearing ages in a *particular* year. For certain reasons parents might decide to postpone some births but eventually have the same number of children they would have had otherwise. This process might show up as a decline of the TFR. An extreme example occurred in Japan in 1966, the year of the white horse. Because it is believed that a female child born in the year of the white horse will grow up to be ill-tempered, and no one will want to marry her, the total fertility rate in 1966 was 1.6 compared with 2.1 and 2.2 in 1965 and 1967, respectively.

Table 1-2   Age Composition of the Female Population, Belgium and Greece, 1965 (in %)

Age Group	Belgium	Greece	Difference
0-4	7.9	8.2	+ 0.3
5-9	7.7	8.1	+ 0.4
10-14	7.3	7.9	+ 0.6
15-19	7.2	8.1	+ 0.9
20-24	5.7	6.7	+ 1.0
25-29	6.1	8.1	+ 2.0
30-34	6.6	8.3	+ 1.7
35-39	6.8	8.0	+ 1.2
40-44	7.0	6.0	- 1.0
45-49	4.7	5.3	+ 0.6
50-54	6.2	5.9	- 0.3
55-59	6.3	5.1	- 1.2
60-64	6.1	4.5	- 1.6
65-69	5.2	3.6	- 1.6
70+	9.2	6.2	- 3.0

Source: Statistical Office of the United Nations. *Demo-graphic Yearbook 1970.* New York, 1971, pp. 304, 305, 330, 331.

Table 1-3 Fertility Characteristics, Costa Rica, 1967 (real and assumed)

Age Group	Female Population	Live Births	Age-Specific Fertility Rates	Age-Specific Fertility Rates (fertility pattern of Belgium 1967)	Live Births (with Belgian fertility pattern)
15-19	79865	8813	.1103	.0836	6677
20-24	63315	17620	.2783	.3887	24611
25-29	51860	14585	.2812	.3760	19499
30-34	44440	10235	.2303	.2129	9461
35-39	38795	7569	.1951	.1034	4011
40-44	32250	2760	.0856	.0280	903
45-49	26720	381	.0143	.0025	67
TOTAL		61963	1.1951 x 5	1.1951 x 5	65229
TOTAL FERTILITY RATE			5.9755	5.9755	
CRUDE BIRTH RATE		61963/1590 = 38.97		65229/1590 = 41.02	

Source: Direccion General de Estadística y Censos. *Estadística Vital 1967*. Costa Rica, p. 14.

A measure sharing the pros and cons of the TFR is the *gross reproduction rate* (GRR). The TFR refers to the total number of children, that is, sons and daughters, whereas the GRR includes only the number of daughters born in a specific year. A simple way of computing the GRR is to multiply the TFR by the proportion of female births among live-born children, which is a reasonably stable ratio. The GRR of Costa Rica in 1967 was 2.9; that is, our hypothetical woman living through her childbearing years subject to the maternity rates of 1967 would bear almost 3 female children during her lifetime (Table 1-4, column 2). The GRR for Belgium in 1967 was 1.2; that is, the level of fertility was such that if this level persisted over the 35 years it would take a group of 15-year-old women to complete their reproductive life, these women would bear slightly more than 1 daughter each.

Another method to derive the GRR yields the same result if accurate data are used. First, *age-specific maternity rates*, or the number of female children born per woman of a certain age group, are computed. Subsequently, these rates are added, then multiplied by five if the rates are for 5-year age groups (Table 1-4, columns 3 and 4). This method is applied in the present project.

Before expanding the present discussion, let us summarize observations that can be made about fertility. Crude birth rates at a certain point in time are the result of an interaction of at least three factors: the level of fertility, the age structure of the population (especially of its female component), and the age distribution of fertility. The crude birth rate is an adequate measure of fertility when comparing populations of different fertility levels (39 in Costa Rica versus 15 in Belgium). Where crude birth rates are of a similar order of magnitude (18.7 in Greece versus 15.3 in Belgium), the level of fertility (as expressed by the TFR, which in 1967 was equal in Belgium and in Greece) need not differ, but a difference of the crude birth rates can be caused by differences of the age structure (a larger proportion of women in the main childbearing ages in Greece compared to Belgium.) It is not hard to imagine a situation in which differing fertility levels would result in equal crude birth rates due to different age structures. A third factor, the age distribution of fertility, can also cause a difference in the value of the crude birth rate. The crude birth rate in Costa Rica would have been 41, not 39, if the age distribution of fertility were that of Belgium. We can conclude that the crude birth rate reflects "obvious" differences of fertility adequately. Crude birth rate differences of smaller magnitudes (say up to +20%) can be caused

Table 1-4 Methods of Computing the Gross Reproduction Rate, Costa Rica, 1967

Age Group	Female Population	Age-Specific Fertility Rates	Female Live Births	Age-Specific Maternity Rates
	(1)	(2)	(3)	(4) = (3)/(2)
15-19	79865	.1103	4293	.0538
20-24	63315	.2783	8582	.1355
25-29	51860	.2812	7104	.1370
30-34	44440	.2303	4986	.1122
35-39	38795	.1951	3686	.0950
40-44	32250	.0856	1344	.0417
45-49	26720	.0143	186	.0070
TOTAL	61963	1.1951	30181	.5822
		x 5		x 5
TOTAL FERTILITY RATE		5.9755		
		x .487		
GROSS REPRODUCTION RATE		2.9101		2.9110

Source: Dirección General de Estadística y Censos. Estadística Vital, 1967. Costa Rica, pp. 14, 23.

by differences of the female age structure and/or of the age patterns of fertility, not necessarily by the level of fertility. Both the TFR and the GRR, on the other hand, can conceal differences of the age patterns of fertility and do not reflect differences of the age structure at all. A comparison of age-specific fertility rates in conjunction with a comparison of the age structure is needed to reveal the possible influence of the age patterns of fertility.

Each of the factors mentioned can be subject to further investigation. For example, the level of total fertility can depend on marriage patterns and on fertility behavior within marriages and consensual unions, if most children in a society are born in marriages and consensual unions. These and other analytical aspects are not covered in this discussion, because it is one layer beyond the level of interaction employed in the methodology of the present project.

What kind of observations can one make about changes of fertility measures through time? One would expect changes of fertility levels in time to be reflected in the crude birth rate trends. But how can changes of the age distribution of the population influence the crude birth rate trends? Will they reinforce or dampen trends of fertility levels? Can changes of the age patterns of fertility influence crude birth rate trends?

In the long run the decisive factor shaping the crude birth rate seems to be the level of fertility (Figures 1-5 and 1-6). The basic trends of the crude birth rate and the TFR during most of the time span covered in the figures were similar in both the United States and Taiwan.

At the same time, however, there were periods during which the crude birth rate trend differed from the TFR trend, during most of the 1950s in the United States, for instance. It is during such periods that changes in the age structure of the population and/or changes of the age patterns of fertility are so significant that they reinforce, dampen, or even offset a fertility level trend. In other words, changes of the age structure and/or of age patterns of fertility alone can cause a decline or an increase in the crude birth rate, holding the level of fertility constant. In real life, however, changes of the age structure and of age patterns of fertility occur simultaneously with changes of fertility levels, and a separate analysis of each factor can provide information whether changes of the age structure, for example, have reinforced or cancelled a fertility level decline or increase.

Figure 1-5 shows that in the United States the shapes of the crude birth rate curve and the TFR curve were similar until the late 1940s.

Thereafter the TFR kept increasing, and toward the end of the 1960s it stabilized around 3.7 (Table 1-5). In contrast, the crude birth rate was stable from 1951 through 1957, but thereafter declined. Clearly, the direction of the crude birth rate trend differed from that of the level of fertility (TFR) trend from 1951 till the late 1950s. In this particular case changes of the age structure of the female population were the main reason for the difference of the crude birth rate and the TFR trends (Table 1-6). The proportion of the female population in almost all reproductive age groups was smaller in 1960 compared with 1950. Moreover, in the 20 to 29 age group, in which over 60% of fertility occurs, there were 1.1 million fewer women in 1960.

To put it differently, the small cohort of women born during the

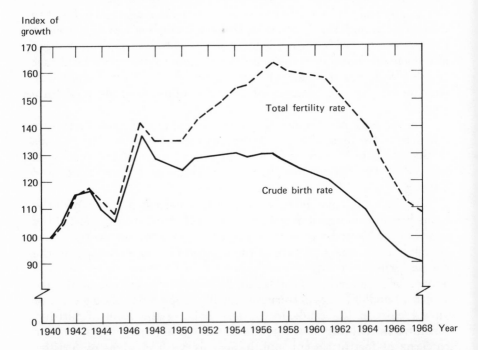

Figure 1–5. Total fertility rate and crude birth rate trends, United States, 1940–1968 (1940 = 100). Data for 1940–1958 are based on births adjusted for underregistration; 1959–1968 are based on registered births. Source: U.S. Department of Health, Education, and Welfare. *Vital Statistics of the United States, 1968.* Rockville, Md.: Public Health Service, 1970, pp. 1–4, 1–7.

1930s constituted the bulk of the childbearers around 1960, and although their fertility was significantly higher than around 1950, the crude birth rate was lower in 1960 compared with 1950. Because changes of the age patterns of fertility were of minor significance during this period, age-structural changes actually caused a decline of the crude birth rate, although the fertility level increased.

In Taiwan with small exceptions the TFR declined throughout the 1950s and 1960s. Basically, all changes of the age structure up to the end of the 1960s went in the direction of reinforcing the fertility decline (Table 1-7), that is, a decrease in the proportion of most age

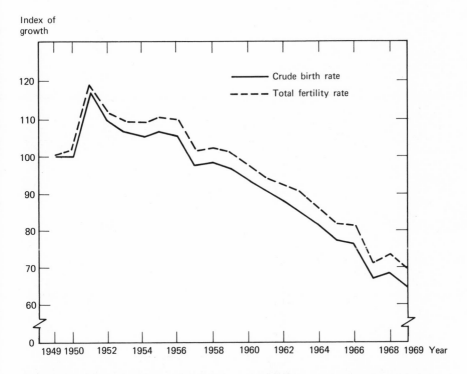

Figure 1-6. Crude birth rate and total fertility rate trends, Taiwan, 1949–1969 (1949 = 100). Sources: Council for International Economic Cooperation and Development, *Taiwan Statistical Data Book 1969*, Republic of China, 1969, p. 5. Department of Civil Affairs, *1969 Taiwan Demographic Fact Book: Republic of China*, Nantou, Taiwan, November 1970, p. 17.

groups of women of reproductive age. The decline of the crude birth rate could have been even larger than it actually was had there been no changes in the age patterns of fertility. Age-specific fertility rates declined at all ages, but the decline was much faster in the older age

Table 1-5   Total Fertility Rates and Crude Birth Rates, United States, 1940-1968[a]

Year	Total Fertility Rate	Crude Birth Rate
1940	2.30	19.4
1941	2.40	20.3
1942	2.63	22.2
1943	2.72	22.7
1944	2.57	21.2
1945	2.49	20.4
1946	2.94	24.1
1947	3.27	26.6
1948	3.11	24.9
1949	3.11	24.5
1950	3.09	24.1
1951	3.27	24.9
1952	3.36	25.1
1953	3.42	25.1
1954	3.54	25.3
1955	3.58	25.0
1956	3.69	25.2
1957	3.77	25.3
1958	3.70	24.5
1959	3.71	24.3
1959	3.67	24.0
1960	3.65	23.7
1961	3.63	23.3
1962	3.47	22.4
1963	3.33	21.7
1964	3.20	21.0
1965	2.93	19.4
1966	2.74	18.4
1967	2.57	17.8
1968	2.48	17.5

[a]1940-1959 births adjusted for under-registration; 1959-1968 registered births.

Source: U.S. Department of Health, Education, and Welfare, *Vital Statistics of the United States, 1968*. Rockville, Maryland: Public Health Service, 1970, pp. 1-4, 1-7.

Table 1-6   Age Composition of the Female Population, United States, 1950 and 1960
(in thousands and %)

Age Group	In Thousands			In Percent		
	1950	1960	Difference	1950	1960	Difference
Under 5	7927	9935	+ 2008	10.4	11.0	+ 0.6
5-9	6485	9139	+ 2654	8.5	10.1	+ 1.6
10-14	5459	8208	+ 2749	7.2	9.0	+ 1.8
15-19	5305	6555	+ 1250	7.0	7.2	+ 0.2
20-24	5875	5501	- 374	7.7	6.1	- 1.6
25-29	6270	5505	- 765	8.3	6.1	- 2.2
30-34	5892	6070	+ 178	7.8	6.7	- 1.1
35-39	5729	6370	+ 641	7.5	7.0	- 0.5
40-44	5134	5899	+ 765	6.8	6.5	- 0.3
45-49	4544	5503	+ 959	6.0	6.1	+ 0.1
50-54	4144	4858	+ 714	5.5	5.4	- 0.1
55-59	3605	4291	+ 686	4.8	4.7	- 0.1
60-64	3022	3725	+ 703	4.0	4.1	+ 0.1
65 and over	6473	9041	+ 2568	8.5	10.0	+ 1.5
TOTAL	75864	90600	+14736	100.0	100.0	--

source: U.S. Department of Commerce, Bureau of the Census. *Historical Statistics of the U.S.: Continuation to 1962 and Revisions.* Washington: Government Printing Office, February 1965.

Table 1-7   Age Composition of the Female Population,
             Taiwan, 1949, 1959, 1969 (in thousands and %)

Age Group	1949	1959	1969	Difference 1949-1959	Difference 1959-1969
In Thousands					
0-4	519	921	921	+ 402	- -
5-9	483	799	977	+ 316	+ 178
10-14	439	504	918	+ 65	+ 414
15-19	385	474	799	+ 89	+ 325
20-24	332	431	499	+ 99	+ 68
25-29	274	379	468	+ 105	+ 89
30-34	220	328	426	+ 108	+ 98
35-39	201	269	374	+ 68	+ 105
40-44	163	213	321	+ 50	+ 108
45-49	129	193	261	+ 64	+ 68
50-54	101	150	203	+ 49	+ 53
55-59	79	114	180	+ 35	+ 66
60-64	68	84	134	+ 16	+ 50
65-69	54	59	94	+ 5	+ 35
70+	53	89	125	+ 36	+ 36
TOTAL	3500	5007	6700	+1507	+1693
In %				*In Percentage Points*	
0-4	14.8	18.4	13.7	+ 3.6	- 4.7
5-9	13.8	15.9	14.6	+ 2.1	- 1.3
10-14	12.6	10.1	13.7	- 2.5	+ 3.6
15-19	11.0	9.5	11.9	- 1.5	+ 2.4
20-24	9.5	8.6	7.4	- 0.9	- 1.2
25-29	7.8	7.6	7.0	- 0.2	- 0.6
30-34	6.3	6.5	6.4	+ 0.2	- 0.1
35-39	5.7	5.4	5.6	- 0.3	+ 0.2
40-44	4.7	4.2	4.8	- 0.5	+ 0.6
45-49	3.7	3.8	3.9	+ 0.1	+ 0.1
50-54	2.9	3.0	3.0	+ 0.1	- -
55-59	2.3	2.3	2.7	- -	+ 0.4
60-64	1.9	1.7	2.0	- 0.2	+ 0.3
65-69	1.5	1.2	1.4	- 0.3	+ 0.2
70+	1.5	1.8	1.9	+ 0.3	+ 0.1
TOTAL	100.0	100.0	100.0	- -	- -

Source: Department of Civil Affairs. *1969 Taiwan Demographic Fact Book: Republic of China.* Nantou, Taiwan, November 1970, pp. 2-3.

groups than for women in their twenties (Figure 1-7). Had the fertility decline been equally spread out among the age groups, crude birth rate would have fallen even more.

A further feature of the age structure should be observed. Since trends of the crude birth rate do depend not only on the level of fertility but also on changes of the age structure, future birth rate trends will depend on the number of women who enter the childbearing ages. In Taiwan the proportion of females between ages 5 and 19 in 1969 was substantial (Figure 1-8). Ten years later, in 1979, these women will be 15 to 29 years old, that is, they will be in their primary childbearing years; this fact will influence the future level of the crude birth rate. If, for instance, the TFR and the age pattern of fertility were to remain constant during the 1970s, the crude birth rate would increase by about 10% in 1980 compared with 1970 as a result of the relative increase of women of reproductive age.

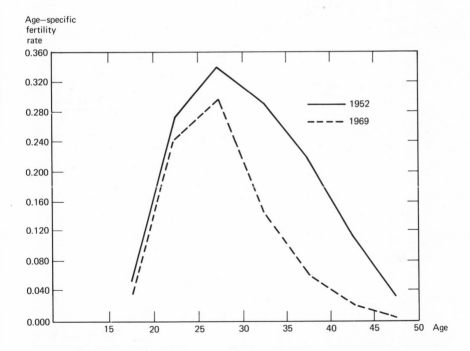

Figure 1-7. Age-specific fertility rate, Taiwan, 1952, 1969. Source: Department of Civil Affairs, *1969 Taiwan Demographic Fact Book: Republic of China*, Nantou, Taiwan, November 1970, pp. 16–17.

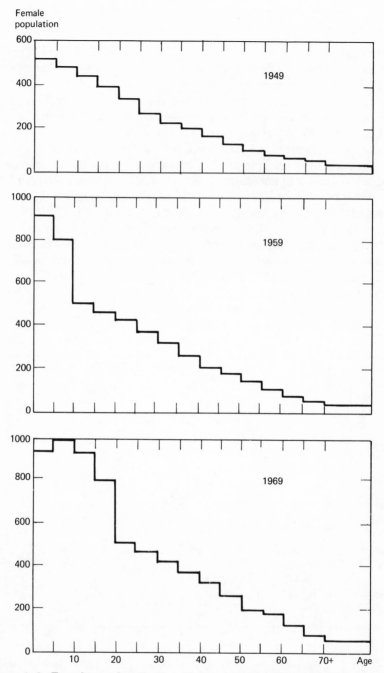

Figure 1–8. Female age distribution, Taiwan, 1949, 1959, 1969 (in thousands). Source: Department of Civil Affairs, *1969 Taiwan Demographic Fact Book: Republic of China*, Nantou, Taiwan, November 1970, pp. 2–3.

To summarize, crude birth rate trends, especially in the long run, reflect and express real changes of fertility behavior. If changes of the age structure and/or of the age patterns of fertility occur simultaneously with fertility level trends, the former will modify and at times even offset the fertility level trends.

A crude birth rate trend of a distinctly different direction than the fertility level trend can be caused either by a decrease (as in the United States in the 1950s) or an increase of the proportion, possibly even of absolute numbers, of women in the ages when most children are born. Because the crude birth rate trend is influenced by the age structure, it is useful to observe the size of cohorts below the childbearing ages who will enter into the scene in the future.

A change in time of age patterns of fertility can also modify the crude birth rate trends. Provided there are no major irregularities in the age structure of a population, the crude birth rate will be lower than otherwise if more children are born to older mothers; the crude birth rate will be higher than otherwise if more children are born to younger mothers (Taiwan in 1969 compared with 1949).

3. A DISCUSSION OF THE AGE STRUCTURE OF A POPULATION

As was demonstrated in previous sections, the age structure can be an important factor in shaping the values and trends of the crude death rate and the crude birth rate. What actually matters is whether there are large or small proportions of the population at ages where the respective level of "behavior" is high or low. For example, a large proportion of people in their twenties will affect the overall death rate negatively because mortality is usually very low in this age group; it can influence the crude birth rate in an upward direction because most people have children in their twenties.

Changes of the age structure over time affect trends of the crude death rate and the crude birth rate. The crude death rate can increase merely because a population is growing older; that is, the proportion of old people will increase, although the level of mortality may remain unchanged. Consequently one would want to know: how is the age structure of a population formed? What are the demographic factors causing the age structure to change?

Up to now we have considered the age distribution as a datum and have noted how the impact of differences in age distribution can affect either the crude birth rate or the crude death rate. Now let us consider how the age distribution itself arises. Essentially, the *age distribution* is a record of past fertility, modified somewhat by past mortality. Specifically, the amount, and thus proportion, of persons of a specific age in a particular year is the result of how many children were born Y years ago and how many of these survived. For instance, there were 3.8 million 22-year-old Americans in 1969 (July 1); these are the survivors (plus immigrants) of the cohort born between July 1, 1946 and June 30, 1947. There were, however, only 3.5 and 2.8 million 21- and 23-year-old Americans in 1969 (Figure 1-9). The three 1-year birth cohorts were all subject to similar health conditions during their life up until 1969; that is, the probability of dying and surviving for the three cohorts was very similar. Obviously the reason that there were so many 22-year-old persons in 1969 must have been that more children were born between July 1, 1946 and June 30, 1947 than in the immediately preceeding and following years (Figure 1-5).

Demographers have proven[2] that it is mainly the past levels and trends of fertility and not of mortality that shape the age structure of a

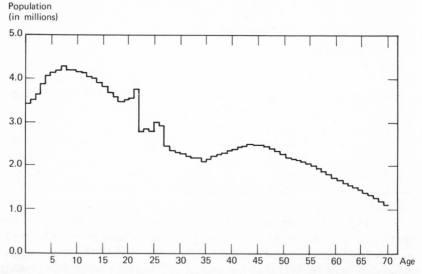

Figure 1–9. Age composition of United States population (in millions), July 1, 1969 (by single years of ages up to age 70). Source: U.S. Department of Commerce, Bureau of the Census, "Estimates of the Population of the United States, by Age, Race, and Sex: July 1, 1967 to July 1, 1969," *Current Population Reports*, Series P-25, 441, Washington: Government Printing Office, 1970.

population. Take, for example, Belgium and the Netherlands. Both populations have had similar mortality trends and levels. The proportion of those born in the nineteenth century and still alive in 1965 is very similar in both countries, and yet of the total population there were only 10% of persons of 65 and more years of age in the Netherlands in 1965, but 15% of such people in Belgium in 1965. This is so because fertility for several decades has been higher in the Netherlands compared with Belgium; and therefore the age structure of both countries is different (Figure 1-10).

That fertility trends act as the main factor shaping the age structure can be demonstrated also on two populations with clearly distinct mortality trends, but similar fertility levels. The Ivory Coast and Costa Rica, for instance, around 1965 had a difference of the expectation of life at birth of about 30 years (around 40 years versus almost 70), but their age structures were very similar (Figure 1-11), because both populations had a history of high fertility.

Only a few illustrations of how fertility and mortality affect the shape of age structures have been presented. An important point is to realize that health conditions and thus the probability of surviving

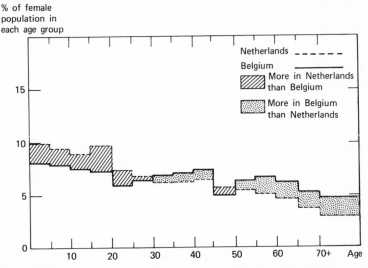

Figure 1-10. Female age distribution, Netherlands and Belgium, 1965. Sources: Centraal Bureau voor de Statistiek, *Population, Marriages, Divorces, Births, Deaths, Internal and External Migration 1946–1965 incl.* Gravenhage, 1966, p. 4. Statistical Office of the United Nations, *Demographic Yearbook 1970,* New York, 1971, pp. 304–305.

% of female
population in
each age group

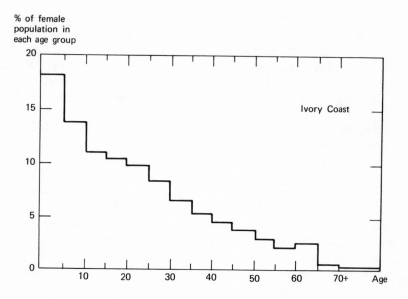

% of female
population in
each age group

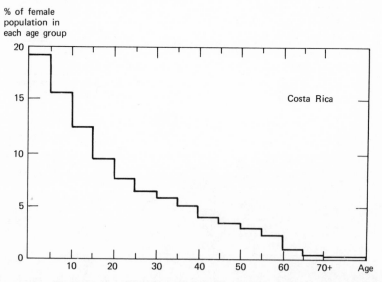

Figure 1–11. Female age distribution, Ivory Coast and Costa Rica, 1965. Sources: Ricardo Jiménez Jiménez et al, "Proyección de la Población de Costa Rica por Sexo y Grupos de Edad, 1965–1990." *Revista de Estudios y Estadísticas*, No. 8 (October 1967), p. 43. Louis Roussel, *Côte D'Ivoire 1965, Population-Etudes Regionales 1962–65—Synthése.* Juillet 1967, p. 82.

determine the average expectation of life of individual people in specific populations. But the age composition of the whole population is mainly determined by fertility levels and trends. High levels of fertility will produce young age structures, low levels of fertility result in old age structures, and fertility fluctuations will cause dents and bulges in the age structure. Exceptionally, high mortality of a specific age group can cause a dent in the age structure, for instance, high male mortality in a major war.

4. A DISCUSSION OF THE CRUDE RATE OF NATURAL INCREASE

A further aspect of population that is of major interest is its rate of growth. It was estimated that the population of Belgium was 9,554,000 at the beginning of 1967 and 9,609,000 at the end of that year. During 1967 the population grew by 0.6% (9609/9554 = 1.0058). We had, however, established earlier that the rate of natural increase was 0.3% in Belgium in 1967. The explanation for this discrepancy is that 0.3% includes *only* natural increase, that is, births minus deaths; whereas 0.6% is total population growth, that is, including gains due to net migration—immigration minus emmigration (Table 1-8).

In the context of the present study attention is devoted only to the *rate of natural increase*. This can be arrived at either by relating the

Table 1-8   Components of Population Growth, Belgium, 1967

Item	In Thousands
Population, Jan. 1, 1967	9554
During 1967	
Births	+146
Deaths	-115
Immigrants	+ 64
Emigrants	- 40
Population, Dec. 31, 1967	9609
Rate of growth	9609/9554 = 1.0058 (0.6%)

Source: Statistical Office of the United Nations. *Demographic Yearbook 1970.* New York, 1971, pp. 302, 623, 657, 769, 797.

absolute value of the natural increase, that is, births minus deaths (146 − 115 = 31), to the total population (usually mid-year: 9580; 31/9580 × 100 = 0.3%); or by subtracting the crude death rate from the crude birth rate (15.3 − 12.0 = 3.3/10 = 0.3%).

Of course, for the planet as a whole the population growth rate and the rate of natural increase are equal, because there is no net migration on or off the earth. Although for short periods of time and for specific countries net migration can cause the rate of natural increase and the population growth rate to differ sharply, for most large nations, particularly those with high rates of natural increase, net migration is not a large component of population growth. In countries with low rates of natural increase, net migration can become a more significant part of population growth.

Because the crude rate of natural increase is a measure derived from the crude birth rate and the crude death rate, its value is necessarily an outcome of the interaction of various factors that have been discussed: the level of fertility and the level of mortality, as well as the age structure and the age patterns of fertility. Some examples are given in Table 1-9.

- High fertility countries have high rates of natural increase (Ivory Coast and Costa Rica versus Belgium and Greece).
- A high fertility and low mortality country has a higher rate of natural increase than a country with high fertility and high mortality (Costa Rica versus Ivory Coast).
- The rate of natural increase of two countries with a similar level of fertility and a similar level of mortality can differ quite significantly (0.3% in Belgium versus 1.0% in Greece), if, for instance, their age structures are significantly different. The age structure of Greece in 1967 was favorable to a relatively high crude birth rate and to a relatively low crude death rate; the reverse situation holds in Belgium.

5. THE NET REPRODUCTION RATE

A rather complex demographic measure reflecting both current fertility and mortality conditions is the *net reproduction rate* (NRR). It is a hypothetical construction along the lines of the total fertility rate and gross reproduction rate. On the basis of the age-specific fertility rates, the total fertility rate (gross reproduction rate) presents information on how many children (daughters) would be born per

Table 1-9 Selected Demographic Measures, Belgium, Greece, Ivory Coast, and Costa Rica, 1967 (unless otherwise stated)

Country	Crude Rate of Natural Increase (in %)	Crude Birth Rate (per thousand)	Crude Death Rate (per thousand)	Total Fertility Rate	Female Expectation of Life at Birth (e_0^0)
Belgium	0.3	15.3	12.0	2.4	73.5 (1959-1963)
Greece	1.0	18.7	8.3	2.4	70.7 (1960-1962)
Ivory Coast	2.3[a]	46.0[a]	22.7[a]	6.4[b]	35.0 (both sexes 1957-1958)
Costa Rica	3.2	39.0	7.1	6.0	64.8 (1962-1964)

[a]United Nations estimates for 1965-1970.
[b]Author's estimate.

Sources: See Tables 1-1, 1-3, 1-4. Statistical Office of the United Nations. *Demographic Yearbook 1970.* New York, 1971, pp. 619-623, 653-657, 712, 716, 724.

woman if they would be subject to current age levels of fertility. The NRR introduces a further component; it estimates how many of these daughters would survive to the age their mothers were at the time of observation by the help of current age-specific mortality rates. Thus a value is computed that gives the number of daughters who would be born per woman and survive at least to the age of their mother at the time of their own birth. In other words, it is the number of daughters who could themselves become mothers. The NRR also approximates the rate at which the current generation of mothers is being replaced by a future generation of potential mothers.

There are two main ways of arriving at the NRR, both of which reach the same value:

1. The GRR, is multiplied by the probability of surviving from birth to the mean age of childbearing; for example, in Costa Rica in 1967 the GRR was 2.9, the probability of surving to age 29 was 0.89, and the product of these two components was 2.6, which is the NRR.

2. The age-specific maternity rates (i.e., the female age-specific fertility rates) are multiplied by the probability of surviving from birth to the respective age (midpoint of age group), and the products, for each age group are added up and multiplied by five (Table 1-10).

Data in Table 1-11 provide an idea of actual NRR values. In countries with low fertility and low mortality the NRR is close to the value of 1.0 (1.1 in Belgium). In countries with high fertility and low mortality the NRR is high (2.6 in Costa Rica). In countries with high fertility but also high mortality, fewer daughters are likely to survive than in the former countries (1.8 in the Ivory Coast).

The information provided by the NRR should not be overrated. The NRR, the TFR, and the GRR are hypothetical structures with limitations as described by Notestein:

These measures summarize a single year's experience for the population of all ages as if it were the experience of a single birth class (cohort) that has passed through all ages. They are hypothetical values like the readings on a car's speedometer. The latter does not tell you how far you have come during the last hour, or how far you will go in the next hour. It gives you the highly hypothetical information that if you had travelled during the past hour at precisely the rate you are travelling now you would have by the end of an hour, travelled the indicated distance.[3]

The level of fertility (expressed in terms of the TFR or the GRR) corresponding to an NRR of 1.0 is often referred to as *fertility at the replacement level*. Since the value of the NRR is dependent not only on

Table 1-10 Methods of Computing Net Reproduction Rate, Costa Rica, 1967

Age Group	Age-Specific Maternity Rates (1)	Age-Specific Survival Rates[a] (e_0 = 68 years) (2)	Product of Preceding Columns (3) = (2) x (1)
15-19	.0538	.90503	.0487
20-24	.1355	.90048	.1220
25-29	.1370	.89472	.1226
30-34	.1122	.88799	.0996
35-39	.0950	.88009	.0836
40-44	.0417	.87013	.0363
45-49	.0070	.85705	.0060
TOTAL	.5822 x 5		.5188 x 5
GROSS REPRODUCTION RATE	2.9110 x .89472		
NET REPRODUCTION RATE	2.6045		2.5940

[a]Probability of surviving from birth to the midpoint of the age group.

Sources: See Tables 1-3 and 1-4. Ansley J. Coale and Paul Demeny. *Regional Model Life Tables and Stable Populations.* Princeton: Princeton University Press, 1966, pp. 675, 676.

fertility but also on mortality conditions, this concept must be handled with caution. Fertility at the replacement level expressed in terms of the TFR would have been 2.1 in Belgium at the end of the 1960s, but around 3.5 in the Ivory Coast. In both countries, because of totally different mortality conditions, the NRR would have been equal to 1.0, had the total fertility rate been 2.1 and 3.5, respectively.

Fertility at the replacement level (NRR = 1 in conjunction with specific mortality conditions) is often associated with an immediate cessation of population growth. As has been demonstrated, the level of fertility is, however, not the only factor shaping the crude birth rate and thus the rate of population growth. The age composition of a population and age patterns of fertility—which are not a component of the NRR—interact with the level of fertility, and this interaction produces a certain crude birth rate. Thus whether a population continues to grow even after achieving an NRR equal to 1.0 depends on these additional factors (the age structure, age patterns of fertility). As will be demonstrated, most populations of the world will continue to grow, even if they immediately attain an NRR of 1.0.

6. STABLE AND STATIONARY POPULATIONS

On a year-to-year basis populations are subject to fluctuating rates and structures, and it is necessary to describe their actual demographic state and trends in detail. For instance, fertility trends and ensuing irregularities of the age structure in the United States in the twentieth century were of such a nature that it would be difficult to summarize them concisely.

Theoretically one can imagine more settled situations: combinations of constant levels of fertility and constant levels of mortality result in populations growing at a specific constant rate of growth, and because of the constancy of the factors of growth, the age structure would not undergo any changes. Such cases are designated as *stable populations*. Although there is scarcely any firm statistical evidence, in premodern times most populations, in the long run, were probably subject to relatively constant high fertility and high mortality levels and thus grew at moderate rates of growth with fairly stable age structures.

In particular instances the number of births might have equalled the number of deaths. Thus the crude birth rate would have been equal to the crude death rate. There would have been no growth, and the age structure would have been constant over time. Such a situation is called a *stationary population*. Because living, health, and hygienic conditions have changed during the process of modernization, mortality has declined considerably and thus a low mortality, stationary population can be attained only with low fertility. Ideally such a population will have a constant age structure and constant age-specific mortality and fertility rates; its NRR will be equal to 1.0; if mortality conditions will be of the current advanced type (female expectation of life at birth around 75 years) the crude birth rate and the crude death rate will be around 13 per thousand population; there would be no population growth; and the age structure would be an old one and remain constant over time. A few European countries, including Belgium, are coming close to the described stationary state.

What kind of demographic trends are needed to reach a stationary state in the widely varying populations of the contemporary world? How can individual populations move from their current situation to the ideal stationary state? What will the interaction of demographic variables be like on this path toward a stationary population? At least part of the answers to these questions can be found in the following chapters.

Table 1-11   Total Fertility Rates, Gross Reproduction Rates (GRR), and Net Reproduction Rates (NRR), Belgium, Ivory Coast, and Costa Rica, 1967

Country	Total Fertility Rate	GRR	NRR
Belgium	2.4	1.2	1.1
Ivory Coast	6.4[a]	3.1[a]	1.8[a]
Costa Rica	6.0	2.9	2.6

[a]Author's computation.

Sources: See Tables 1-8 and 1-9. Statistical Office of the United Nations. *Demographic Yearbook 1969.* New York, 1970, pp. 675, 676.

NOTES

1. Ansley J. Coale and C. Y. Tye, "The Signifiance of Age Patterns of Fertility in High Fertility Populations," *Milbank Memorial Fund Quarterly*, Vol. 39, No. 4 (October 1961), 631–646.
2. Ansley J. Coale, "How the Age Distribution of a Human Population Is Determined," *Cold Spring Harbor Symposia on Quantitative Biology*, Vol. XXII (1957), pp. 83–89.
3. Unpublished manuscript.

2 The Methodology

1. THE TECHNIQUES

This study employed most of the basic techniques generally used to compute population projections (see Appendix 1 for a technical exposition of the mechanism). The current size of a population and its age structure are projected into the future on the basis of certain assumptions about the course of age-specific mortality and fertility rates.

The initial population is divided by 5-year age groups and is moved ahead 5 years at a time. All projections start in 1965 and continue by 5-year intervals through 2160. In most of the tables in this book data are presented in 5-year or 10-year intervals through 2050, then in intervals of 25 years.

As a rule, all population units (countries, regions, major areas, the

35

whole world) are treated uniformly. The starting point of the projections is always 1965; the general nature of the underlying assumptions is the same—although these assumptions naturally differ in absolute level for each unit—and the basic series of tables are the same for all units. One could have chosen a different approach and, for example, begun the projections of each population from the date for which the most reliable basic data were available. A generally uniform treatment for all populations was chosen in order to minimize the complexity of the project and to ensure comparability.

The projections were set up with the following features:

1. Once the current characteristics of a population (age structure, level and age pattern of mortality, level and age pattern of fertility) have been established, small changes in the fertility or mortality assumptions permit computations of any number of desired alternative projections. This feature is utilized throughout the project. Five projections based on differing rates of fertility decline constitute the backbone of the main set of projections for each population. In addition, several modified sets of projections based on variations in the fertility and mortality assumptions have been computed (see Chapter 6).

2. The interrelations of important demographic variables are explicitly expressed and published in a fairly simple manner. For example, one can visualize the size of the total population implied by certain trends in average number of children per family; one can see what kind of annual rates of population change correspond to certain levels of crude birth rates; and one can judge the nature of fertility change needed to attain a certain desired total population size at a specific date in the future.

3. The mortality and fertility assumptions of the first period (1965–70) are as realistic as possible, so that the estimated population size and structure for 1970 is the actual starting point. The assumptions are the same for all projections of a certain population in the 1965–70 period. In this way it is possible to demonstrate vividly the difference between current properties of any given population unit and future developments, especially in those alternatives where major changes are assumed (for instance, one can compare the real 1965–70 growth rate with growth rates of subsequent periods of alternative projections).

It is important to mention that all computations were done with female populations only; data for the total population are obtained by doubling the projected female population. Use of female populations cuts down considerably the amount of work and computer time and yet has negligible influence on the results. Trends of population growth and trends of fertility characteristics are hardly affected. The crude birth rate, however, is usually somewhat underestimated, and the relative proportions of some age groups of the total population might differ by a few tenths of a percent from a possible projection of both sexes.

Further, migration was not taken into account. It is recognized that in a specific country and specific period, international migration can play a significant role in population development.[1] However, it was felt that in the long run migration in most countries would probably not play a major role in the development of total numbers of respective populations (this does not mean that internal migration will be insignificant). Further, it certainly does not seem probable that the total world population could be influenced by either in- or out-migration during the foreseeable future. Finally, the inclusion of any migration assumptions would significantly increase the complexity of the project.

A selected number of basic factors of population growth form the basis of this study, specifically fertility levels and age patterns, mortality levels and age patterns, and the age structure of population units. Other demographic and nondemographic factors, such as the proportion of women married (de facto), the average age at marriage, the type and amount of labor force participation of women, the level of education, all of which are certainly relevant phenomena influencing fertility behavior, have not been taken into account. The main objective of this project is to illustrate demographic trends, especially fertility trends, that have to be generated to approach stationary populations, not to investigate how specific changes in fertility can be induced or influenced. Besides, the inclusion of such components would have increased the complexity of the project beyond reasonable bounds.

2. FERTILITY ASSUMPTIONS

The variations of fertility assumptions constitute the basic analytical framework of the whole study. With the aim of illustrating the various population-growth consequences of extremely fast and varying degrees of moderate fertility decline that would ultimately lead to non-growing populations, it was decided to compute five different projections for each population unit.

One projection differs from another by length of period of fertility decline (0, 10, 30, 50 or 70 years) and therefore also by speed of fertility decline. In the main set, or standard series, of projections fertility is assumed to decline from its current level to a level that corresponds to a net reproduction rate (NRR) of 1.0. Once an NRR of 1.0 is reached, it is assumed to remain at this level throughout the rest of the projection.

In the standard series of projections fertility is assumed to decline at a linear rate; that is, the assumed fertility decline is divided equally among the number of 5-year periods over which fertility is decreasing. However, the indicator that is assumed to decline linearly is not the NRR but the corresponding gross reproduction rate (GRR). This technique seems to be justified because a linear decline of the NRR would mean an irregular decline of the GRR and because the GRR (as opposed to the NRR) does not contain the element of mortality considerations and is the rate that is a closer approximation of actual fertility behavior of women; thus it seems more appropriate to manipulate the GRR and not the NRR.

The specific procedure in constructing the standard series was as follows. For each projection the current (1965–70) GRR was compared with the GRR of a population when it reaches an NRR of 1.0; for example, in Projection Three it is the period 2000–05. The decline in the GRR over that time was equally divided into 5-year periods (e. g., see Table 2-1.[2]

In the standard series for the first projection it is always assumed that the NRR declines immediately, for example, in the period 1970–75, to a level of 1.0. For Projection Two it is assumed that an NRR of 1.0 is reached in 1980–85; for Projection Three, in 2000–05; for Projection Four, in 2020–25; and for Projection Five, in 2040–45.

For each unit the current age-specific fertility rates are estimated with the highest possible degree of accuracy. Since the basis for the projections is the female population, age-specific maternity rates are actually used. These have exactly the same pattern as age-specific fertility rates. In the standard series these age-specific fertility rates are then applied throughout the projections, but deflated in accordance with the respective nature of the fertility decline. This might seem to be a shortcoming of the project, because trends of certain age-specific fertility rates over time can be different from trends of overall fertility. Changes in the age patterns of fertility in the long run can have an impact on population growth; the order of magnitude of its

Table 2-1   Assumptions of Gross Reproduction Rate (GRR) and Net Reproduction Rate (NRR)
             Decline Underlying Standard Series of Projections for Population of Less Devel-
             oped Regions, 1965-2150

Period	Projection 1		Projection 2		Projection 3		Projection 4		Projection 5	
	GRR	NRR	GRR	NRR	GRR	NRR	GRR	NRR	GRR	NRR
1965-1970	2.800	2.073	2.800	2.073	2.800	2.073	2.800	2.073	2.800	2.073
1970-1975	1.299	1.000	2.275	1.752	2.563	1.973	2.643	2.035	2.683	2.066
1975-1980	1.261	1.000	1.751	1.389	2.325	1.844	2.486	1.972	2.565	2.035
1980-1985	1.226	1.000	1.226	1.000	2.088	1.703	2.329	1.900	2.448	1.997
1985-1990	1.202	1.000	1.202	1.000	1.850	1.539	2.172	1.807	2.331	1.938
1990-1995	1.179	1.000	1.179	1.000	1.613	1.368	2.016	1.709	2.213	1.877
1995-2000	1.158	1.000	1.158	1.000	1.376	1.188	1.859	1.605	2.096	1.810
2000-2005	1.138	1.000	1.138	1.000	1.138	1.000	1.702	1.495	1.979	1.739
2005-2010	1.119	1.000	1.119	1.000	1.119	1.000	1.545	1.381	1.862	1.663
2010-2015	1.101	1.000	1.101	1.000	1.101	1.000	1.388	1.260	1.744	1.584
2015-2020	1.085	1.000	1.085	1.000	1.085	1.000	1.231	1.135	1.627	1.500
2020-2025	1.074	1.000	1.074	1.000	1.074	1.000	1.074	1.000	1.510	1.405
2025-2030	1.064	1.000	1.064	1.000	1.064	1.000	1.064	1.000	1.392	1.309
2030-2035	1.056	1.000	1.056	1.000	1.056	1.000	1.056	1.000	1.275	1.208
2035-2040	1.048	1.000	1.048	1.000	1.048	1.000	1.048	1.000	1.158	1.105
2040-2045	1.040	1.000	1.040	1.000	1.040	1.000	1.040	1.000	1.040	1.000
2045-2050	1.034	1.000	1.034	1.000	1.034	1.000	1.034	1.000	1.034	1.000
2070-2075	1.034	1.000	1.034	1.000	1.034	1.000	1.034	1.000	1.034	1.000
2095-2100	1.034	1.000	1.034	1.000	1.034	1.000	1.034	1.000	1.034	1.000
2120-2125	1.034	1.000	1.034	1.000	1.034	1.000	1.034	1.000	1.034	1.000
2145-2150	1.034	1.000	1.034	1.000	1.034	1.000	1.034	1.000	1.034	1.000

impact is tested in Chapter 6. The analysis of the impact of changes of fertility patterns is intentionally postponed for separate treatment so that the consequences of fertility level trends can be illustrated with greater clarity.

Several questions remain to be answered:

- Why was the NRR of 1.0 chosen as the level at which fertility of populations would stabilize for the standard series of projections?
- Why it decided to have a projection in which the NRR would drop to 1.0 immediately (i.e., in the 1970–75 period) as the lower limit and a slow fertility decline as the upper limit of the projections?
- Why was a linear rate of fertility decline assumed for the standard series of projections?

The choice of an NRR of 1.0 was somewhat arbitrary, but it does seem to be the "natural" choice for several reasons.

1. There is a relative consensus that populations sooner or later must stop growing. If a population adopts and maintains a fertility pattern roughly corresponding to an NRR of 1.0, this population will ultimately cease to grow, and it will develop into a stationary population (provided, of course, mortality patterns also stabilize). To put it differently, to choose an NRR that would settle at a level significantly above 1.0 results in a constantly growing population, and the application of such an assumption would never result in a stationary population.

2. An NRR below 1.0 could have been chosen for the standard series. This would imply not only a nongrowing population but eventually even a population of declining size. There is no reason why this should not happen, and this alternative will also be explored. However, the history of modern times seems to indicate that nations become extremely concerned once their NRR declines below 1.0 and seek to maintain a fertility level of at least replacement. As a matter of fact, only in exceptional cases have nations in modern times maintained levels of fertility below replacement for an "extended" period of time.

In sum, for all practical purposes only a sustained NRR of 1.0 results eventually in a stationary population.

The choice of the five velocities of fertility decline to an NRR of 1.0 was guided by the intention to present a range of alternatives that would be meaningful both for more developed and less developed countries and regions. Projection One, in which the NRR declines without delay to 1.0, illustrates for certain more developed countries a high but achievable rate of decline. For the less developed countries it illustrates unachievable population growth trends.

For the upper limit the choice was extremely difficult. One obvious possibility would have been assumptions of constant current mortality and fertility levels. This idea was discarded for the standard series because it would never result in a stationary population. Nevertheless, in Chapter 6 some population growth consequences of possible constant fertility are explored. Further, the results to be obtained under such assumptions have been worked out elsewhere.[3] Lastly, it seems that the assumptions of slowly declining fertility employed in our project are even more powerful in conveying the message of the population growth consequences of slow fertility decline in the less developed countries.

The assumption of a linear decline of the GRR is believed to be just as good as any other. It was purely an arbitrary choice for the standard series of projections. In the analysis the version of a constant rate of fertility decline is also discussed. As seen from the vantage point of our research, the differences are not very meaningful. Suffice it to mention now that in the first projection there is no difference whatsoever, because with the immediate adoption of an NRR of 1.0, there is no difference between a linear and constant rate of fertility decline.

3. MORTALITY ASSUMPTIONS

In almost all series of projections a single set of mortality assumptions is applied. This is true for the standard series and for most of the variations analyzed in Chapter 6. Because, however, future mortality trends as applied in these projections are challengeable, some alternative mortality assumptions are used in Chapter 6. Thus in most projections it is presumed that mortality will decline further. It is assumed that in the near future the current speed of mortality decline of a population will be maintained and that after 10, 15, or 20 years this speed of mortality decline will become gradually smaller.

Each projection begins with a set of age-specific survival rates, based on an estimate of current mortality. Beyond 1970, appropriate Coale-Demeny life tables[4] are applied.

A rough idea of the nature of mortality assumptions can be gained from Table 2-2, in which mortality levels are expressed by the female expectation of life at birth (e_0^o). It is assumed that the female expectation of life will not go beyond 77.5 years (level 24 of the Coale-Demeny model life table) and that most of the decline of mortality will occur within the twentieth century. Small mortality

Table 2-2   Mortality Assumptions for Major Areas and Regions (in female e_0^o) and Family of Model Life Table Applied

	1965-1970	2000-2005	2045-2050	Family of Model Life Table
WORLD	56.5	68.0	75.0	west
MORE DEVELOPED REGIONS	72.5	76.0	77.5	west
LESS DEVELOPED REGIONS	51.0	63.5	74.0	west
A. *EAST ASIA*	54.5	65.5	74.5	west
1. *Mainland Region*	52.0	66.0	74.0	west
2. *Japan*	73.0	76.5	77.5	west
3. *Other East Asia*	62.0	70.0	76.0	west
B. *SOUTH ASIA*	51.0	66.0	74.0	west
4. *Middle South Asia*	50.0	65.0	73.5	west
5. *South-East Asia*	52.0	67.0	74.5	west
6. *South-West Asia*	53.0	68.0	74.5	west
C. *EUROPE*	73.0	76.5	77.5	west
7. *Western Europe*	73.5	77.0	77.5	west
8. *Southern Europe*	72.0	75.5	77.5	south
9. *Eastern Europe*	72.5	76.0	77.5	east
10. *Northern Europe*	74.0	77.5	77.5	west
D.11. *U.S.S.R.*	72.5	76.0	77.5	west
E. *AFRICA*	44.5	59.5	72.0	west
12. *Western Africa*	41.0	60.0	71.0	west
13. *Eastern Africa*	44.0	61.0	72.0	west
14. *Middle Africa*	41.0	60.0	71.0	west
15. *Northern Africa*	51.5	66.0	74.0	west
16. *Southern Africa*	50.0	64.5	73.5	west
F.17. *NORTH AMERICA*	72.5	76.0	77.5	west
G. *LATIN AMERICA*	62.5	70.0	76.0	south
18. *Tropical South America*	61.5	70.5	76.0	south
19. *Middle America (mainland)*	62.5	70.0	76.0	south
20. *Temperate South America*	66.5	72.5	77.0	south
21. *Caribbean*	60.0	71.0	75.5	south
H. *OCEANIA*	68.5	73.0	77.0	west
22. *Australia & New Zealand*	74.0	76.0	77.5	west
23. *Melanesia*	48.5	63.5	73.5	west
24. *Polynesia & Micronesia*	63.0	70.0	75.0	west

declines are assumed to occur even during the next century. The average world female expectation of life at birth is assumed to stabilize at 75.0 years, with an average of 77.5 years for the more developed regions and 74.0 for the less developed regions by the middle of the twenty-first century.

Why is mortality assumed to decline further? Mortality could have been assumed to remain at the current level, and the difference of the future population growth consequences of varying fertility developments would have been almost as clear. However, the assumption of mortality decline gives some projections more than merely an analytical and illustrative value. Provided that a certain pattern of fertility decline is considered feasible, the corresponding population growth is shown with a relatively high degree of resemblance to assumed, real, future developments.

Why, then, is there only one set of mortality assumptions for a given population? Several considerations justify the use of one set of mortality assumptions for most projections. In the absence of major wars and other unexpected disasters, the limits of probable future mortality development are comparatively narrow. Within these limits differences in mortality conditions—especially once mortality levels become comparatively low—have a relatively small impact on the rate of population growth.[5] Finally, within broad limits mortality can be fairly well predicted. Having these circumstances in mind, it seemed reasonable in most projections to apply one set of mortality assumptions, not several alternatives.

The fact that in the majority of the projections one set of mortality assumptions was used should not imply that the estimated trends are the ones that will actually occur. In some countries they might turn out to be more erratic than in others. Mortality might even take a course absolutely different from what has been assumed. However, a detailed investigation of population-growth consequences of alternative mortality developments will have to await a different occasion.

4. SOURCES AND QUALITY OF DATA

The sources of data are listed at the end of the book. Nevertheless it seems useful to add a general comment, although to many it may sound self-evident. There is a considerable variety in the quality of the "input" data; in addition, unfortunately, there is an inverse relation between the quality of the data and the need for the kind of knowledge that this study intends to provide. To put it differently, at times the information about the current demographic properties of a population was extremely scanty, and yet it was felt that the country involved should not be excluded from the analysis. There was no other choice than to resort to the best estimates we could find or make, usually with the help of regional experts.

The quality of the information on current demographic characteristics has been rated into three broad groups: (1) reliable data, (2) fairly reliable data, and (3) unreliable data. The dividing lines were roughly the following: If the available information was based on a reasonable, comprehensive system of vital registration and censuses, the population was considered to fit into group (1). Information based on a mix of less reliable censuses and vital registration but possibly linked with some fairly reliable sample surveys would qualify for group (2). Anything below that would be classified as group (3). Since much of the important information about the current demographic characteristics of a population is presented in the analytical tables, the reader can check to what degree the data applied in this study match more recent information and can judge whether the analysis of a specific unit has a sound starting point.

The main source of data for the "non-country" population units—that is, for the regions, major areas, the more and less developed regions, and the whole world—are published and unpublished data of the United Nations Population Division that were made available for this study.

5. GEOGRAPHICAL SCOPE

Projections were computed for the world population, for the population of the less developed regions as a whole, for the population of the more developed regions, for 8 major areas, and for 24 regions of the world[6] (see Figure 2-1). In addition to these aggregate units, about 60 "country studies" were carried out.

The 8 major areas were the following:

A. East Asia   E. Africa
B. South Asia   F. Northern America
C. Europe   G. Latin America
D. U.S.S.R.   H. Oceania

Major areas, regions, and countries (see Figure 2–1) are labeled by

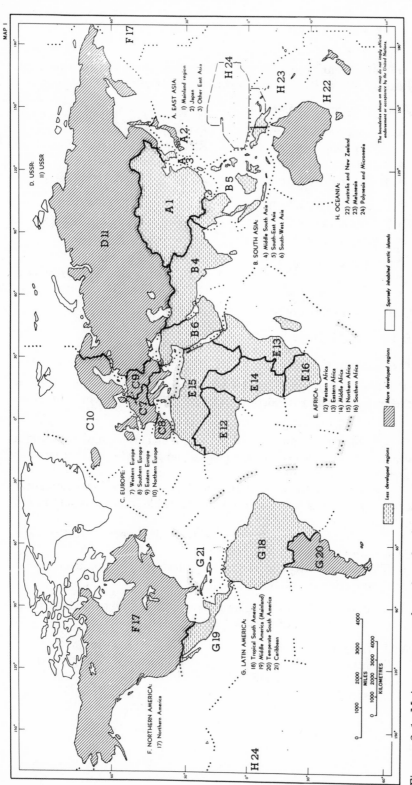

MAP 1

A. EAST ASIA:
  1) Mainland region
  2) Japan
  3) Other East Asia

B. SOUTH ASIA:
  4) Middle South Asia
  5) South-East Asia
  6) South-West Asia

C. EUROPE:
  7) Western Europe
  8) Southern Europe
  9) Eastern Europe
  10) Northern Europe

D. USSR:
  11) USSR

E. AFRICA:
  12) Western Africa
  13) Eastern Africa
  14) Middle Africa
  15) Northern Africa
  16) Southern Africa

F. NORTHERN AMERICA:
  17) Northern America

G. LATIN AMERICA:
  18) Tropical South America
  19) Middle America (Mainland)
  20) Temperate South America
  21) Caribbean

H. OCEANIA:
  22) Australia and New Zealand
  23) Melanesia
  24) Polynesia and Micronesia

More developed regions

Less developed regions

Sparsely inhabited arctic islands

The boundaries shown on this map do not imply official
endorsement or acceptance by the United Nations.

MILES
0   1000   2000   3000   4000

KILOMETRES
0   1000 2000 3000 4000

Figure 2–1. Major areas and regions by levels of economic and social development. Source: United Nations, map no. 1620, October 1965.

capital letters and numbers in the same way as in the U.N. publication, *World Population Prospects as Assessed in 1963.*

The 24 regions consisted of:

A.1	East Asia—mainland region	
A.2	Japan	
A.3	Other East Asia	
B.4	Middle South Asia	
B.5	South-East Asia	
B.6	South-West Asia	
C.7	Western Europe	
C.8	Southern Europe	
C.9	Eastern Europe	
C.10	Northern Europe	
D.11	U.S.S.R.	
E.12	Western Africa	

E.13   Eastern Africa
E.14   Middle Africa
E.15   Northern Africa
E.16   Southern Africa

F.17   Northern America

G.18   Tropical South America
G.19   Middle America (mainland)
G.20   Temperate South America
G.21   Caribbean

H.22   Australia and New Zealand
H.23   Melanesia
H.24   Polynesia and Micronesia

Candidates for the country studies were chosen for some kind of special interest and/or importance according to the following criteria:

1. Size of the population.

2. Organized private and/or government action implementing a population policy—this could be a population policy to either restrict or enhance population growth.

3. Countries with no explicit population policy—however, other government or private action has a considerable impact on population development.

4. The country being a reasonably typical representative of a group of countries.

5. The availability of reasonably accurate information about current population characteristics.

The countries chosen were as follows (the number in parenthesis indicates the reliability of the data, as discussed previously):

A.11   Hong Kong (1)
A.2   Japan (1)
A.3   Republic of Korea (South Korea) (2)
A.3   Republic of China (Taiwan) (1)

B.4   India (3)
B.4   Bangladesh (3)
B.4   Pakistan (3)
B.4   Iran (3)

B.4	Ceylon (2)	E.12	Ivory Coast (3)
B.5	Philippines (3)	E.12	Liberia (3)
B.5	Thailand (2)	E.13	Tanzania (3)
B.5	West Malaysia (2)	E.13	Kenya (3)
B.5	Singapore (3)	E.13	Mauritius (2)
B.6	Turkey (2)	E.15	United Arab Republic (3)
B.6	Israel	E.15	Morocco (3)
	Total population (1)	E.15	Algeria (3)
	Jewish population (1)	E.15	Tunisia (3)
	Non-Jewish population (1)	E.16	Swaziland (2)
C.7	German Federal Republic (1)	F.17	United States (1)
C.7	France (1)	F.17	Canada (1)
C.7	Netherlands (1)		
C.7	Belgium (1)	G.18	Brazil (3)
C.7	Austria (1)	G.18	Colombia (2–3)
C.8	Italy (2)	G.18	Peru (3)
C.8	Yugoslavia (1)	G.18	Venezuela (2–3)
C.8	Greece (1)	G.19	Mexico (2–3)
C.9	Poland	G.19	El-Salvador (3)
C.9	Czechoslovakia (1)	G.19	Honduras (3)
C.9	Hungary (1)	G.19	Costa Rica (1–2)
		G.20	Argentina (2–3)
C.10	England and Wales (1)	G.20	Chile (2)
C.10	Sweden (1)	G.21	Cuba (2)
C.10	Denmark (1)	G.21	Dominican Republic (3)
		G.21	Puerto Rico (1)
D.11	U.S.S.R. (2)	G.21	Trinidad and Tobago (2)
E.12	Nigeria (3)		
E.12	Ghana (3)	H.22	Australia (1)

Detailed analytical tables for the above-listed populations are published by the Population Council, New York.

6. THE LOGIC OF THE SET OF ANALYTICAL TABLES

For each population unit there is at least one set of analytical tables (see Appendix 2). This set consists of nine tables. They are designed to give (1) a sufficient idea of the input data and the applied mortality and fertility assumptions, and (2) a comprehensive illustration of future demographic developments determined by the assumed fertility (and mortality) behavior of the respective population.

Five of the nine tables provide information about the interaction of various demographic measures (such as size of population, vital rates, reproduction rates) for one specific projection. Four tables compare the differing behavior of one or more specific demographic measures of the respective five projections.

Data for any particular year refer to the middle of that year. Data for a specific period refer to the period between the middle of the year at the beginning of that period to the middle of the year at the end of the period (for instance, 1965–70 means mid-1965 to mid-1970).

Table A compares the growth of the size of the whole population under review between the five projections both in absolute and relative numbers.

Tables B through F furnish information—each table for a single projection—on the possible developments of the female crude birth and death rates, the average annual growth rate, the gross and net reproduction rates, the total fertility rate, female expectation of life at birth, and the absolute size of the population. Table B is for the projection with the most rapid fertility decline, Table F for the one with the slowest fertility decline, and Tables C, D, E are the intermediate ones.

Table G compares the developments of average annual growth rates between the five projections.

Table H compares the evolution of the average annual increments of population in absolute numbers among the five projections.

Table I provides comparative information on the age structure of the respective population. The age groups were chosen to enable the reader to combine them into meaningful combinations, for example, children of school age, women in the reproductive ages, the potential labor force, the economically dependent population (ages 0–15, 65+). To this end it was deemed necessary to provide eight age groups, and space limitations dictated publishing the information only for 8 selected years (1970, 1985, 2000, 2015, 2030, 2045, 2060, and 2075).

The majority of the sets of tables is of the "standard" type; that is, a linear fertility decline is assumed. Once an NRR of 1.0 is achieved, it is maintained indefinitely; the periods in which this reproductive level is reached (determining the difference between the individual projections) are 1970–75, 1980–85, 2000–05, 2020–25, and 2040–45. The sets of tables are distinguished by a short description of the main assumptions in the second line of the title, for instance, linear decline of fertility to NRR level of 1.0 (this is the main set), or temporary increase in fertility followed by decline to NRR of 1.0.

NOTES

1. Cf. Nathan Keyfitz, "Migration as a Means of Population Control," *Population Studies*, Vol. 25, No. 1 (March 1971), pp. 63–72, and Ansley J. Coale, "Alternative Paths to a Stationary Population," paper prepared for the Commission on Population Growth and the American Future, unpublished manuscript (May 1971).

2. After the NRR reaches the 1.0 level the GRR continues to decline moderately as long as mortality continues to decline. Otherwise, the NRR would rise again.

3. Cf. Projections of the United Nations among which there is always a set with constant fertility and constant mortality assumptions. See United Nations, *World Population Prospects as Assessed in 1963* (New York: 1966). See also National Academy of Sciences-National Research Council, *The Growth of U.S. Population* (Washington, D.C.: 1965), p. 1: "If present fertility and mortality trends persist our population will surpass the present world population in a century and a half."

4. Ansley J. Coale and Paul Demeny, *Regional Model Life Tables and Stable Populations* (Princeton: Princeton University Press, 1966). For the aggregate population units the model life tables were applied even for the 1965–70 period. The same is true for the countries with unreliable current life tables.

5. A. J. Coale, "Increases in Expectation of Life and Population Growth," *International Population Conference, Vienna 1959* (Vienna: I.U.S.S.P., 1959), pp. 36–41.

6. This classification was worked out by the Population Division of the United Nations and used, for instance, in *World Population Prospects as Assessed in 1963*, Population Studies No. 41, United Nations Publication, Sales No.: 66.XIII.2 (New York: 1966). In this report it is stated that "at the present juncture, it is most pertinent to distinguish two major types only, namely, those of regions and countries regarded, by various criteria, as 'developed' and 'developing.' No other criterion, be it *per capita* income, urbanization, literacy, industrialization, etc., defines this dichotomy so sharply as the level of fertility. With exceedingly few exceptions, it can be said that where the gross reproduction rate is greater than 2.0, the country is a 'developing' one, and where it is less, the country is 'developed' " (see p. 3). And further, "the basic scheme of geographical classification used. . .refers to eight

major areas so drawn as to obtain somewhat greater homogeneity [than the conventional division of the earth into continents] in sizes of population, types of demographic circumstances, and accuracy of demographic statistics. Six of the major areas are further subdivided into regions. In this manner, a total of twenty-four regions is arrived at. . ." (see p. 8).

3 Growth Alternatives of the World Population

AN ABSTRACT OF FINDINGS

World population in 1970 was probably in the vicinity of 3.6 billion inhabitants—1.1 billion were living in the more developed countries and 2.5 billion in the less developed countries. According to the estimates that have been used, this population had a crude birth rate of 33 per thousand population, a crude death rate of 13, and an annual rate of natural increase of 2.0%. Of course in the more developed countries these rates are quite different from the rates in the less developed countries. In the former, in the late 1960s the birth rate was around 18 per thousand population, the death rate about 10 per thousand population, and the annual growth rate about 0.8%. In the less developed countries the birth rate was probably over 40, the death rate around 15, and the rate of population growth about 2.6% a year.

Almost 70 million people were being added to the world population in each of those years. Of these about 9 million belonged to the more developed countries and over 60 million to the less developed regions.

On the average women were probably bearing almost 5 children, which is an expression of the fact that in the more developed regions women were bearing an average of 2 to 3 children each, whereas in the less developed regions the average number of children born per woman was between 5 and 7. The estimated world net reproduction rate (NRR) equaled 1.9, which means that under the given fertility and mortality conditions almost 2 daughters per woman would survive into the reproductive ages. In the more developed regions the NRR of the late 1960s was probably in the order of 1.2 to 1.3; in the less developed regions, about 2.1.

Also, the age structure of the population of the more developed and of the less developed regions differed from each other significantly. In the former about 26% of the population in 1970 were children under 15 years, and about 11% were people older than 65 years. In the less developed regions probably about 42% of the population were under 15 years, and only about 3% were above the age of 65. Because twice as many people lived in the less developed regions as in the more developed regions, the age structure of the world population was closer to that of the former—37% of the world population was probably under 15 years and 5 to 6% over 65 (see Figure 3-1). The median age of the world population in 1970 was 22 years, in the less developed regions 19 years, and in the more developed regions 31 years.

Let us now explore how these populations would grow under varying assumptions of fertility and mortality decline on their path to eventual stationarity. It almost goes without saying that a country considered one of the more developed regions or of the less developed regions at the outset remains so through the entire period of the projections. For example, even though Taiwan may one day attain the demographic features of Japan, it remains in the group of the less developed regions throughout the projections.

1. ALTERNATIVES OF WORLDWIDE POPULATION GROWTH

It is almost self-evident that the speed of fertility decline exerts a meaningful effect on population growth (see Table A, World Total, Standard Set; the detailed tables for this section are in Appendix 2). Provided the average fertility conditions changed so substantially that the NRR declined from its estimated current (1965–70) level of 1.9 to a

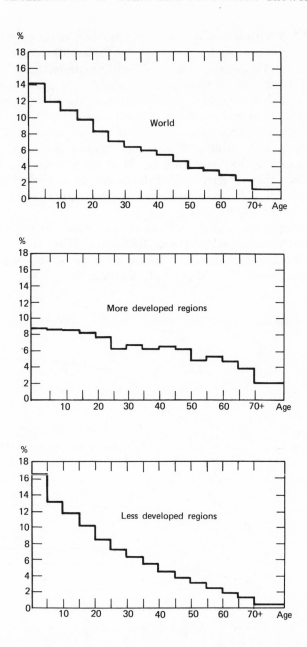

Figure 3-1. Age structure of the world, more developed regions and less developed regions, 1970.

level of 1.0 within a few years, the present world population of 3.6 billion would increase by about 50% by the middle of the next century and would settle at around 5.6 to 5.7 billion inhabitants. If, however, a world fertility decline were brought about very gradually so that in, say, 70 years an NRR of 1.0 were attained, then by the middle of the twenty-first century world population would be about 3.5 times its current size. In this case the world would have about 13 billion inhabitants by the middle of the twenty-first century, and by the end of that century world population would settle at over 15 billion. Quite clearly the nature of current and short-term fertility developments can make a large difference in terms of the future size of the world population (see Figure 3-2).

It should be noted that even the most improbable fertility developments—for instance, a decline of the NRR to a level of 1.0, that is, to a replacement level, within a few years—would still cause a significant growth of total population numbers.

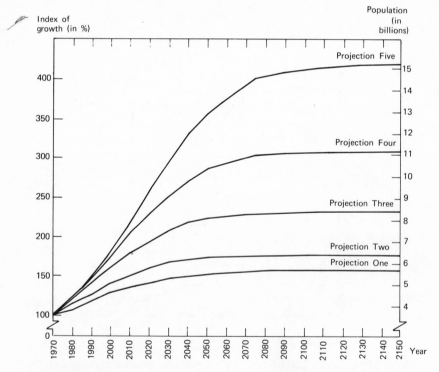

Figure 3-2. Growth of world population, Projections One to Five, standard set, 1970–2150 (in absolute numbers and in percentages).

As is generally recognized, it is practically impossible to predict future fertility trends. It is, however, possible to proclaim with absolute certainty that even if there were a significant change of world average fertility, it would certainly not be possible to attain an NRR of 1.0 before 1975. Without doubt, the forecast of Projection One (see Tables A and B, World Total, Standard Set), describes an unattainable situation. Therefore, by the year 2000, world population, in the absence of major catastrophes, will be at least 30% larger than it is now; that is, it will number at least 4.7 billion inhabitants. And by the same reasoning, world population will still be growing in the first half of the next century and will exceed 5.6 to 5.7 billion inhabitants before leveling off, by the year 2100.

With almost the same amount of confidence it seems reasonable to assume that a world NRR of 1.0 will not be reached by the beginning of the 1980s. One can therefore conclude that the population growth forecast by Projection Two of the World Standard Set still may be unrealistically low, although it implies a minimum of 5 billion inhabitants in the world around the year 2000 and a minimum of 6.4 billion by the year 2100.

An assumption of fertility decline to an NRR of 1.0 by the end of this century (Projection Three) seems plausible but not necessarily realistic within lines of current experience and thinking. This implies, for example, that the average number of children would have to decline from a level of almost 5 per family to significantly less than 3 per family by the year 2000. The world crude birth rate, which is estimated to be around 33 at present, would drop to about 20 per 1000 population around the year 2000. If such developments were achieved, that is, if by the end of the century almost all countries throughout the world were to adopt a fertility behavior that is currently typical for many of the developed countries, world population would number at least 6 billion inhabitants around the year 2000. Even this may seem to many an "optimistic" estimate of world population growth in the near future. If the NRR of 1.0 achieved by 2000 were maintained during the twenty-first century a population numbering over 8 billion would be reached by the middle of that century and would stabilize shortly afterward.

If the assumptions underlying Projection Four of the standard set were realized, that is, if an NRR of 1.0 were not reached before the end of the first quarter of the twenty-first century, the size of the world population would be above 6 billion at the beginning of the twenty-first century and then would continue to grow to a level of between 10 and 11 billion inhabitants.

The hypothetical projection that assumes the most gradual fertility decline within the standard set (Projection Five) would yield a world population of around 6.7 billion by the year 2000, a total world population of 14 billion during the second half of the next century, and ultimately, over 15 billion. Yet the fertility decline of this projection, albeit very gradual (NRR = 1.0 by 2040) is not negligible (see Figure 3-3 and Table F, World Total, Standard Set), and it is not without precedent. It is similar to that of currently more developed countries at the beginning of this century; for example, it is similar to the fertility trend of the United States between 1905 and 1940 (Table 3-1).

Even Projection Five assumes fertility and mortality declines that may prove to be unrealistically large. As far as the mortality assumptions are concerned, one can assume with a fair degree of confidence that, at least in the short run, mortality on the average will not increase or remain at current levels; in the long run, however, it is impossible to predict even the direction of mortality trends. With twentieth-century experience of mortality trends in mind, the applied assumptions of mortality decline are conservative. The applied fertility assumptions—even those of Projection Five—are not neces-

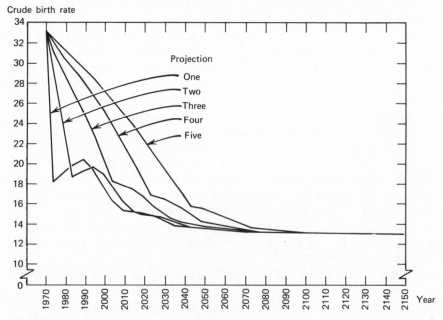

Figure 3-3. Development of crude birth rates of world population, Projections One to Five, standard set, 1970–2150.

sarily an overestimation of real future fertility developments. They might easily be underestimating future fertility levels. According to the "medium" variant of the official United Nations population projections prepared in 1968, the growth of the total world population is between Projection Four and Projection Five (see Table 3-2).

This point is raised to make it clear that we do not consider either Projection Three the most probable path of future demographic developments or Projection Five the maximum limit of future population growth. It is most fortunate that in the absence of major catastrophes it is possible to outline, even though inaccurately, the

Table 3-1   Gross Reproduction Rates (GRR), and Net Reproduction Rates (NRR), United States, Actual, 1905-1940, and World, Assumed, 2005-2040

U.S.: Actual			World: Projection Five		
Period	GRR	NRR	Period	GRR	NRR
1905-1910	1.793	1.336	2005-2010	1.628	1.516
1930-1935	1.108	0.984	2030-2035	1.201	1.158
1935-1940	1.101	0.978	2035-2040	1.116	1.079

Source: U.S. Department of Commerce, Bureau of the Census. *Statistical Abstract of the United States, 1969.* Washington: Government Printing Office, p. 51.

Table 3-2   Size of Total Population According to United Nations "Medium" 1968 Projection and Projections 4 and 5, World, Standard Set, 1965-2000 (in millions)

	1965	1970	1980	1990	2000
U.N. "medium" projection	3289	3632	4457	5438	6494
Projection 4	3289	3645	4436	5378	6422
Projection 5	3289	3645	4460	5473	6670

Sources: United Nations, Population Division. *World Population Prospects, 1965-2000, as Assessed in 1968.* ESA/P/WP.37, 17 December 1970, p. 14. Table F, World, Standard Set.

minimum limits of future world population growth at least for the next, say, two to three decades (see Projections One and Two of World Total, Standard Set). We did not make a similar attempt to delineate maximum limits of future population growth because we found it impossible to assess any maximum limits of average fertility developments for the next few decades. In Chapter 6, however, some population growth consequences of other fertility assumptions are explored, inter alia, the population growth consequences of constant fertility.

As has been demonstrated, Projection Two (Table C, World Total, Standard Set) is still a minimum-limit projection, and the chances of future world population growth taking this course are almost zero. Thus it would be unwise to expect annual average growth rates of the world population to be significantly below 1.0% around the end of this century. Projection Three leads us to believe that the annual growth rates might be in the vicinity of 1.0% by the year 2000. Projections Four and Five indicate that the more gradual assumptions of fertility decline lead to almost no changes in the growth rates of the world population for at least the next two decades (Table G, World Total, Standard Set). According to Projection Four a gradual decline of the growth rate could be expected after 1985; whereas Projection Five suggests a persistence of the 2% annual rates of growth throughout the rest of the twentieth century, with very gradual declines to be expected by the turn of the century.

In terms of annual average increments of population in absolute numbers (Table H, World, Standard Set) the projections indicate that it would not be reasonable to assume any decline of these absolute increments for quite some time. Only according to the minimum-limit projections could one expect that the annual increments of world population would decline below the current level of 60 to 70 million inhabitants per year. Already according to Projection Three one can anticipate a probability of a slight growth of the annual absolute increment of population. Projection Five shows the possibility of these increments increasing quite rapidly throughout the rest of the century—it is quite conceivable that as early as in the 1980s world population would be growing by 100 million persons annually.

A decrease of the world average crude birth rate below the level of 20 during this century does not seem possible. Such a situation could be brought about only if fertility declined so rapidly that the NRR dropped to a 1.0 level by the early 1980s. The fertility decline of Projection Three implies a decrease of about 2 points in the crude birth rate every 5 years; thus around the end of this century the crude birth rate would be in the low 20s. A comparatively slow trend of fertility decline suggests the average world crude birth rate to be in the upper 20s even toward the end of the twentieth century.

Figure 3-3, depicting the crude birth rate trends of the five projections, gives a superficial idea of how the current age structure of the world population is a factor pushing the crude birth rate (and also the growth rate) in an upward direction. This is clearly demonstrated by Projections One and Two. In these the NRR is assumed to reach the 1.0 level during the 1970–75 and 1980–85 periods, respectively, and from then on remain at this level. As a result of the first rapid changes of fertility conditions the crude birth rates naturally would also show an initial rapid decline. However, when the NRR reaches the 1.0 level the crude birth rate does not remain at the attained level. According to Projection One, the crude birth rate would increase by 2 points within 15 years. The young age structure of the world population, which provides for a large influx of women into the childbearing ages, will tend to push the crude birth rates and the average growth rates upward, offsetting declines of the fertility level.

The age structure of any population unit not only influences future growth of the respective population but responds, in turn, to the nature of population growth. In the case of the world population- —provided our estimates are not too far from reality—the 1970 age structure can be labeled as a young one. Probably about 37% of the world population is under 15 and only about 5% so far is 65 years or older (see Figure 3-1). If future fertility and mortality conditions develop along the lines of Projection Five (Table 1, World, Standard Set, and Figure 3-4, the current age structure of the world population will change only very insignificantly for quite a long time. The faster the fertility decline, the larger the changes of the age structure to be expected. Changes of the age structure implied by Projections One and Two are enormous, however unrealistic. According to Projection Two, for example, around the turn of the century roughly 25% of the population will be younger than 15 and 7% older than 65 years.

It would be erroneous to assume that the trend of the crude death rates will be identical in all the projections because the underlying mortality assumptions are the same in all projections. The assumption of declining mortality (expressed in the increase of the expectation of life at birth) is one important factor determining the level and trend of the crude death rates. The other factor of equal significance is the changing age structure. As has been demonstrated, the age structure of the world population not only changes in time but also varies simultaneously from one projection to another. Both elements—the

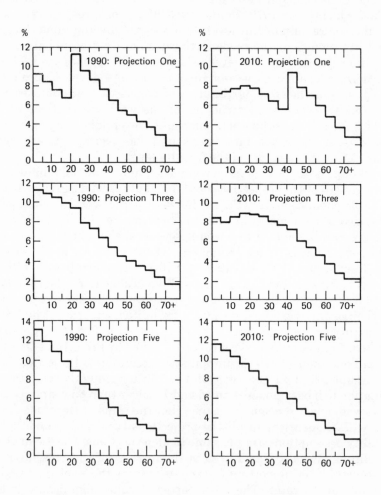

Figure 3–4. Changes of age structure of world population, Projections One, Three, and Five, standard set, 1970–2050.

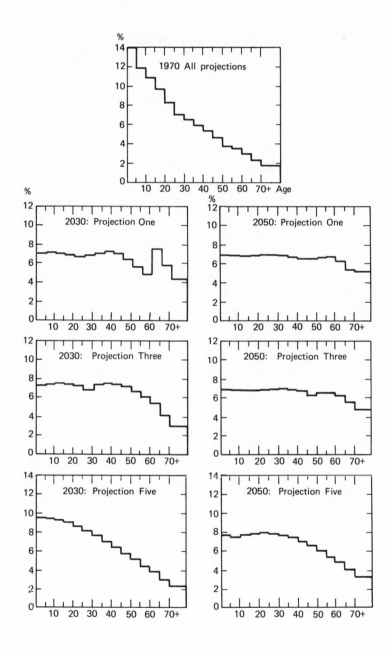

decline of mortality and the age structure changes—have a considerable influence on the level and trend of the crude death rates.

The world average crude death rate will have a tendency to decline in the short run no matter what kind of fertility (and thus age structure) changes occur. Later on—depending on how fast the aging process continues—the crude death rate will increase until it reaches the 13 per thousand level[1] (see Tables B–F, World Total, Standard Set, and Figure 3-5). According to Projection One, the crude death rate will at first decline quite rapidly, but it will not go below 10 per thousand because the effect of an aging population will set in soon afterward and will cause the crude death rate to rise after a comparatively short period of decline. The "temporary" decline of the crude death rate around the middle of the twenty-first century envisaged by this projection is due to the assumed drop in fertility in the early 1970s, which leads to a relatively small cohort of persons being born during the 1970s and reaching the high mortality ages in the middle of the twenty-first century. In other words, in the case of Projection One, the dip in the crude death rate would be a result of age-structure changes, because it is assumed that by the middle of the twenty-first century mortality would reach its lowest level.

Provided world fertility were to decline fairly gradually (Projection Five), the world average crude death rate would decline for quite a long period of time and go as low as 7 to 8 per thousand population. The

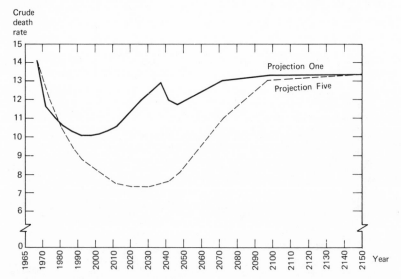

Figure 3–5. Changes of crude death rate of world population, Projections One and Five, 1965–2050.

crude death rate would start to rise when relatively large cohorts reached the older ages and would continue to rise quite rapidly after the middle of the next century in line with a rather fast aging process.

It has been mentioned several times that the projections differ from each other predominantly as a result of varying fertility assumptions. Therefore, the behavior of the individual demographic characteristics and measures are obviously related to the varying fertility assumptions of the individual projections. It might, however, be useful to give an example of how all the demographic phenomena are interrelated. Take, for instance, Projection Two of the World Standard Set. If an NRR of 1.0 were to be attained during the early 1980s, rapid changes in the childbearing behavior would have to take place, especially in the developing countries of the world. Within 10 to 15 years the world population on the average would have to adopt a 2-child family pattern. The average annual growth rate of the world population would rapidly decline from its current 2% to 1%; however, it would remain at 1% for about two decades—roughly throughout the 1980s and 1990s—before a further decrease of the average annual growth rates could be expected. The crude birth rates would take a similar course of rapid decline to 20 per thousand population and remain at this level throughout the rest of this century.

Should we assume the data of Projection Three to materialize, the transition from the current world average of 5 children being born per woman to a global average of 2 children per woman could take 3 decades. In this case, the average annual growth rates would gradually decline, reach the 1% level at the beginning of the twenty-first century, and remain slightly under this level for about two decades. Around 65 to 75 million people would be added to the world population each year throughout the rest of the twentieth century, and by the year 2000 there would be a total of about 6 billion inhabitants. The crude birth rate would also gradually decline, by 4 points each decade, and reach 20 per thousand by the year 2000.

Looking at Projection Three from the vantage point of assessing goals of future population size and future population growth features, one can assert:

- If total world population is not to exceed 6 billion inhabitants in the year 2000, an average world NRR of 1.0 has to be reached around the end of this century.
- If the average annual growth rate of world population is to decrease to a 1% level by the year 2000 and thereafter remain under this level, the average number of children born per woman has to decline quite rapidly—almost by 1 child each

decade. The world population would have to adopt the average 2-child family pattern by the beginning of the twenty-first century. An *average* 2-child family does permit individual variation—provided there is a high proportion of childless women and women with 1 child; other women can bear 3, 4, or more children.

- If a crude birth rate of 20 per thousand population is to prevail throughout the world by the year 2000, the just-mentioned basic condition of a significant decline of average family size (expressed in the achievement of an NRR of 1.0 by the year 2000) has to be reached.

A schematic idea of the interrelationships of future population size and speed of growth on the one hand and short-term changes in the level of fertility and reproduction on the other hand is presented in Table 3-3. It summarizes some important points that have been made. Extremely fast and sharp changes of world average fertility behavior would have to be generated to have a world population of 5 billion or less around the year 2000. If such a fertility decline could be attained at all, world population could settle at about 6 billion inhabitants. Less rapid fertility declines will generate significantly larger population numbers, especially in the long run. Developments along the lines of Projections Three, Four, and Five would generate total population numbers between 5.9 and 6.7 billion for the year 2000. These differences in the total population numbers need not be considered very large. However, the difference in the speed of growth even around the end of this century between, for instance, Projections Five and three is already considerable—a 2.0% as opposed to a 1.2% average annual rate of growth.

The long-term consequences of differences in speed of short-term fertility decline are especially large. The relatively fast fertility decline assumptions of Projection Three would generate a 8.2 and 8.4 billion world population for the years 2050 and 2100, respectively; the moderate fertility decline assumptions of Projection Five would generate a world population of 13.0 and 15.1 billion inhabitants for the year 2050 and 2100.

A general conclusion seems to emerge: short-term growth of the total number of the world population seems to be predetermined to fairly narrow limits; that is, within realistic possibilities, no matter what course of development fertility decline takes in the short run, the differences in numbers of the total population will not be great throughout the next one or two decades. The farther into the future

Table 3-3 Changes of Total World Population, Crude Birth Rates, Average Annual Growth Rates, and Average Annual Increments, Projections 1-5, 1970-2100

Year	Total Population (in billions)	Crude Birth Rate	Average Annual Growth Rate	Average Annual Increment (in millions)	Period	Net Reproduction Rate	Total Fertility Rate
IN 1970	3.6	33	2.0	68	1965-1970	1.9	4.7
IF IN	*CHARACTERISTICS BELOW ARE TO BE ACHIEVED*				*THEN IN*	*RATES BELOW ARE NECESSARY*	
PROJ. 1 2000	4.7	18	0.8	37	1970-1975	1.0	2.5
2050	5.6	14	0.2	9	1980-1985	1.0	2.4
2100	5.7	13	0.0	0	1990-1995	1.0	2.3
PROJ. 2 2000	5.1	19	1.0	49	1970-1975	1.6	3.9
2050	6.3	14	0.1	7	1980-1985	1.0	2.4
2100	6.4	13	0.0	0	1990-1995	1.0	2.3
PROJ. 3 2000	5.9	21	1.2	70	1970-1975	1.8	4.4
2050	8.2	14	0.3	21	1980-1985	1.6	3.7
2100	8.4	13	0.0	0	1990-1995	1.3	2.9
PROJ. 4 2000	6.4	25	1.7	106	1970-1975	1.8	4.5
2050	10.5	14	0.5	50	1980-1985	1.7	4.0
2100	11.2	13	0.0	2	1990-1995	1.6	3.6
PROJ. 5 2000	6.7	28	2.0	124	1970-1975	1.9	4.6
2050	13.0	16	0.8	97	1980-1985	1.8	4.2
2100	15.1	13	0.0	5	1990-1995	1.7	3.9

one looks the bigger the differences can be. The nature of short-term demographic, especially fertility, developments are very significant for the long-term growth of world population. Future population numbers depend heavily on the nature of current static and dynamic demographic properties of the world population.

Many doubts can be expressed concerning the validity of the preceding conclusions and the described alternative trends of world population development due to the heterogeneity of the world population. A small, nevertheless meaningful, first step in answering these doubts is to subject the populations of the more developed regions and of the less developed regions of the world to the same type of analysis that we have just done for the total world population.

A question it might be well to answer at this stage is whether the hypothetical projections of the parts add up to the whole. By and large the answer is yes. Usually the size of the total population at any point in the future differs little from the sum of the parts of the population unit according to the same projection in the same year. This is especially true of Projections One, Two, and Three. It is only in Projection Four and especially Projection Five that the differences become larger. Because most of the differences are trivial, the question shall not be explored further here.[2]

2. POPULATION GROWTH ALTERNATIVES OF THE MORE DEVELOPED REGIONS OF THE WORLD

The overall low level of fertility and mortality in conjunction with the old age structure of the population of the more developed regions are the main reasons why their potential population growth properties are of a distinctly different nature, not only in comparison with the less developed regions but also to the total world population. As a matter of fact, even the standard set of hypothetical projections can and must be interpreted in a different way. Whereas in the instance of the total world population, past and current experience was good enough evidence to identify Projections One and Two as clearly being minimum-level projections, this is certainly not so in the case of the population of the more developed regions.

It can well be imagined that the average NRR of the more developed regions could almost immediately, that is, within a few years, decline to a 1.0 level. An economic, social, political, or environmental crisis or an increased "population growth concern" could very well cause such fertility (and possibly even mortality) developments that the NRR would rapidly drop to the 1.0 value during the early 1970s. Several countries (Japan, Hungary, and Czechoslovakia) did achieve an NRR close to 1.0 during the 1960s. Thus the trends of Projection One can be considered as a realistic alternative for the more developed regions. (The possibility of an immediate cessation of population growth is discussed in Chapter 6.)

Further, Projection One of the standard set for the population of the more developed regions shows that even an immediate decline of the NRR to 1.0 does not entail an immediate cessation of population growth. The general, rapid adoption of the 2-child family pattern in the developed countries would slow down the current speed of population growth from an average annual rate of almost 0.9% to 0.5% for about two decades. However, the population of the more developed regions would probably continue to grow until sometime in the middle of the next century.

A more general observation is the fact that, as far as the developed countries are concerned, any kind of a fertility decline—slow or fast—to a 1.0 NRR would not make a large difference in terms of total population growth throughout the rest of the twentieth century. A rapid fertility decline would generate a population of around 1.3 billion in the year 2000, whereas a slow decline of fertility would generate a population of over 1.4 billion in these countries. Naturally, an unexpected rise in fertility—which is not at all impossible in the developed countries, as many of them actually have pronatalistic (implicit or explicit) population policies—would bring about a population growth well above the numbers outlined by Projection Five. Thus Projection Five is by no means to be considered a maximum-level projection and—as was indicated earlier—Projection One of the standard set cannot be considered a minimum-limit projection for the more developed regions. However, there does seem to be some justification for considering these projections as limits of "reasonable" expectations. This justification is based on the experience of the last 10 to 20 years: considering the population of the more developed countries as a whole, it is unlikely that the NRR will decline below the 1.0 level, because in some countries where this has happened strong pronatalistic countermeasures have been taken. Their overall impact in most countries has not brought large increases in fertility,[3] but neither did fertility decline further. Moreover, in several of the larger developed countries the NRR in the late 1960s was still discernibly above the

1.0.[4] At the same time, precisely in these countries, fertility has been decreasing in recent years; thus far there is no reason to believe that this trend will be reversed. Therefore, provided no unexpected fertility developments occur in these countries, that is, provided that on the average fertility gradually declines further but not significantly beyond the NRR level of 1.0 by the year 2000 there is a good chance that the population of the developed countries will be only 15 to 25% larger than its current size.

The varying fertility decline assumptions of Projections One to Five would yield more obvious differences in population size by the middle of the twenty-first century, when according to the assumptions of an NRR of 1.0 by 1970–75 in Projection One, the population of the more developed regions would be about 27% larger than it is now, but according to Projection Five (NRR = 1.0 in 2040–45) the population of these regions would be 65% above the 1970 size (see Table A, More Developed Regions, Standard Set). According to Projection One, the population of the more developed regions would eventually settle at a level less than 30% larger than its present size, and according to Projection Five it would be almost 75% larger.

It is almost "by definition" that the differences in population growth consequences of alternative paths of fertility decline in the more developed regions of the world will be relatively small because on the average, especially in the major countries, the reproduction levels of these populations are already comparatively close to replacement levels.

The current average annual growth rate of the population of the more developed regions is already under 1%, in fact probably under 0.9% per year. Our set of hypothetical projections indicates that the growth rate probably will not reach the 0.5% level soon (see Table G, More Developed Regions, Standard Set). By the year 2000, however, the growth rate could easily decline below 0.5% and even approach zero by the middle of the twenty-first century.

Our analysis further shows that the average annual absolute increments of the population of the more developed regions are not likely to increase significantly. At present, roughly 9 to 10 million inhabitants are added annually to the population of the developed countries. Even according to Projective Five, which can almost be interpreted as a projection assuming an unchanged level of fertility in the developed countries during the next decade or two, the average, annual, absolute increments of population would rise only slightly above the 10 million level; however, they would remain there for several decades. According to Projection Three, average annual increments of population of the more developed regions would more or less remain at current levels throughout the rest of this century, then start to decline. Projections One and Two indicate an immediate decline of the annual increments of population. According to Projection One, for the most of the next 30 years the absolute annual increments would be in the order of 6 million inhabitants.

No substantial changes in the crude vital rates of population movements seem to be ahead throughout the rest of this century in the more developed regions under the range of assumptions involved in the standard series of the projections. Even if an NRR of 1.0 were attained in the beginning of the 1970s, the crude birth rate would drop by about 3 points but then would remain at the 15 to 16 per thousand population level for over two decades. Possible changes of the crude death rates are even less dramatic. There is a high probability (in the absence of major wars and natural catastrophes and in the absence of a major medical breakthrough, say, in the treatment of heart disease or cancer) that the crude death rate will be very stable for the rest of the century—on the average around 10 per thousand population.[5] During the twenty-first century both the crude birth rates and the crude death rates are likely to settle around 13 per thousand population, provided the NRR stabilizes at the replacement level.

The age structure of the population of the more developed regions is already a comparatively old one. Even the fastest alternative of fertility decline would not bring forth very dramatic changes in the age structure—at least not by the end of the twentieth century; however, the aging of populations of the more developed regions is likely to continue. According to this projection, for all practical purposes a stationary age structure will be attained by the middle of the next century. With such a stationary age structure (i.e., one generated by low mortality and low fertility) each 5-year age group characteristically comprises around 6.3% of the total population up to the age of 50, and thereafter the percentage of each group gradually becomes smaller. The main change such a stationary age distribution would bring is a decrease in the proportion of persons under the age of 25 in favor of those over 50; the proportion of people between the ages of 25 and 50 would be similar to what it is now (see Table I, More Developed Regions, Standard Set, and Figure 3–6).

The following broad conclusions for the population of the more developed regions can be drawn with a fair amount of confidence: the population of the developed countries cannot be expected to stop growing altogether within the next three decades or so; however, the population growth of these countries will be moderate, if fertility and mortality do not deviate significantly from their current level and trends. The total population of the more developed regions will probably be around 20% larger than it is now by the end of this

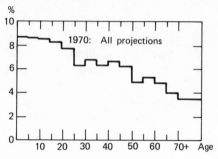

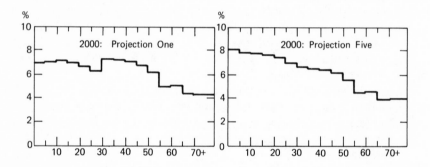

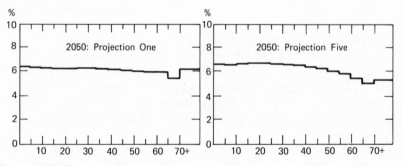

Figure 3–6. Changes of age structure of population of more developed regions, Projections One and Five, standard set, 1970–2050.

century. Provided that during the rest of this century the average childbearing pattern of the population of the more developed countries follows that of the 1960s, it can be assumed that around the middle of the twenty-first century the total population of the more developed countries will not be more than 60% larger than it is now. Indeed, there is a high probability that it will be only 30 to 50% larger than it is in 1970. The population will probably grow from its current total of over 1.1 billion to about 1.5 to 1.7 billion inhabitants by the year 2050. The average annual growth rates, which are currently under 0.9% per year, will probably continue to decline throughout the rest of this century, but there is a high probability that they will not decline below the 0.5% level. Such a decline can be expected around the turn of the century. By the middle of the twenty-first century, even with a very gradual decline of fertility (Projection Five), the average annual growth rates will be negligible. Average annual absolute increments of population in the more developed regions are not likely to be much higher than 10 million per year nor much less than 7 million per year up to the end of this century. A continuation of the aging process can be expected, with over 18% of this population being over 65 years of age by the middle of the twenty-first century compared with the current 10 to 11%.

3. POPULATION GROWTH ALTERNATIVES OF THE LESS DEVELOPED REGIONS OF THE WORLD

In 1970 almost 70% of the world population lived in the less developed regions. No wonder, therefore, that many of the population growth features that have been revealed for the total world population become even more prominent when the population of the less developed regions is analyzed separately.

The inherent growth potential of the two major parts of the world population is such that the proportion of the population currently living in the less developed regions is bound to increase rapidly in the near future (see Table 3-4). By the end of the twentieth century the proportion of the population of the less developed regions will certainly not be less than 75% and might even be close to 80% of the total world population. Various combinations of population growth of the less developed regions and of the more developed regions are depicted in Table 3-4. It is only in the practically impossible combination, that is,

Table 3-4 Changes in Composition of World Population by Development Status, Selected Projections, 1970-2100

	Proj.	1970 Population		2000 Population		2050 Population		2100 Population	
		In Millions	In %	In Millions	In %	In Millions	In %	In Millions	In %
More Developed	1	1122	31	1305	28	1423	26	1427	25
Less Developed	1	2530	69	3427	72	4136	74	4251	75
WORLD TOTAL		3652	100	4732	100	5559	100	5678	100
More Developed	3	1122	31	1388	23	1610	20	1623	19
Less Developed	3	2530	69	4528	77	6525	80	6763	81
WORLD TOTAL		3652	100	5916	100	8135	100	8386	100
More Developed	5	1122	31	1431	21	1853	14	1952	12
Less Developed	5	2530	69	5259	79	11591	86	13863	88
WORLD TOTAL		3652	100	6690	100	13444	100	15815	100
More Developed	1	1122	31	1305	22	1423	18	1427	17
Less Developed	3	2530	69	4528	78	6525	82	6763	83
WORLD TOTAL		3652	100	5833	100	7948	100	8190	100
More Developed	5	1122	31	1431	24	1853	22	1952	22
Less Developed	3	2530	69	4528	76	6525	78	6763	78
WORLD TOTAL		3642	100	5959	100	8378	100	8715	100
More Developed	1	1122	31	1305	20	1423	11	1427	9
Less Developed	5	2530	69	5259	80	11591	89	13863	91
WORLD TOTAL		3652	100	6564	100	13014	100	15290	100

Projection One for both the less developed regions and the more developed regions, that the proportion of the less developed regions is below 75% in the year 2000. In the other projections the proportion of the population of the less developed regions for the year 2000 is between 76% and 80% of the total.

Throughout the twenty-first century the proportion of the "third world" population will increase further. Around the middle of the twenty-first century the proportion of the less developed regions is likely to be between 80 and 90%; and, provided the world population and its major components will stabilize within the limits assumed by our projections, the proportion of the less developed regions will increase only marginally thereafter.

The significance of this trend is that future world population growth will increasingly be determined by the nature of population growth in the less developed regions.

The growth potential of the population of the less developed regions is of an absolutely different order of magnitude from that of the more developed regions (see Table 3-5 and Figure 3-7). Even with a

Table 3-5   Indices of Population Size (1970 = 100), More Developed Regions and Less Developed Regions, Projections 1-5, 1980-2050

Period in Which NRR of 1.0 Is Reached

	1970-1975	1980-1985	2000-2005	2020-2025	2040-2045
	Proj. 1	Proj. 2	Proj. 3	Proj. 4	Proj. 5
More Developed Regions					
1980	105.4	107.3	108.4	108.7	108.9
2000	116.3	119.0	123.7	126.3	127.5
2050	126.8	132.0	143.5	154.7	165.1
Less Developed Regions					
1980	109.3	119.5	125.9	127.7	128.6
2000	135.4	148.8	179.0	198.2	207.9
2050	163.5	188.3	257.9	349.4	458.2

merely negligible fertility decline in the more developed regions, their population would still grow more slowly than the population of the less developed regions, even assuming an inconceivably sharp fertility decline there. The population of the more developed regions—even if it achieved an NRR of 1.0 as late as in the middle of the next century—would grow by less than 30% by the year 2000 and to around

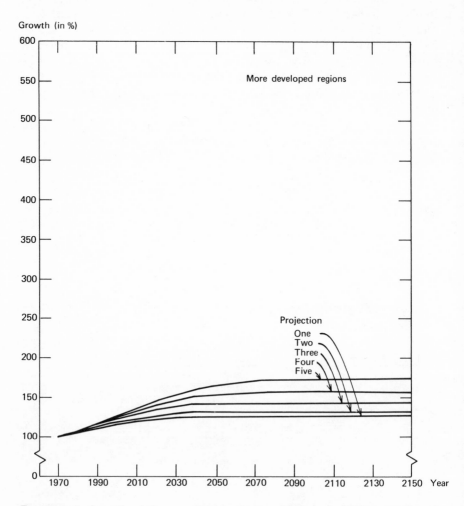

Figure 3–7. Growth of the population of more developed and less developed regions, Projections One to Five, standard set, 1970–2150 (1970 = 100).

70% by the second half of the twenty-first century. Population growth of such a low order is unimaginable for the less developed regions. Even if one would assume that an NRR of unity could be achieved as early as in the 1980s—which is out of the question—their population would grow by about 50% by the year 2000 and by about 90% by the year 2050.

The more plausible alternative population projections of the less developed regions indicate that its population might double in size by

Growth (in %)

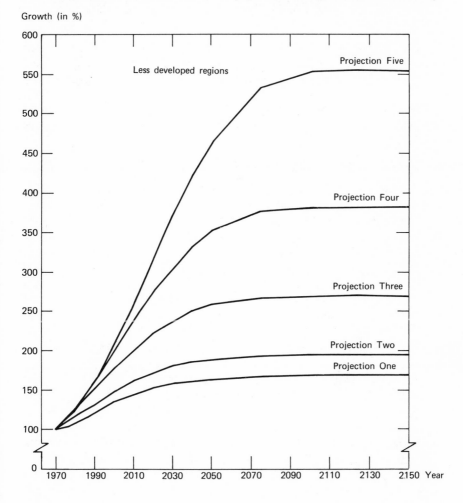

Figure 3–7 (continued).

the end of the current century and that by the middle of the next century a growth factor of 3.5 to 4.5 is more likely than a growth factor of around 2.5.

It is striking that the speed of fertility decline in the less developed regions is the prime determinant of their long-term population growth. This is not so evident when comparing the possible sizes of the population of the less developed regions of Projections Three, Four, and Five for the year 2000, but it becomes very clear later on (see Table A, Standard Set, Less Developed Regions) that:

- Provided a fairly rapid fertility decline takes place throughout the rest of the twentieth century and the less developed regions achieve an average NRR of 1.0 by the year 2000, the population of the less developed regions in the year 2000 will be only about 80% larger than in 1970, and by the middle of the twenty-first century it will be about 2.5 times larger than it is now.
- Provided a less rapid, nevertheless meaningful, fertility decline occurs and the less developed regions achieved an NRR of unity around the year 2020, then their total population would be about 2.0 and 3.5 times the current size by the year 2000 and 2050,
- With a rather moderate, nevertheless not improbable, fertility decline, and assuming these regions achieve an NRR of unity around the middle of the twenty-first century, the less developed regions would more than double their populations by the year 2000; by the second half of the next century this population might reach 4 to 5 times its current

One implication of the above findings cannot be stressed enough: long-term population growth of the less developed regions depends heavily upon fertility changes of the near future. This is so because current high fertility is producing future large stocks of child bearers. Even if fertility is drastically reduced, say, at the beginning of the twenty-first century, large cohorts of child bearers produced as a result of high fertility in the 1970s and 1980s will ensure fast population growth. A rapid fertility decline can provide such conditions that the population of the less developed regions will not necessarily be larger than 2.5 times its current size by the year 2050. If, however, the fertility decline of these regions during the next two to three decades is slow, their population will reach 3.5 to 4.5 or more times its current size. (Of course, constant fertility, that is, no decline, would bring about even larger populations.) It seems most improbable that the population of the less developed regions will ultimately be less than double its 1970 size, because this would require an NRR of unity to be reached in the early 1980s and to settle down at this level. The absolute impossible is expressed by Projection One, which is based on the assumption that an NRR of 1.0 is reached immediately, that is, in the early 1970s.

The above trends of population growth could be influenced by unexpected mortality trends. It is possible, for example, that mortality in some parts of the less developed regions will not decline to the current levels of the more developed regions or might even increase as a result of political frictions, lack of food, ecological disasters, epidemics, and so on. Whether this would be directly treaceable to any disequilibrium caused originally by fast population growth will probably always be disputable.

The average annual growth rates of the population of the less developed regions are currently around 2.5% (see Table G, Standard Set, Less Developed Regions). If fertility in the less developed regions declines slowly (Projection Five), the annual growth rates will remain practically unchanged for two decades or so. In this case, the growth rates will still be above 2.0% during the beginning of the twenty-first century. According to the assumptions of Projection Three (NRR = 1.0 by the year 2000) the annual population growth rates will not decline below 2% before the late 1980s and at the beginning of the next century will still be above 1.0%. To expect a decline of the annual growth rate in the less developed regions below the 1% level before the beginning of the next century is out of the question, as indicated by Projections One and Two.

The average annual increment of the population of the less developed regions is about 60 million persons at present. The absolute increments can undoubtedly be expected to increase, at least in the near future. According to the "optimistic" assumptions of Projection Three, the annual increments will probably increase to the 70 million level in the 1980s, and after that will start to decline quite rapidly to the 50 million level at the beginning of the next century, where they will stay for about two decades. According to Projections Four and Five, the increases of the annual average increments will be quite substantial. As a matter of fact, the moderate fertility decline of

Projection Five implies a doubling of the annual increments by the beginning of the twenty-first century.[6] These increments would remain at a high level for most of the first half of the twenty-first century and only toward the middle of that century start to decline.

Unless average fertility levels throughout the less developed areas of the world remain practically constant—which does not seem to be the most probable path of future development—meaningful changes of the crude birth and death rates can be expected to occur. In other words, real events indicate, and there exists a fairly general consent about the fact, that the developing countries will undergo a demographic transition. It is not at all clear to what extent this transition will resemble the demographic transition of the currently more developed countries—where, as is generally acknowledged, there are also several variations. That the demographic transition of most of the less developed countries is going to be different from that of the more developed countries seems to be fairly obvious. On the average, death rates are currently at a relatively low level and, because they are coupled with birth rates of a relatively high level, in many less developed countries population growth rates are or will be of an unprecedented magnitude. Thus, provided that we accept the future occurrence of the demographic transition in the less developed regions as a working hypothesis, the question remains whether this transition is going to be fast or slow. Since we have dismissed Projections One and Two (NRR = 1.0 by 1970–75 and 1980–85, respectively) as being unrealistic, we can consider Projection Three (NRR = 1.0 by 2000–05) as an appropriate illustration of a fast demographic transition of the less developed regions and Projection Five (NRR = 1.0 by 2040–45) as a fair example of a comparatively slow demographic transition in the less developed regions.

The future demographic transition of the less developed regions will be, by definition, expressed more pungently in the trend of the crude birth rates than in that of the crude death rates, because the latter have already advanced a not insignificant distance along the lines of the demographic transition. In the event that Projection Three became the reality for these regions the crude birth rate would decrease rapidly, as depicted in Figure 3-8. This would be the result of significant changes in childbearing behavior (see Table D, Standard Set, Less Developed Regions).

The decline of the crude birth rate envisioned by Projection Five is slower but still not insignificant (see Table F, Standard Set, Less Developed Regions, and Fig. 3-8).

The decline of the crude death rates during the rest of the

twentieth century would be fairly similar, irrespective of whether Projection Three or Projection Five became the reality.[3] However, the crude death rates would decline over a longer time and to a lower level and, during the first half of the twenty-first century, would start

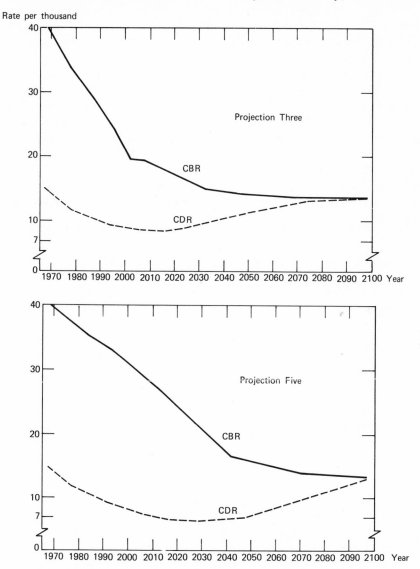

Figure 3–8. Crude birth rates (CBR) and crude death rates (CDR), less developed regions, Projections Three and Five, 1965–2100.

increasing considerably later according to Projection Five than according to Projection Three, because of differing changes of the age structure of the populations.

A natural result of the differing changes in the crude birth rate and the crude death rate according to Projection Three and Projection Five is significantly different rates of natural increase. These rates would be considerably larger if future events proceed as outlined by Projection Five than if by Projection Three.

The age structure of the population of the less developed regions is currently a very young one. Almost 42% of the population is under 15 years of age (see Table I, Standard Set, Less Developed Regions and Table 3-6), and only around 3% of the population is over 65 years of age; the median age of the population is about 19 years. Obviously the speed of the aging process of this population will depend on the speed of fertility decline in these less developed regions. A faster fertility decline will cause a faster aging of the population. Nevertheless, in comparison with the more developed regions, the population of the less developed regions will remain a young one throughout the rest of the

Table 3-6   Age Structure of the Population of Less Developed Regions (in percentages and in millions), Projections 3 and 5, 1970-2030

	0-14		15-44		45+	
	Proj. 3	Proj. 5	Proj. 3	Proj. 5	Proj. 3	Proj. 5
In Percentages						
1970	41.6	41.6	42.9	42.9	15.5	15.5
1985	38.2	40.7	45.3	43.5	16.5	15.8
2000	31.4	38.2	49.2	45.1	19.4	16.7
2015	24.8	34.8	49.5	46.2	25.7	19.0
2030	22.8	30.4	44.1	47.0	33.1	22.6
In Millions						
1970	1052	1052	1087	1087	391	391
1985	1349	1498	1601	1601	583	583
2000	1423	2011	2229	2372	876	876
2015	1318	2514	2626	3335	1367	1367
2030	1366	2829	2642	4376	1982	2111

twentieth century. Even according to the "optimistic" assumptions of Projection Three—which anticipates substantial changes in the age structure of the less developed regions—in the year 2000 over 30% of the population will still be under 15 years of age. According to Projection Five the proportion of the lowest age groups will be decreasing at an even slower rate.

An important feature of the probable age structure changes is that there will be a transitory stage between the typical young and old age structure in which there will be an unusually large proportion of middle-aged people. Whether this will be considered a fortunate or unfortunate state of affairs will depend on the prevailing social conditions. What is clear from a formal demographic point of view is that this will entail a decrease in the proportion of dependent people, an increase in the proportion of the potential labor force, and a high proportion of women in their childbearing ages.[7] Eventually, for all practical purposes, the age structure of the population of the less developed regions should become very similar to the age structure of the population of the more developed regions.

NOTES

1. This is the level predetermined by the given mortality level (female $e_0^0 =$ 75.0) and the chosen reproduction rate (NRR = 1.0) once the population attains the features of a stationary population.

2. Some of the problems and considerations involved are as follows: Theoretically, the correct way of computing our projections would have been to compute projections of the smallest population units and add these up to the higher aggregates (countries into regions, major areas, development status areas, world). If such a procedure were used, by definition there would not have been the fact of sums of parts not equaling the aggregates. Such a procedure is, however, not possible if for no other reason than we do not have data for all countries.

   Once separate projections are made for parts and aggregates, some differences are inevitable, because all the inputs of the projections cannot be properly apportioned. For example, the mortality assumptions for the year 2000 are $e_0^0 = 68.0$ for the world, 76.0 for the more developed regions, and 63.5 for the less developed regions. The estimate of the world e_0^0 should, however, be weighed by the proportions of the population in the more developed regions and less developed regions in the year 2000; but since projections are not yet computed at the time when assumptions are assessed it is not possible to weigh the components of the assumptions.

   In order to be able to compute and publish all the information (the time series of the vital rates, reproduction rates, age structure) the theoretically correct way of computing the projections would have required infinitely more work and resources (especially computer time), which would not justify the trivial improvements in the quality of the projections.

In conclusion, the trends and interrelationships provided by the separate projections for the aggregates are absolutely sufficient for the purposes of this study, that is, as illustrations of the differing population growth consequences of varying fertility and mortality assumptions for different populations.

3. Romania seems to be an exception, at least in the short run, that is, a time horizon of 2 to 4 years. Romania's drastic revision of the abortion legislation can be considered an extreme case, which, in addition, was not expected by the public.

4. See *United Nations Demographic Yearbook 1969*, pp. 474–476.

5. This does not mean that in individual countries or areas it cannot be substantially higher. For instance, in West Berlin—because of the old age structure of the population—the crude death rate is approaching the 20 per thousand population level (*United Nations Demographic Yearbook, 1969*, pp. 586.)

6. It is necessary to call attention to the fact that the data on the average annual increments of Projection Five for the less developed regions after the turn of the century reflect one of the shortcomings of the projections. As pointed out earlier, the summations of parts of a specific population unit do not always correspond to the projections of the respective population unit, and this fact applies especially to Projection Five. In the case of the average annual increments, the marginal nature of these data make this shortcoming conspicuous. Thus not only do the average annual increments of the more developed regions and the less developed regions for the same period and projection not add up to the respective annual average increment of the world population, but in Projection Five in the middle of the twenty-first century the average annual increments of the less developed regions are somewhat larger than the corresponding increments of the world population, although the increments of the more developed regions are not negative. Nevertheless, even in this case the trends indicated by the data are certainly in the correct direction; they are not misleading but merely imperfect.

7. Note that a higher proportion, say, of the population between 15 and 44 in Projection Three in the year 2000 compared with Projection Five in the same year does not mean that the absolute number of population according to Projection Three would be higher than in Projection Five (see Table 3-6). On the contrary, the absolute numbers of all age groups grow faster or at least not slower in Projection Five than in Projection Three and so, for instance, in the year 2000 the 15-to-44 age group would be about 6 to 7% larger according to Projection Five than according to Projection Three (2370 million as opposed to 2230 million persons).

4 Population Growth Alternatives of the Major Areas

AN ABSTRACT OF FINDINGS

Many of the major areas are demographically relatively homogeneous. They consist either of more developed or less developed countries. The three exceptions are East Asia, Latin America, and Oceania. The fertility indicators of Table 4-1 illustrate this point quite distinctly. For example, the gross reproduction rate (GRR) in Europe, U.S.S.R. and North America is between 1.2 and 1.4; in Oceania, East Asia, and Latin America it is 1.7, 2.2, and 2.7, respectively, and in South Asia, and Africa, 3.0 and 3.1.

The crude birth rates range from 17 to 19 per thousand population in the more developed major areas and from 38 to 45 in the less developed major areas. In Oceania, where most of the population lives in the more developed countries, the birth rate is 24 per thousand population; on the other hand, in East Asia and Latin America, where the majority of the population lives in countries that are classified as less developed, the birth rate is 34 and 38 per thousand, respectively.

Table 4-1 Basic Demographic Measures of the Eight Major Areas, 1965-1970

	Female Crude Birth Rate	Female Crude Death Rate	Total Fertility Rate	Gross Reproduction Rate	Net Reproduction Rate	Total Population at End of Period (in thousands)	Female Average Annual Rate of Growth (in %)	Female Expectation of Life at Birth
WORLD TOTAL	33	13	4.7	2.3	1.9	3645[a]	2.0	56.5
MORE DEVELOPED REGIONS	18	10	2.7	1.3	1.3	1122	0.9	72.5
LESS DEVELOPED REGIONS	41	15	5.7	2.8	2.1	2530	2.6	51.0
EAST ASIA	34	13	4.5	2.2	1.7	941	2.0	54.5
SOUTH ASIA	43	15	6.2	3.0	2.2	1103	2.8	51.0
EUROPE	18	11	2.7	1.3	1.2	474	0.7	73.0
U.S.S.R.	17	9	2.5	1.2	1.2	260	0.8	72.5
AFRICA	45	20	6.4	3.1	2.1	344	2.5	44.5
NORTH AMERICA	19	9	2.9	1.4	1.3	228	1.0	72.5
LATIN AMERICA	38	9	5.5	2.7	2.3	283	2.9	62.5
OCEANIA	24	10	3.5	1.7	1.6	19	1.4	68.5

[a]Summations of major areas and/or of more developed regions and less developed regions do not equal world total (for details see note 2 of Chapter 3).

A similar but not so conspicuous distinction can be observed in the levels of mortality (female e_0^0). As a matter of fact (provided current estimates are close to reality), mortality is probably higher in East Asia than it is in Latin America.

The crude death rates for most of the major areas are between 9 and 11 per thousand population. The crude death rates for East and South Asia are not too much higher. However, the crude death rate of Africa is double that of the more developed regions. For example, the crude death rate of Europe (and Oceania) is higher than that of Latin America, although the expectation of life is quite distinctly lower in Latin America, because of quite different age structures in these two major areas. The small differences of the crude death rates between most of the major areas reflect the interaction of the mortality levels and the age structures. Usually, higher levels of mortality (low e_0^0) are coupled with young age distributions and vice versa, and therefore the crude death rates are pulled downward in the former and upward in the latter. Compare also, North America and Latin America: the level of mortality as indicated by the e_0^0 is distinctly different, and yet the crude death rate is the same, evidently because of differences of the age structures.

Because mortality (especially the crude death rate) has been decreasing in recent decades and because fertility in most less developed countries has changed much less, if at all, there is a great difference between the population growth rates of the individual major areas. The annual rates of natural increase in the major areas with exclusively or predominantly more developed countries are between 0.7% and 1.4%; whereas in the major areas with exclusively or mainly less developed countries these rates range from 2.0% to 2.9% per year.

As was indicated in Chapters 1 and 2 the current demographic properties of populations will undoubtedly be instrumental in shaping future population growth, and this will make itself visible also in the global distribution of population. Both of these items are dealt with below.

It should again be brought to the reader's attention that there are certain discrepancies between the projections of the total world population and the summations of the projections of the populations of the major areas (see Table 4-2). The order of difference seems to be of a "permissible" size. Some reasons for the discrepancies have been listed in footnote 2 of the previous chapter.

In conjunction with Table 4-3, one can compare the population growth potential of the major areas. A general observation about the

Table 4-2 Population Growth of Eight Major Areas and a Comparison with the Independent Projections of World Population Growth (in millions), Projections 1-5, 1965-2150

| | Major Areas | | | | | | | | Sum of Major Areas | World Population | Difference | |
	A East Asia	B South Asia	C Europe	D USSR	E Africa	F North America	G Latin America	H Oceania			In Absolute Numbers	In %
						Projection 1						
1965	852	981	445	230	303	214	246	18	3289	3289	0	0.0
1980	1026	1207	490	275	373	243	316	20	3950	3933	17	0.4
2000	1229	1522	527	302	464	277	405	23	4749	4746	3	0.1
2050	1448	1854	565	327	565	312	494	27	5592	5592	0	0.0
2100	1482	1889	566	328	582	313	503	27	5690	5691	-1	0.0
2150	1480	1886	566	327	581	312	502	27	5681	5684	-3	-0.1
						Projection 2						
1965	852	981	445	230	303	214	246	18	3289	3289	0	0.0
1980	1091	1333	499	278	409	249	348	21	4228	4213	15	0.4
2000	1314	1687	540	307	510	286	447	25	5116	5116	0	0.0
2050	1605	2163	589	335	649	329	575	29	6274	6286	-12	-0.2
2100	1647	2211	591	336	671	331	588	30	6405	6417	-12	-0.2
2150	1645	2207	591	336	670	330	587	30	6396	6407	-11	-0.2
						Projection 3						
1965	852	981	445	230	303	214	246	18	3289	3289	0	0.0
1980	1130	1413	504	279	432	253	367	21	4399	4387	12	0.3
2000	1485	2079	561	314	620	302	540	27	5928	5922	6	0.1
2050	2002	3077	641	353	899	368	797	35	8172	8172	0	0.0
2100	2062	3166	645	355	934	372	823	36	8393	8389	4	0.1
2150	2060	3163	645	355	933	372	824	36	8388	8382	6	0.1

Table 4-2 (continued)

	Major Areas										Difference	
	A East Asia	B South Asia	C Europe	D USSR	E Africa	F North America	G Latin America	H Oceania	Sum of Major Areas	World Population	In Absolute Numbers	In %
Projection 4												
1965	852	981	445	230	303	214	246	18	3289	3289	0	0.0
1980	1141	1436	505	280	439	254	372	22	4449	4436	13	0.3
2000	1592	2339	572	318	693	310	598	28	6450	6422	28	0.4
2050	2487	4350	692	371	1244	406	1077	41	10668	10473	195	1.9
2100	2647	4711	708	376	1351	418	1172	43	11426	11169	257	2.3
2150	2646	4709	708	376	1350	418	1174	43	11424	11165	259	2.3
Projection 5												
1965	852	981	445	230	303	214	246	18	3289	3289	0	0.0
1980	1146	1447	506	280	442	255	375	22	4473	4460	13	0.3
2000	1646	2469	578	320	729	315	626	29	6712	6670	42	0.6
2050	3011	5916	739	387	1664	444	1396	47	13604	13025	579	4.4
2100	3448	7170	778	401	2003	475	1683	52	16010	15102	908	6.0
2150	3456	7196	779	401	2008	476	1696	53	16065	15148	917	6.1

data of Projection One is that in any major area even with the immediate achievement of a net reproduction rate (NRR) of 1.0 some population growth follows. As was pointed out earlier, however, to bring about an NRR of 1.0 within the next few years might be quite feasible for any population unit that has passed through the whole or a part of the demographic transition but is out of the question for population units that have yet to make a more or less substantial part

Table 4-3   Indices of Population Size (1970 = 100) of Eight Major Areas, Projections 1-5, 1970-2150

	A East Asia	B South Asia	C Europe	D USSR	E Africa	F North America	G Latin America	H Oceania	World
				Projection 1					
1970	100	100	100	100	100	100	100	100	100
2000	131	138	111	116	135	122	143	126	130
2050	154	168	119	126	164	137	174	145	153
2100	157	171	119	126	169	137	177	147	156
2150	157	171	119	126	169	137	177	147	156
				Projection 2					
1970	100	100	100	100	100	100	100	100	100
2000	140	153	114	118	148	125	158	133	140
2050	171	196	124	129	188	144	203	158	172
2100	175	201	125	129	195	145	207	160	176
2150	175	200	125	129	195	145	207	160	176
				Projection 3					
1970	100	100	100	100	100	100	100	100	100
2000	158	189	118	121	180	132	191	146	162
2050	213	279	135	136	261	162	281	189	224
2100	219	287	136	137	271	163	291	193	230
2150	219	287	136	137	271	163	291	193	230
				Projection 4					
1970	100	100	100	100	100	100	100	100	100
2000	169	212	121	122	201	136	211	153	176
2050	264	394	146	143	362	178	380	222	287
2100	281	427	149	145	392	184	414	233	306
2150	281	427	149	145	392	184	415	233	306
				Projection 5					
1970	100	100	100	100	100	100	100	100	100
2000	175	224	122	123	212	138	221	156	183
2050	320	536	156	149	483	195	493	254	357
2100	367	650	164	154	582	209	594	282	414
2150	367	653	164	154	583	209	599	283	416

of that transition. Hence one can say that Projection One may describe the lower, "optimistic" limit of population growth for the areas that consist of more developed countries, predominantly (or exclusively), and Projection Three, for the areas that consist of less developed countries mainly (or wholly) (see the left section of Figure 4-1).

From the above it is possible to make the following observations. The population growth potential of Europe and the Soviet Union is of the lowest order of magnitude, and it is possible that the population of these areas will not grow more than by about 20 to 30% over its current size during the next 50 or so years. The population growth potential of North America is slightly larger, and its population might expand about 30 to 40% within the next 50 to 70 years. One has to be somewhat more cautious with a similar conjecture for Oceania because roughly one-quarter of its current population lives in less developed countries; nevertheless, with this in mind a reasonable interpretation of the data might be that the population of Oceania could grow by 50% or more during the coming 50 to 70 years. The major area of East Asia can also be considered a heterogeneous area because, at least from a demographic point of view, around 20% of its population is (or will soon be) living in developed countries. If we do apply Projection Three as an indicator of the minimum of the population growth potential of this area the message is that its population need not more than double during the coming 50 to 100 years. As far as South Asia, Africa, and Latin America are concerned, it is reasonable to anticipate that their populations could triple during the next 50 to 100 years (provided mortality continues to fall and this trend is not reversed in the future).

A further interpretation of the data in Table 4-3 is that the population of Europe and the Soviet Union is not likely to grow by more than about 50 to 60% during the first half of the next century unless an unexpected significant upward turn occurs in fertility trends. Similarly, a growth factor of around 2.0 to 2.5 seems to be a reasonable upper estimate for the populations of North America and Oceania for most of the next century. It is not at all unrealistic, however, to assume that the population of East Asia, that is, Mainland China, might become three to four times its current size within the next century. Finally, South Asia, Africa, and Latin America may easily reach four to six times their current size within the next 100 years (see Figure 4-1).

It might be worthwhile to give two examples of the nature of the changes that are likely to occur:

1. Even if most populations grow along the "optimistic" lines of Projection Three, by the year 2000 the combined population of East

and South Asia would be as large as that of the entire world now.

2. In 1965 the populations of the Soviet Union, Africa, North America, and Latin America were each between 200 and 300 million inhabitants. By the middle of the next century the population of Africa and of Latin America probably will each be two to four times larger than that of the Soviet Union or North America at that time.

Naturally such unevenness in speed of population growth will

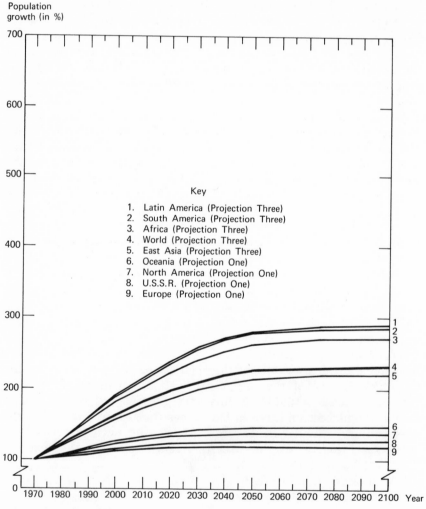

Figure 4–1. Possible low and high paths to future population growth (in %) (1970 100), by major areas, 1970–2100.

make itself visible in a changing relative distribution of population over the globe (see Table 4-4). For an illustration of the trends of changes in the spatial distribution of the world population resulting from the differing potentials of natural increase (i.e., not taking into account any possible major migratory movement) one can consult Projection Four. Should future population growth proceed along the lines of this projection, which is quite possible, the proportion of the population living in South Asia, Africa, and Latin America would

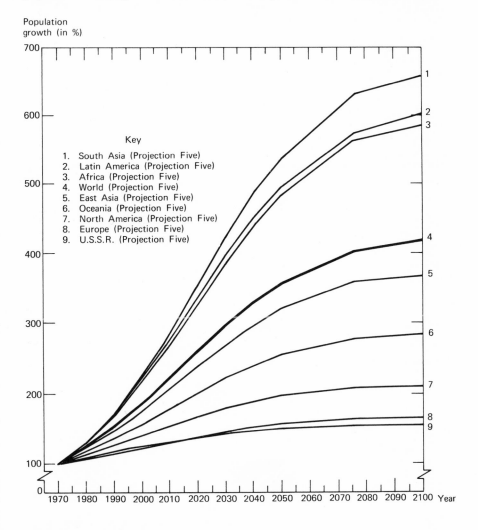

Population growth (in %)

Key
1. South Asia (Projection Five)
2. Latin America (Projection Five)
3. Africa (Projection Five)
4. World (Projection Five)
5. East Asia (Projection Five)
6. Oceania (Projection Five)
7. North America (Projection Five)
8. Europe (Projection Five)
9. U.S.S.R. (Projection Five)

Figure 4–1 (continued).

increase from about 30 to 40%, 9 to 12%, and 7 to 10% of the world total, respectively (see Figure 4-2). The proportion of the population living in East Asia may become even slightly smaller than it is currently, and this might also be true for Oceania. The proportion of the population of Europe, the Soviet Union, and North America would decrease quite visibly: from 14 to 6%, from almost 8 to 4%, and from almost 7 to between 4 and 5%, respectively.

Table 4-4   The Distribution of World Population into Eight Major Areas, Projections 1-5, 1965-2150 (in %)

	A East Asia	B South Asia	C Europe	D USSR	E Africa	F North America	G Latin America	H Oceania	Sum of Major Areas
				Projection 1					
1965	25.8	29.1	13.9	7.6	9.2	6.6	7.4	0.5	100.0
1980	26.0	30.5	12.4	7.0	9.4	6.2	8.0	0.5	100.0
2000	25.9	32.0	11.1	6.4	9.8	5.8	8.5	0.5	100.0
2050	25.9	33.2	10.1	5.8	10.1	5.6	8.8	0.5	100.0
2100	26.0	33.2	10.0	5.8	10.2	5.5	8.8	0.5	100.0
2150	26.0	33.2	10.0	5.8	10.2	5.5	8.8	0.5	100.0
				Projection 2					
1965	25.8	29.1	13.9	7.6	9.2	6.6	7.4	0.5	100.0
1980	25.8	31.5	11.8	6.6	9.7	5.9	8.2	0.5	100.0
2000	25.7	33.0	10.5	6.0	10.0	5.6	8.7	0.5	100.0
2050	25.6	34.5	9.4	5.3	10.3	5.2	9.2	0.5	100.0
2100	25.7	34.5	9.2	5.2	10.5	5.2	9.2	0.5	100.0
2150	25.7	34.5	9.2	5.2	10.5	5.2	9.2	0.5	100.0
				Projection 3					
1965	25.8	29.1	13.9	7.6	9.2	6.6	7.4	0.5	100.0
1980	25.7	32.1	11.4	6.4	9.8	5.8	8.3	0.5	100.0
2000	25.0	35.1	9.5	5.3	10.5	5.1	9.1	0.4	100.0
2050	24.5	37.7	7.8	4.3	11.0	4.5	9.8	0.4	100.0
2100	24.6	37.7	7.7	4.3	11.1	4.4	9.8	0.4	100.0
2150	24.6	37.7	7.7	4.3	11.1	4.4	9.8	0.4	100.0
				Projection 4					
1965	25.8	29.1	13.9	7.6	9.2	6.6	7.4	0.5	100.0
1980	25.6	32.3	11.3	6.3	9.9	5.7	8.4	0.5	100.0
2000	24.7	36.3	8.9	4.9	10.7	4.8	9.3	0.4	100.0
2050	23.3	40.8	6.5	3.5	11.6	3.8	10.1	0.4	100.0
2100	23.2	41.2	6.2	3.3	11.8	3.6	10.3	0.4	100.0
2150	23.2	41.2	6.2	3.3	11.8	3.6	10.3	0.4	100.0
				Projection 5					
1965	25.8	29.1	13.9	7.6	9.2	6.6	7.4	0.5	100.0
1980	25.6	32.3	11.3	6.3	9.9	5.7	8.4	0.5	100.0
2000	24.5	36.8	8.6	4.8	10.9	4.7	9.3	0.4	100.0
2050	22.1	43.5	5.4	2.8	12.2	3.3	10.3	0.4	100.0
2100	21.5	44.8	4.9	2.5	12.5	3.0	10.5	0.3	100.0
2150	21.5	44.8	4.8	2.5	12.5	3.0	10.6	0.3	100.0

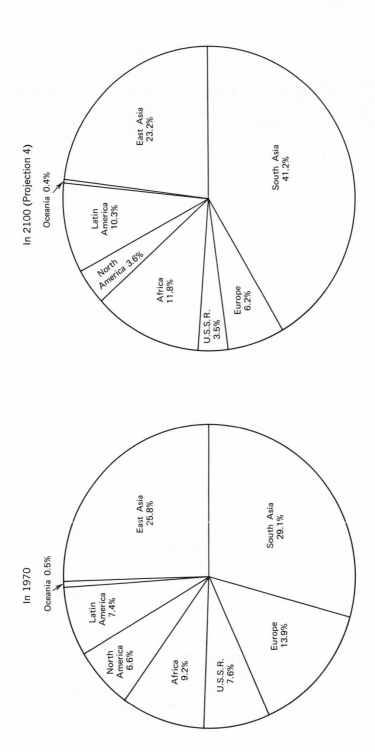

Figure 4–2. World population, proportions by major areas, actual (1970) possible (2100).

5 Population Growth Alternatives of Selected Countries

It is not possible to discuss in detail the population growth alternatives in every country. This chapter merely gives a rough idea of the kind of developments that could occur within the major areas. The preceding chapter sketched hypothetical trends and interrelations, with each major area acting as a unit. The present chapter is a reminder that a continent, major area, or any other supranational region is an artifact consisting of national populations whose developments may vary significantly.

Since the possible paths toward stationarity depend significantly on the contemporary demographic features of nations, these are at first briefly touched upon, and thereafter potential trends of a few typical national populations are discussed. The reader may take notice only of the section that is of interest to him, and bypass the other sections. The detailed projections of national populations as listed in Section 5,

Chapter 2, are published in a separate volume and are also available separately for each country upon request from the Population Council.

1. POPULATION GROWTH ALTERNATIVES OF COUNTRIES OF EUROPE, THE U.S.S.R., NORTH AMERICA, AND OTHER MORE DEVELOPED COUNTRIES

Almost all the more developed countries have—by world standards —arrived at a demographic situation of low fertility and low mortality (Tables 5-1 and 5-2). Within the major areas named in the title of this section there are some exceptional countries, such as Albania, and even within large countries there are certain regions, such as the Soviet Central Asian Republics, or ethnic or cultural groups with relatively high fertility and occasionally even above-average mortality. However, during the 1960s most of these demographically pretransitional populations seem to have started to experience a fertility decline. In this section we omit such countries as Albania or Chile, which are formally considered to be a part of the demographically more developed countries, inclusion of which would bring confusion to the overall analysis.

The gross reproduction rates (GRR) of the more developed countries are in the order of 1.0 to 1.4, and none of these countries seems to have a crude birth rate above 20 per thousand population. The female life expectancies are almost all above 72.0 years, and the crude death rates range from about 7 to 13 per thousand population.

Annual rates of natural increase are around 0.4% in countries that have a history of low fertility and therefore have "older" populations, and around 1.0%, for instance, in countries where the post-World War II baby boom was of a more sustained nature or where fertility is still relatively high.

It is interesting to observe two absolutely opposed viewpoints regarding future population growth that have been voiced in several more developed countries (and occasionally in a single country):

1. Population growth is considered to aggravate many aspects of life—environmental pollution, depletion of resources, urban congestion, among others—and it is therefore postulated as desirable that population growth be halted as soon as possible. An articulate new organization with such views in the United States has even adopted the name Zero Population Growth (ZPG).

2. Governments and/or individuals of some developed countries

Table 5-1 Basic Demographic Measures for Selected Regions and Countries of Europe, 1965-1970

	Female Crude Birth Rate	Female Crude Death Rate	Total Fertility Rate	Gross Reproduction Rate	Net Reproduction Rate	Total Population in 1970 (in millions)	Female Average Annual Rate of Growth (in %)	Female Expectation of Life at Birth
C. EUROPE	18	11	2.7	1.3	1.2	474	0.7	73.0
C.7. WESTERN EUROPE	17	12	2.7	1.3	1.3	152	0.5	73.5
German Fed. Rep.	16	12	2.5	1.2	1.2	63	0.4	73.5
France	16	12	2.6	1.3	1.3	51	0.5	73.5
Netherlands	19	8	2.8	1.4	1.3	13	1.1	76.5
Belgium	15	12	2.4	1.2	1.1	10	0.3	73.5
Austria	16	13	2.6	1.3	1.2	8	0.3	73.5
C.8. SOUTHERN EUROPE	19	9	2.7	1.3	1.2	132	1.0	72.0
Italy	17	9	2.5	1.2	1.1	56	0.8	73.5
Yugoslavia	19	9	2.6	1.3	1.1	21	1.0	66.5
Greece	17	8	2.4	1.2	1.1	9	0.9	74.0
Albania	35	9	5.6	2.7	2.4	2	2.7	67.0
C.9. EASTERN EUROPE	17	10	2.5	1.2	1.2	107	0.7	72.5
Poland	16	8	2.3	1.1	1.1	34	0.8	73.0
Czechoslovakia	15	10	2.1	1.0	1.0	15	0.4	73.5
Hungary	14	11	2.0	1.0	0.9	11	0.3	72.0
C.10. NORTHERN EUROPE	17	12	2.7	1.3	1.3	83	0.5	74.0
England & Wales	16	12	2.6	1.3	1.2	50	0.4	75.0
Sweden	15	11	2.3	1.1	1.1	8	0.4	76.0
Denmark	18	10	2.6	1.3	1.2	5	0.8	75.0
Ireland	22	11	3.9	1.9	1.8	3	1.1	72.5

Table 5-2 Basic Demographic Measures for Non-European Demographically Developed Regions and Countries, 1965-1970

	Female Crude Birth Rate	Female Crude Death Rate	Total Fertility Rate	Gross Reproduction Rate	Net Reproduction Rate	Total Population in 1970 (in millions)	Female Average Annual Rate of Growth (in %)	Female Expectation of Life at Birth
A.2. *JAPAN*	18	7	2.1	1.0	1.0	106	1.1	73.5
D.11. *U.S.S.R.*	17	9	2.5	1.2	1.2	260	0.8	72.5
F.17. *NORTHERN AMERICA*	19	9	2.9	1.4	1.3	228	1.0	72.5
United States	17	9	2.6	1.3	1.2	206	0.8	74.0
Canada	18	7	2.6	1.3	1.2	21	1.1	74.5
G.20. *TEMPERATE SOUTH AMERICA*	26	9	3.7	1.8	1.6	39	1.7	66.5
Argentina	22	8	3.0	1.5	1.3	24	1.4	70.5
Chile	28	9	3.8	1.9	1.6	10	1.9	64.0
H. *OCEANIA*	24	10	3.5	1.7	1.6	19	1.4	68.5
Australia	20	8	3.0	1.4	1.4	12	1.2	75.0

fear that current population growth is too low and are afraid that demographic trends could lead to a decrease of population, which is considered undesirable.

To get an idea about the extent to which these concerns are warranted in the more developed countries, let us compare the Netherlands and Hungary—each one from the opposite end of the spectrum.

The Netherlands, with about 13 million inhabitants in 1970, has a relatively high fertility among more developed countries. Its total fertility rate (TFR) in the late 1960s was 2.8. Hungary, with about 10.5 million inhabitants, had an estimated average TFR of 2.0. The crude birth rate in the Netherlands was about 19 per thousand population and in Hungary, 14 per thousand population in the late 1960s.

The mortality differences were significant within the context of the more developed countries—the Netherlands had a female e_0^0 of 76.5 years and Hungary of 72.0 years; the female crude death rate was 8 per thousand population in the former and almost 11 in the latter.

There is also a distinct difference in the age structures of both countries—over 50% of the Netherlands' population is under 30 and the corresponding proportion for Hungary is only about 43%.

The differences of the basic demographic characteristics of the two countries are reflected both in the differences of their NRR—about 1.3 in the former and 0.9 in the latter—as well as in the rates of natural increase—1.1% per year in the Netherlands compared with 0.3% in Hungary. Moreover, the current demographic features together with future fertility and mortality trends will be reflected in future population growth. If one grafts the same type of fertility and mortality assumptions onto the current demographic structures of both of these populations, it is possible to observe the varying population growth implications inherent in the current demographic features (Table 5-3).

Let us assume that an NRR of 1.0 is attained immediately and thereafter maintained indefinitely in both countries. In the Netherlands, this would necessitate a sharp fertility decline; the TFR would have to fall from its 1965–70 average of 2.8 to 2.1. In Hungary fertility would have to increase slightly; the 1965–70 TFR of 2.0 would have to increase to 2.1 to 2.2, because the estimated average 1965–70 NRR in Hungary was below 1.0. Thus if an NRR of 1.0 were attained in both countries immediately, the population of Hungary would grow by 7% by the year 2000 and by 11% by the year 2050; the Dutch population would grow by 21% and by 32% by the years 2000 and 2050,

Table 5-3   Indices of Population Growth (1970 = 100), Netherlands and Hungary, Projections 1 and 5, Standard
Set, 1970-2100

	Netherlands		Hungary	
	Projection 1 (NRR = 1.0 in 1970-1975)	Projection 5 (NRR = 1.0 in 2040-2045)	Projection 1 (NRR = 1.0 in 1970-1975)	Projection 5 (NRR = 1.0 in 2040-2045)
1970	100	100	100	100
2000	121	136	107	104
2050	132	183	111	103
2100	132	194	112	101

respectively. The population growth potential inherent in the current demographic features of the Dutch population is significantly larger than that of the Hungarian population. This factor is even more evident if one compares the population growth consequences of a slow approach to the NRR of 1.0 in both countries (Projection Five in Table 5-3). If fertility declines very slowly in the Netherlands before it reaches a value corresponding to the NRR of 1.0, the Dutch population might grow by almost 40% by the year 2000, and it might almost double by the end of the next century. If, however, fertility in Hungary very slowly increases to the level corresponding to an NRR of 1.0, the Hungarian population would grow only by about 4% by the year 2000 and by the second half of the next century would start to decline in size. (A discussion of the population growth consequences of attaining and maintaining an NRR of 0.9 is included in Chapter 6.)

The applied fertility and mortality assumptions would also be reflected in the trends of the crude vital rates: the crude birth rates, death rates and rates of natural increase (Table 5-4). A transition toward the stationary, nongrowing situation is detectable in all cases. Such a state, where the e_0^0 is 77.5 years, is characterized by a crude birth rate of 13, a crude death rate of 13, and a zero rate of population growth (excluding the effects of migration). Naturally, in Hungary, where the demographic reality is already close to such a situation, future changes will be minimal, if the underlying fertility and mortality trends stabilize. In the Netherlands, the crude birth rate would decline rapidly or slowly depending on the speed of fertility

Table 5-4 Crude Female Vital Rates, Netherlands and Hungary, Projections 1 and 5, Standard Set, 1965-2100

	Netherlands			Hungary		
	Crude Birth Rate	Crude Death Rate	Rate of Natural Increase	Crude Birth Rate	Crude Death Rate	Rate of Natural Increase
			Projection 1			
			(NRR = 1.0 in 1970-1975)			
1965-1970	19	8	1.1	14	11	0.3
1995-2000	14	9	0.5	14	12	0.2
2025-2030	13	12	0.1	13	13	0.0
2045-2050	13	13	0.0	13	13	0.0
			Projection 5			
			(NRR = 1.0 in 2040-2045)			
1965-1970	19	8	1.1	14	11	0.3
1995-2000	18	9	0.9	13	13	0.0
2025-2030	15	10	0.5	13	14	-0.1
2045-2050	14	11	0.3	13	13	0.0

decline. The crude death rate in the Netherlands would increase rapidly or slowly depending on changes in the age structure.

Within the range of the applied fertility and mortality assumptions, changes of the age structures are bound to occur (Figure 5-1). In general, both populations will proceed along the path of aging—the proportions of their young age groups will decline, and the proportions of their old age groups will increase. Since the transition of the age structure to a stationary state is more advanced in Hungary than in the Netherlands, the probability and the magnitude of changes in the latter is likely to be larger than in the former. At present the Netherlands has almost 27% of its population in the 0–14 age group and 11% of age 65 and over; 20% of the Hungarian population is in the 0–14 age group, and 13% is of age 65 and over. Once a nongrowing population (with low mortality) is achieved, the age groups 0–14 and 65+ are likely to be of a similar size—both somewhat less than 20% of the total population. Changes of the age structure will be reflected in changes of the median age of the population—in the Netherlands the median age of the female population is currently 29 years, in Hungary close to 36 years; both would ultimately have a female median age of over 39 years.

The discussed trends give an idea of the kind of population growth that can be expected in the more developed countries in the coming century or so. They should, however, not be treated as predictions. Fertility or mortality trends other than those underlying the standard set could occur.

This discussion of the population growth alternatives of the Netherlands and Hungary is an illustration that can be applied to most of the more developed countries. Somebody may, however, wonder why at times there are two countries that have, say, almost identical current fertility levels, yet their growth rates differ significantly, and the outlined hypothetical future patterns of population growth also differ. A particularly vivid example of such a situation is Japan compared with Hungary.

Why do Hungary and Japan have almost identical fertility (TFR) and mortality (e_0^0) levels and yet very different rates of natural increase? Among the factors that cause this seeming contradiction, the differences of the age structures are probably the most important. For instance, the 20–29 age group of women (which in both countries bear the majority of the children) is significantly smaller in Hungary than in Japan—14% compared with 19% of the total population. On the other hand, the 65+ age group (which is subject to high mortality) is

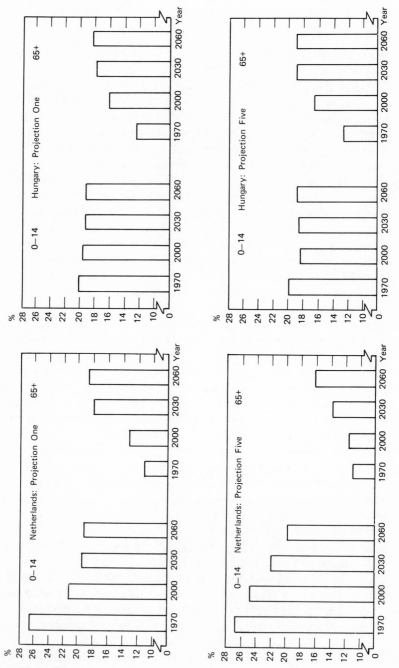

Figure 5-1. Proportions of specified age groups (in %), the Netherlands and Hungary, Projections One and Five, standard set, 1970–2060.

larger in Hungary than in Japan—13% compared with 8% of the total population.

Also, because of age-structural differences, the outlook for future population growth in Hungary differs from that in Japan. If both of these countries would attain and maintain the NRR of 1.0, Hungary would grow by 7% by the year 2000 and 11% by the year 2050. Japan's population, however, would grow by 23 and 30%, respectively. One important reason for this is again the different proportions of women who will enter into the childbearing ages during the coming decades. Let us take only those who are already born. In Hungary in 1970, the 0–14 age group comprised 20% of the total population; whereas in Japan it was over 23%.

The hypothetical population growth patterns of the Netherlands and Hungary illustrate the borderline and yet typical patterns. Such countries as Australia, the United States, and Canada have a demographic situation similar to that of the Netherlands and thus similar alternatives of future development. Countries such as Belgium, Czechoslovakia, and Sweden are approaching a demographic situation like that of Hungary and therefore have similar prospects for population growth. Clearly, the hypothetical population growth prospects of other more developed countries are between these two groups.

To summarize, in several countries, if an NRR of 1.0 were realized immediately and maintained, population would grow thereafter only very slowly; examples are Austria, Hungary, England and Wales, and Sweden (see Table 5-5). In other countries, even if an NRR of 1.0 were attained instantly and maintained thereafter, population would grow appreciably—by some 20% by the year 2000; examples are Japan, the Netherlands, Yugoslavia, Poland, the United States, Canada, and Australia.

Some of the more developed countries would experience little population growth even if only trivial changes in fertility behavior occurred; Hungary, Sweden, and Czechoslovakia are such countries. Other countries might double their size within the next five to seven decades—Australia, Canada, the United States, and the Netherlands.

Based on the analysis of the standard set of projections one can deliver at least some general statements referring to the earlier-mentioned concerns: the wish to halt population growth immediately and the fear of a decline in population growth if current trends and levels of fertility persist.

Very much depends on which countries one has in mind. As we

Table 5-5 Indices of Population Size (1970 = 100), More Developed Regions and Countries, Projections 1 and 5, Standard Set, 1970-2100

	Total Population in 1970 (in millions)	Projection 1 (NRR = 1.0 in 1970-1975)				Projection 5 (NRR = 1.0 in 2040-2045)			
		1970	2000	2050	2100	1970	2000	2050	2100
A.2. JAPAN	105.8	100	123	130	131	100	124	133	134
C. EUROPE	474.0	100	111	119	119	100	122	156	164
C.7. WESTERN EUROPE	151.8	100	108	114	115	100	118	150	158
German Fed. Rep.	63.2	100	103	106	106	100	109	129	134
France	51.2	100	111	117	118	100	121	153	160
Netherlands	13.1	100	121	132	132	100	136	183	194
Belgium	9.8	100	106	112	112	100	112	130	134
Austria	7.8	100	103	109	109	100	112	139	146
C.8. SOUTHERN EUROPE	132.4	100	117	126	126	100	125	155	163
Italy	55.9	100	113	119	120	100	119	139	143
Yugoslavia	20.9	100	122	135	137	100	129	156	163
Greece	9.2	100	117	122	122	100	119	130	132
Albania	2.1	100	141	171	173	100	220	488	585
C.9. EASTERN EUROPE	107.1	100	114	122	123	100	120	145	150
Poland	33.7	100	122	133	133	100	125	146	149
Czechoslovakia	14.8	100	112	120	120	100	112	117	117
Hungary	10.6	100	107	111	112	100	104	103	101

Table 5-5 (continued)

	Total Population in 1970 (in millions)	Projection 1 (NRR = 1.0 in 1970-1975)				Projection 5 (NRR = 1.0 in 2040-2045)			
		1970	2000	2050	2100	1970	2000	2050	2100
C.10. *NORTHERN EUROPE*	82.5	100	108	115	115	100	119	151	159
England & Wales	50.2	100	106	111	111	100	116	143	151
Sweden	7.9	100	105	108	108	100	109	119	121
Denmark	5.0	100	112	119	120	100	123	154	162
Ireland	3.0	100	120	135	136	100	155	261	291
D.11. *U.S.S.R.*	260.1	100	116	126	126	100	123	149	154
F.17. *NORTHERN AMERICA*	227.7	100	122	137	137	100	138	195	209
United States	205.7	100	122	136	136	100	132	172	180
Canada	20.5	100	128	143	144	100	139	182	190
G.20. *TEMPERATE SOUTH AMERICA*	39.2	100	129	148	150	100	159	255	284
Argentina	24.0	100	125	140	141	100	141	193	208
Chile	9.6	100	138	164	166	100	174	293	329
H.22. *AUSTRALIA & NEW ZEALAND*	14.8	100	123	138	138	100	145	215	234
Australia	11.9	100	123	136	136	100	142	203	218

have seen, in a number of countries future population growth would be
of a trivial size if an NRR of 1.0 is realized. Since this would be a
situation very close to the current ones for Austria, England and
Wales, and Sweden, it can be considered as a realistic possibility. For
Australia, Canada, the United States, the Netherlands, Poland, and
Yugoslavia, if it were desired to cease population growth all together,
it would be necessary to bring about a substantial decline of fertility to
below the level at which NRR = 1.0 (a detailed calculation of the
needed fertility decline is presented in Chapter 6). In other words, in
the latter it would be rather unrealistic to expect an immediate
cessation of population growth.

Our analysis also provides grounds to discuss the fear of
population decline. In almost all more developed countries, provided no
major catastrophes occur, such a fear seems to be unsubstantiated.
Countries like Poland, France, or even Japan have a rather good
guarantee in their current demographic features. The danger of
population decline seems to be a real one (within the next two to three
decades) only in very few countries—in Hungary for instance. Even in
Hungary, however, our analysis indicates that there is a high
probability of population size stabilizing rather than significantly
declining. (More evidence and discussion of this problem is given in
Chapter 6.)

2. POPULATION GROWTH ALTERNATIVES OF COUNTRIES OF EAST ASIA

One quarter of the world population lives in East Asia. East Asia
seems to rank as the most developed among the demographically less
developed major areas. To put it differently, most of the population of
East Asia has started out on the path of demographic transition. Not
only is its mortality declining but also its fertility. In the late 1960s
East Asia had the lowest fertility of the less developed major areas—a
TFR of 4.5, compared with 6.2, 6.4, and 5.5 in South Asia, Africa, and
Latin America, respectively; and the lowest rate of natural in-
crease—2.0% per year as compared with 2.8%, 2.5%, and 2.9% in South
Asia, Africa, and Latin America, respectively.

Within East Asia the current demographic situation of the
countries varies considerably. Japan is (and has been for some years) a
more developed country and therefore has been dealt with in the
preceding section. Countries such as Republic of Korea (South Korea),

Taiwan, and Hong Kong seem to be in the midst of a rapid demographic transition. The scanty evidence and the United Nations estimates indicate that meaningful demographic changes are underway also in the mainland region of which the Chinese People's Republic is the major part.

Data of Table 5-6 indicate that in the late 1960s there probably were no large fertility differences among the individual countries. For example, the total fertility rate for South Korea was 4.9, for Taiwan was 4.4, and for the mainland region was an estimated 4.9 children born per woman of childbearing age. The estimates of the growth rate, however, differ: the mainland region presumably had a natural increase of 2.1% per year, South Korea 2.5%, and Taiwan 2.6% in the 1965–70 period. The main cause of the different population growth rates seems to be the mortality differences: a female expectation of life at birth is equal to 52 years in the mainland region, 65 years in South Korea, and 70 years in Taiwan.

Such was the average situation of the late 1960s. There is, however, reliable evidence that fertility is rapidly declining in Taiwan and South Korea. Preliminary data for 1970 indicate that the rate of natural increase was around 2.2% per year in Taiwan[1] and 2.0% in South Korea[2] as compared with the 1965–70 averages of 2.5 and 2.6%, respectively. Whether there is a similar situation in the Chinese People's Republic is not known. Even if the downward trend of fertility in the mainland region were moderate, the situation of the East Asian countries is still unique. By standards of the less developed regions the fertility in these countries is low; moreover, there is evidence that it is declining. This observation is of utmost importance, especially because it cannot be made about any other significant part of the less developed regions.

Let us compare the population growth alternatives of the above-mentioned countries with the corresponding population growth alternatives of the less developed countries as a whole (Table 5-7). Formally, the growth potential of Taiwan, for example, is almost the same as that of the total of the less developed regions. The important difference, however, is that the current demographic situation and trend in South Korea and Taiwan enable us to assume that real future development may proceed somewhere along the paths illustrated by Projections Two or Three. However, so far this seems very unlikely for the majority of the less developed countries. In other words, an order of difference between the population growth prospects for most of the less developed countries on the one hand and for the countries of East Asia on the other can be imagined by comparing Projection Four of the former to, say, Projection Three of the latter. There is reason to believe that in most less developed countries population might double by the year 2000 and grow by a factor of 3.5 or so by the year 2050. On the other hand, it is quite possible that the countries of East Asia will grow only by about 40 to 80% by the year 2000 and that by the year 2050 they will not increase by more than a factor of about 2.5.

If the current trends of fertility decline in the countries of East Asia continue and if they ultimately stabilize at a level roughly corresponding to an NRR of 1.0, all basic demographic characteristics will naturally be affected (for changes of the crude vital rates see Table 5-8).

The type of changes that might occur in the age structure can be illustrated by South Korean data. South Korea currently has a young population (Figure 5-2). Over 40% of its population is under 14 and only 4% over 65 years of age. Clearly the age structure will become older, and the speed of the aging process depends on the speed of fertility decline. Let us briefly follow through time the developments of particular age groups according to Projections Two and Three (Table 5-9). There is a chance that the child age groups might decline even in absolute numbers in the near future (Figure 5-3). After 15 to 20 years this decline of numbers would also affect the young adult age groups. During the nearest 5 to 15 years, however, it is beyond doubt that the young adult age groups (for example, women in their prime childbearing ages) will grow very rapidly; it is precisely their fertility behavior (low or high) that will have long-term population growth consequences.

3. POPULATION GROWTH ALTERNATIVES OF COUNTRIES OF SOUTH ASIA

The major area of South Asia stretches from Turkey and Israel in the west to the Philippines and Indonesia in the east. Its importance for world population growth is underlined by the fact that currently about 30% of the world population lives in this area, which covers less than 12% of the world's land. Most of the population of the area is concentrated in four countries: India, Bangladesh, Pakistan, and Indonesia.

The population of South Asia clearly qualifies as less developed. It has very high fertility, relatively high mortality, and a high rate of

Table 5-6 Basic Demographic Measures for Selected Regions and Countries of East Asia, 1965-1970

	Female Crude Birth Rate	Female Crude Death Rate	Total Fertility Rate	Gross Reproduction Rate	Net Reproduction Rate	Total Population in 1970 (in millions)	Female Average Annual Rate of Growth (in %)	Female Expectation of Life at Birth
A. EAST ASIA	34	13	4.5	2.2	1.7	941	2.0	54.5
A.1. MAINLAND REGION	36	15	4.9	2.4	1.8	773	2.1	52.0
Hong Kong	25	5	4.2	2.1	2.0	4	2.0	73.0
A.2. JAPAN	18	7	2.1	1.0	1.0	106	1.1	73.5
A.3. OTHER EAST ASIA	35	9	5.1	2.5	2.2	61	2.6	62.0
Rep. of Korea	32	7	4.9	2.4	2.1	32	2.5	65.0
Rep. of China (Taiwan)	30	5	4.4	2.1	2.0	14	2.5	70.0

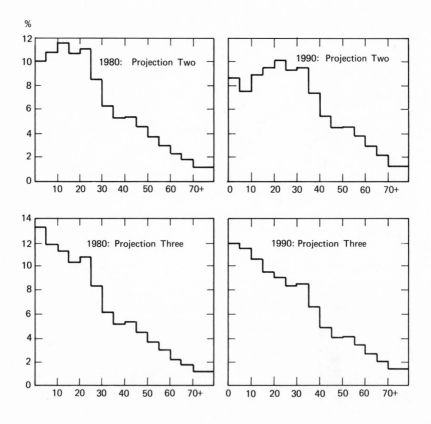

Figure 5–2. Changes of age structure, Republic of Korea, Projections Two and Three, standard set, 1970–2010.

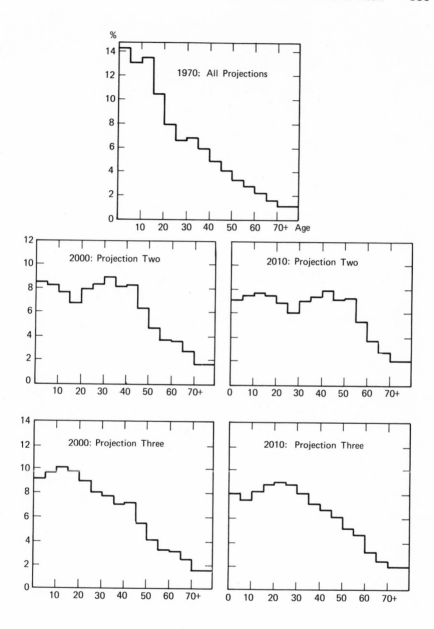

Figure 5–2 (continued).

Table 5-7 Indices of Population Size (1970 = 100), Less Developed Regions, Mainland Region (East Asia), South Korea, and Taiwan, Projections 2, 3, and 4, Standard Set, 1970-2100

	Projection 2 (NRR = 1.0 in 1980-1985)	Projection 3 (NRR = 1.0 in 2000-2005)	Projection 4 (NRR = 1.0 in 2020-2025)
Less Developed Regions			
1970	100	100	100
2000	149	179	198
2050	188	258	349
2100	194	267	378
Mainland Region (East Asia)			
1970	100	100	100
2000	141	162	176
2050	173	221	283
2100	177	227	300
South Korea			
1970	100	100	100
2000	151	178	194
2050	185	247	321
2100	188	253	341
Taiwan			
1970	100	100	100
2000	161	188	204
2050	204	271	348
2100	207	277	371

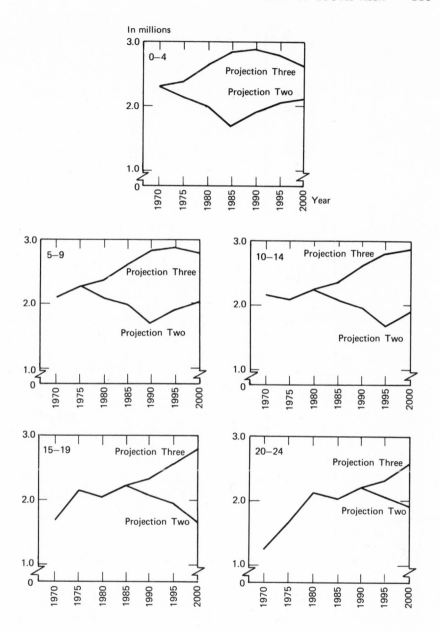

Figure 5–3. Growth (in millions) of selected female age groups, Republic of Korea, Projections Two and Three, standard set, 1970–2000.

Table 5-8   Crude Female Vital Rates, Population of East Asia, Projections 2 and 4, Standard Set, 1970-2050

	Mainland Region			Taiwan			South Korea		
	Crude Birth Rate	Crude Death Rate	Rate of Natural Increase	Crude Birth Rate	Crude Death Rate	Rate of Natural Increase	Crude Birth Rate	Crude Death Rate	Rate of Natural Increase
	Projection 2								
	(NRR = 1.0 in 1980-1985)								
1970	36	15	2.1	30	5	2.6	32	8	2.5
2000	19	10	1.0	18	6	1.2	18	7	1.1
2030	15	11	0.4	14	10	0.4	14	11	0.3
2050	14	13	0.1	13	12	0.1	13	12	0.1
	Projection 4								
	(NRR = 1.0 in 2020-2025)								
1970	36	15	2.1	30	5	2.6	32	8	2.5
2000	26	9	1.7	24	5	1.9	25	6	1.9
2030	17	8	0.8	16	7	0.9	16	8	0.8
2050	15	10	0.5	14	9	0.5	14	9	0.5

Table 5-9 Female Population of Selected Age Groups (in millions) and Annual Growth Rates of Age Groups (in %), Republic of Korea, Projections 2 and 3, 1970-2000

	ABSOLUTE NUMBER						
	1970	1975	1980	1985	1990	1995	2000
Projection 2 (NRR = 1.0 in 1980-1985)							
0-4	2.3	2.1	2.0	1.7	1.9	2.0	2.1
5-14	4.2	4.3	4.3	4.0	3.6	3.5	3.9
15-29	4.0	5.1	5.8	6.4	6.3	6.2	5.7
30-44	2.8	3.0	3.3	3.9	4.9	5.7	6.2
45-64	2.0	2.3	2.7	3.2	3.5	3.9	4.5
65+	0.6	0.7	0.9	1.0	1.2	1.4	1.6
TOTAL	15.9	17.6	19.0	20.1	21.4	22.8	24.1
Projection 3 (NRR = 1.0 in 2000-2005)							
0-4	2.3	2.4	2.6	2.8	2.9	2.8	2.6
5-14	4.2	4.3	4.6	4.9	5.4	5.7	5.6
15-29	4.0	5.1	5.8	6.4	6.6	7.1	7.7
30-44	2.8	3.0	3.3	3.9	4.9	5.7	6.2
45-64	2.0	2.3	2.7	3.2	3.5	3.9	4.5
65+	0.6	0.7	0.9	1.0	1.2	1.4	1.6
TOTAL	15.9	17.8	19.9	22.2	24.5	26.6	28.4

	ANNUAL GROWTH RATE					
	1970-75	1975-80	1980-85	1985-90	1990-95	1995-2000
Projection 2 (NRR = 1.0 in 1980-1985)						
0-4	- 1.6	- 1.2	- 3.3	2.5	1.5	0.5
5-14	0.4	0.1	- 1.4	- 2.2	- 0.4	2.0
15-29	4.8	2.9	1.8	- 0.2	- 0.3	- 1.9
30-44	1.6	1.8	3.1	5.0	2.9	1.9
45-64	3.0	3.3	3.2	2.0	2.2	3.1
65+	3.4	3.0	2.8	3.3	3.4	- 3.6
TOTAL	2.0	1.6	1.1	1.2	1.2	1.1
Projection 3 (NRR = 1.0 in 2000-2005)						
0-4	0.8	2.0	1.5	0.5	- 0.7	- 1.3
5-14	0.4	1.2	1.5	1.8	1.0	- 1.0
15-29	4.8	2.9	1.8	0.6	1.6	1.5
30-44	1.6	1.8	3.1	5.0	2.9	1.9
45-64	3.0	3.3	3.2	2.0	2.2	3.1
65+	3.4	3.0	2.8	3.3	3.4	3.6
TOTAL	2.3	2.3	2.2	2.0	1.7	1.3

population growth. Fertility conditions of most countries are close to the area average of a TFR of over 6.0 (Table 5-10), and the female expectation of life at birth is usually around 50 years. The average annual rates of population growth in almost all countries are within the range of 2.5 to 3.3% per year. Only a few exceptions can be found. Among these exceptions are Ceylon and West Malaysia where both fertility and mortality are lower than elsewhere, and thus the growth rates are still high: 2.5% in Ceylon and 2.9% in West Malaysia.

The investigation of alternative population growth prospects of many countries of this area clearly indicates the unprecedented situations that might occur. Let us take India and Bangladesh. The estimates of current mortality and fertility might, of course, be incorrect, but if one wants to explore the population prospects of these countries there is no other choice but to work with unreliable data. Furthermore, our assumptions on future trends of mortality might be misleading. A single hypothetical trend of mortality decline is applied, and the danger of having incorporated either a too-optimistic or too-pessimistic trend is real. Caution in any interpretation of the computed projections is therefore appropriate. Be that as it may, there is no problem in illustrating the significant differences in the population growth consequences of different trends of fertility decline.

According to our estimates India has relatively low fertility (TFR = 5.6) and high mortality (e_0^0 = 49.0), Bangladesh' fertility seems to be higher (TFR = 6.8) and mortality lower (e_0^0 = 52.0). Whether this corresponds exactly to real differences is by no means certain, but it does give an idea of the order of differences that exist among countries of South Asia. Even if the assumed future fertility and mortality trends applied to both populations are identical, such initial differences (together with differences of other demographic characteristics such as the age patterns of fertility) can cause a significant difference in the population growth potential of these countries (Projection Three, Table 5-11). For instance, assuming that fertility in both countries declined rapidly during the coming decades and an NRR of 1.0 was reached by the end of this century, India's population would grow by less than 80% and Bangladesh' population would more than double. If fertility were to decline slowly (Projection Five, Table 5-11), the population of India would double and that of Bangladesh would grow by a factor of 2.7 by the end of this century. The differences in the long run are even more conspicuous.

Whatever the differences between the countries, the differences in the population growth consequences of varying velocities of fertility

Table 5-10 Basic Demographic Measures for Selected Regions and Countries of South Asia, 1965-1970

	Female Crude Birth Rate	Female Crude Death Rate	Total Fertility Rate	Gross Reproduction Rate	Net Reproduction Rate	Total Population in 1970 (in millions)	Female Average Annual Rate of Growth (in %)	Female Expectation of Life at Birth
B. SOUTH ASIA	43	15	6.2	3.0	2.2	1103	2.8	51.0
B.4. MIDDLE SOUTH ASIA	42	15	6.2	3.0	2.2	735	2.7	50.0
India	40	16	5.6	2.7	2.0	534	2.4	49.0
Bangladesh	44	14	6.8	3.3	2.5	69	3.0	52.0
Pakistan	39	14	6.2	3.0	2.3	57	2.5	53.0
Iran	44	15	6.8	3.3	2.5	28	2.9	52.0
Ceylon	32	7	4.5	2.2	2.0	12	2.5	65.0
B.5. SOUTH-EAST ASIA	43	14	6.2	3.0	2.3	288	2.9	52.0
The Philippines	44	11	6.8	3.3	2.6	38	3.3	55.0
Thailand	40	10	6.2	3.0	2.5	37	3.0	59.5
West Malaysia	35	6	5.3	2.6	2.4	9	2.9	66.5
Singapore	27	4	4.1	2.0	1.9	2	2.3	70.0
B.6. SOUTH-WEST ASIA	43	14	6.4	3.1	2.4	76	2.9	53.0
Turkey	35	13	5.3	2.6	2.1	35	2.2	56.0
Israel (Total)	26	6	3.9	1.9	1.8	2.8	2.0	73.0
Israel:Jewish	22	7	3.2	1.6	1.5	2.4	1.5	73.5
Israel:non-Jewish	45	5	7.4	3.6	3.4	0.3	4.0	70.5

Table 5-11 Indices of Population Size (1970 = 100), India and Bangladesh, Projections 1, 3, and 5, Standard Set, 1970-2100

	India			Bangladesh		
	Projection 1 (NRR = 1.0 in 1970-1975)	Projection 3 (NRR = 1.0 in 2000-2005)	Projection 5 (NRR = 1.0 in 2040-2045)	Projection 1 (NRR = 1.0 in 1970-1975)	Projection 3 (NRR = 1.0 in 2000-2005)	Projection 5 (NRR = 1.0 in 2040-2045)
1970	100	100	100	100	100	100
2000	135	177	206	146	218	269
2050	164	256	455	185	347	764
2100	167	263	542	188	357	961

decline within each country, especially in the long run, are enormous. By the year 2050 the population of India could be 2.5 times or 4.5 times larger than it is, and the population of Bangladesh 3.5 times or 7.6 times its current size, depending on whether fertility decline is fast or slow.

A meaningful observation is that even a rapid fertility decline would bring about unprecedented population densities for these countries. Bangladesh even at present has one of the highest, if not the highest, population densities in the world—485 persons per square kilometer. In comparison, the population densities of Japan and the Netherlands are 290 and 320 persons per square kilometer, respectively. With a rapid fertility decline (Projection Three) by the middle of the next century the population density of India could be 431 and that of Bangladesh 1,700 inhabitants per square kilometer (Table 5-12). With a slow fertility decline (Projection Five) the population density of India could be 750 and that of Bangladesh could theoretically be 3,700 inhabitants per square kilometer. These calculations were, however, computed assuming a gradual mortality decline to a level similar to the current situation in the more developed countries. Would it be possible to maintain low mortality in such an unprecedented situation of population density?

A further aspect that merits exploration is the possible evolution of crude vital rates (Table 5-13). If a rapid fertility decline were to occur (Projection Three), in India the crude birth rate would decline by 5 to 6 points each decade for the remainder of this century; in Bangladesh the overall decline of the crude birth rate would be of a similar magnitude but not so evenly spread out in time. If fertility were to decline moderately (Projection Five), the crude birth rate in India would decline by only 2 to 3 points each decade. In Bangladesh a moderate fertility decline could at first be accompanied even with an increase of the crude birth rate; a decline would not set in before the 1980s.

Remember that the present hypothetical projections are based on a trend of mortality decline which is roughly that of the past two to three decades. If this assumed mortality trend were to materialize, the crude death rates of India and Bangladesh would decline to a level of 9 and 6 per thousand population, respectively, by the end of this century.

An important message of Table 5-13 is the outlined trends of the crude rate of natural increase. In India even a rapid fertility decline (Projection Three) would generate only a moderate decline of the rate of nonmigratory population growth; in Bangladesh it seems that even

Table 5-12 Population Density, India and Bangladesh, Projections 3 and 5, Standard Set, 1970 and 2050

	India		Bangladesh	
	Projection 3 (NRR = 1.0 in 2000-2005)	Projection 5 (NRR = 1.0 in 2040-2045)	Projection 3 (NRR = 1.0 in 2000-2005)	Projection 5 (NRR = 1.0 in 2040-2045)
1970	164	164	485	485
2050	418	744	1679	3700

Table 5-13   Crude Female Vital Rates, India and Bangladesh, Projections 3 and 5, Standard Set,
1965-2000

	India			Bangladesh		
	Crude Birth Rate	Crude Death Rate	Rate of Natural Increase	Crude Birth Rate	Crude Death Rate	Rate of Natural Increase
			Projection 3			
		(NRR = 1.0 in 2000-2005)				
1965-1970	40	16	2.4	44	14	3.0
1975-1980	35	13	2.2	42	11	3.1
1985-1990	29	10	1.9	34	8	2.6
1995-2000	23	9	1.4	25	7	1.8
			Projection 5			
		(NRR = 1.0 in 2040-2045)				
1965-1970	40	16	2.4	44	14	3.0
1975-1980	38	13	2.5	46	11	3.5
1985-1990	35	10	2.5	42	8	3.4
1995-2000	32	9	2.4	38	6	3.2

a rapid fertility decline would not guarantee a decline of the rate of
natural increase during the next 10 and possibly 20 years provided, of
course, mortality also declined. More important, in both countries a
moderate fertility decline (Projection Five) is unlikely to generate any
decline of the rate of natural increase whatsoever, and in Bangladesh
the rate of natural increase might even increase. To put it differently,
a moderate fertility decline in typical countries of South Asia would
not bring about a decline in the rate of natural increase, which in
many countries is close to 3% per year.

The annual increments of population expressed in absolute
numbers are almost inconceivable (Figure 5-4). At present 12 million
persons are added to India's population annually. With a rapid fertility
decline (Projection Three) the annual increment would increase
somewhat and would remain between 13 to 14 million persons
throughout this century. If fertility were to decline moderately
(Projection Five) the annual increment would increase very rapidly. In

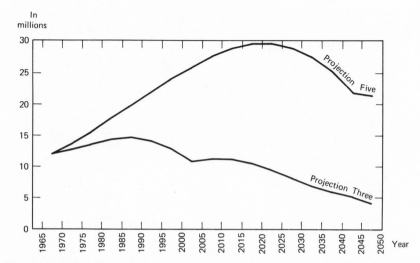

Figure 5–4. Annual increments of population (in millions), India, Projections Three and Five, standard set, 1965–2050.

the beginning of the 1980s, around 18 million people would be added to India's population annually, and in the beginning of the twenty-first century the annual additions of population would be between 25 and 30 million inhabitants.

The age structure of most South Asian populations is extremely young. The population of India, for example, has a median age of around 19 (Table 5-14). One of the important reasons of the built-in inertia of population growth is this young age structure. The 42% of the population under 15 years of age in India are the large cohorts of women that are potential mothers in the coming 15 years. If these mothers continue to have high fertility, they will produce further huge cohorts of potential mothers 15 to 30 years hence. Therefore, if fertility declines moderately (Projection Five), future changes of the age structure throughout this century will be very gradual. The median age of the female population in India around the year 2000 would be only 2 years older than at present: 21 years.

4. POPULATION GROWTH ALTERNATIVES OF COUNTRIES OF AFRICA

About 9% (350 million inhabitants) of the world population presently lives in Africa. Although demographic characteristics of population do

Table 5-14   Median Age of Female Population, India and Bangladesh, Projections 3 and 5, Standard Set, 1970-2050

	India		Bangladesh	
	Projection 3 (NRR = 1.0 in 2000-2005)	Projection 5 (NRR = 1.0 in 2040-2045)	Projection 3 (NRR = 1.0 in 2000-2005)	Projection 5 (NRR = 1.0 in 2040-2045)
1970	19.0	19.0	15.8	15.8
2000	24.4	20.8	21.9	17.8
2050	36.5	31.3	36.8	30.0

differ from country to country and region to region within Africa (Table 5-15), most populations do have typical African features: high fertility and relatively high mortality resulting in growth rates around 2.5% and more.

Provided the estimates that have been assembled are representative and indicative of real situations, the TFR of many African countries are between 6.5 and 7.5. The female expectation of life at birth is probably between 40 and 45 years in the countries of Western, Eastern, and Middle Africa, and around 50 years in Northern and Southern Africa. Rates of natural increase seem to be around 2.5% per year in most parts of Africa, with several exceptions, many of which are in Northern Africa, where the rates of natural increase are often around 3% per year and more.

To illustrate the type of population growth that might occur in Africa in the remainder of this century and to indicate what may happen in the beginning of the twenty-first century, we have decided to discuss the computed hypothetical data for the populations of Ghana and Morocco. One reason for selecting these populations is that their current demographic data are—for African standards—relatively reliable. Secondly, both countries do represent certain general demographic types. In Ghana fertility is high (TFR = 7.0) and so is mortality (female e_0^0 = 41 years); in Morocco fertility is even higher (TFR = 7.4), but mortality is lower (female e_0^0 = 50 years) than in Ghana. Differences in the age structure of the two populations are probably not too large, because both have an estimated median age of under 17 years.

Caution in interpreting our hypothetical projections is necessary, especially in those countries where mortality is very high (the female e_0^0 below 45 years). At the same time, there is less evidence than elsewhere about mortality decline in general and the speed of mortality decline in particular. In most of the other areas of the world there is more evidence about the speed of mortality decline, and because there seems to be an appreciable momentum of mortality decline once it is on its way, assumptions about further mortality decline are fairly well substantiated. These considerations are valid only to a limited extent in many countries of Africa; thus our assumptions of mortality decline in Africa are more dubious than for other areas. As has been noted elsewhere, an attempt to overcome this problem is made in Chapter 6, where other than the standard mortality assumptions are explored.

As can be expected, the growth potential of the African

Table 5-15 Basic Demographic Measures for Selected Regions and Countries of Africa, 1965-1970

	Female Crude Birth Rate	Female Crude Death Rate	Total Fertility Rate	Gross Reproduction Rate	Net Reproduction Rate	Total Population in 1970 (in millions)	Female Average Annual Rate of Growth (in %)	Female Expectation of Life at Birth
E. AFRICA	45	20	6.4	3.1	2.1	344	2.5	44.5
E.12. WESTERN AFRICA	46	22	6.6	3.2	2.0	100	2.4	41.0
Nigeria	56	23	7.0	3.4	2.1	65	3.3	41.0
Ghana	48	22	7.0	3.4	2.1	9	2.6	41.0
Ivory Coast	48	24	6.4	3.1	1.8	4	2.4	38.0
Liberia	47	23	6.3	3.1	1.9	2	2.4	41.0
E.13. EASTERN AFRICA	45	20	6.4	3.1	2.0	99	2.5	44.0
Tanzania	48	23	6.6	3.2	2.0	13	2.5	41.0
Kenya	48	19	6.8	3.3	2.2	11	2.9	45.0
Mauritius	30	8	4.6	2.2	2.0	1	2.2	63.0
E.14. MIDDLE AFRICA	43	23	5.9	2.9	1.8	37	2.0	41.0
E.15. NORTHERN AFRICA	45	15	6.6	3.2	2.4	86	3.0	51.5
United Arab Republic	43	16	6.1	3.0	2.2	33	2.7	50.0
Morocco	51	16	7.4	3.6	2.6	16	3.5	50.0
Algeria	48	16	7.2	3.5	2.6	14	3.2	50.5
Tunisia	44	15	6.8	3.3	2.5	5	2.9	51.5
E.16. SOUTHERN AFRICA	41	16	5.7	2.8	2.0	23	2.4	50.0
Swaziland	45	19	7.0	3.4	2.3	0.4	2.6	45.0

populations is large. If it were at all possible to reduce the current NRR of around 2.0 almost overnight to an NRR of 1.0, the populations of Africa would grow by about 40% by the year 2000 and by about 70% by the middle of the next century (Table 5-16). Because, clearly, such a development cannot be brought about, one can conclude that the growth of African populations is likely to be significantly larger than just stated. The computations indicate that if the fertility decline of African countries is fairly slow (as assumed by Projection Five), by the turn of the century these populations would more than double; in fact, countries with demographic conditions similar to Morocco would have a population 2.5 times their current size; by the middle of the twenty-first century a slow fertility decline could generate populations 5 to 8 times larger than they are at present. The population of Morocco could, for instance, be over 100 million. This would imply a population density of about 260 persons per square kilometer, compared with the current 35.

The complexity of slowing down the rate of population growth in African countries is illustrated by data of Table 5-17. A moderate nevertheless meaningful fertility decline (Projection Five) might be only just enough to keep the growth rates at their current levels for the remainder of this century. Even quite rapid paths of fertility decline would keep the rates of population growth above 2% per year, and at the end of the century they would be in the order of 1.5 to 1.8% per year.

5. POPULATION GROWTH ALTERNATIVES OF LATIN AMERICA

Almost 300 million inhabitants live in Latin America. A large range of demographic variety can be found among the population of Latin America (Table 5-18). Two examples are Argentina, whose demographic features are those of a developed country, and the Dominican Republic, with a crude birth rate close to 50 per thousand population and a crude rate of natural increase between 3.5 and 4.0% per year.

The overall demographic picture of Latin America is determined by the fact that most populations are demographically closer to the situation in the Dominican Republic than to that of Argentina. In comparison with other less developed major areas Latin America has a number of unique features:

1. The lowest average mortality levels: the female life expectan-

Table 5-16 Indices of Population Size (1970 = 100), Ghana and Morocco, Projections 1, 3, and 5, Standard Set, 1970-2050

	Ghana			Morocco		
	Projection 1 (NRR = 1.0 in 1970-1975)	Projection 3 (NRR = 1.0 in 2000-2005)	Projection 5 (NRR = 1.0 in 2040-2045)	Projection 1 (NRR = 1.0 in 1970-1975)	Projection 3 (NRR = 1.0 in 2000-2005)	Projection 5 (NRR = 1.0 in 2040-2045)
1970	100	100	100	100	100	100
2000	136	187	225	141	211	262
2050	168	276	555	175	328	735

Table 5-17   Crude Female Vital Rates, Ghana and Morocco, Projections 3 and 5, Standard Set, 1965-2000

	Ghana			Morocco		
	Crude Birth Rate	Crude Death Rate	Rate of Natural Increase	Crude Birth Rate	Crude Death Rate	Rate of Natural Increase
Projection 3 *(NRR = 1.0 in 2000-2005)*						
1965-1970	48	22	2.6	51	16	3.5
1975-1980	40	16	2.4	40	12	2.9
1985-1990	34	12	2.2	34	9	2.5
1995-2000	25	10	1.5	25	7	1.8
Projection 5 *(NRR = 1.0 in 2040-2045)*						
1965-1970	48	22	2.6	51	16	3.5
1975-1980	44	17	2.7	45	12	3.3
1985-1990	41	13	2.8	42	9	3.3
1995-2000	37	10	2.8	39	7	3.2

cies at birth are 60 or more years, compared with 50 and 45 in South Asia and Africa, respectively.

2. The lowest fertility levels: the TFR is 5.5 compared with 6.2 and 6.4 in South Asia and Africa, respectively.

3. The resulting average rate of population growth is probably the highest in the world, 2.9% per year but South Asia is not far behind, with an estimated annual growth rate of 2.8% and Africa with a growth rate of 2.5%.

4. The NRR is also the highest: 2.3 compared with 2.2 in South Asia and 2.1 in Africa, indicating that the current cohorts of childbearing women are reproducing themselves by this factor of 2.3.

In addition to these static features there is a fair amount of reliable evidence about trends of mortality decline.[3] These lead one to believe that there is a good chance of a further improvement of mortality conditions throughout Latin America. The hypothetical projections here include such an assumption, but to be on the safe side

Table 5-18 Basic Demographic Measures for Selected Regions and Countries of Latin America, 1965-1970

	Female Crude Birth Rate	Female Crude Death Rate	Total Fertility Rate	Gross Reproduction Rate	Net Reproduction Rate	Total Population in 1970 (in millions)	Female Average Annual Rate of Growth (in %)	Female Expectation of Life at Birth
G. *LATIN AMERICA*	38	9	5.5	2.7	2.3	283	2.9	62.5
G.18. *TROPICAL SOUTH AMERICA*								
Brazil	40	9	5.7	2.8	2.3	151	3.1	61.5
Colombia	38	9	5.4	2.6	2.2	94	2.9	63.0
Peru	37	10	5.6	2.7	2.2	21	2.7	60.0
Venezuela	43	11	6.4	3.1	2.5	14	3.2	59.0
	40	6	6.0	2.9	2.6	10	3.4	68.0
G.19. *MIDDLE AMERICA (MAINLAND)*								
Mexico	43	9	6.4	3.1	2.6	67	3.4	62.5
El Salvador	43	8	6.5	3.2	2.7	51	3.5	64.0
Honduras	44	12	6.6	3.2	2.5	3	3.2	57.0
Costa Rica	44	9	6.6	3.2	2.6	3	3.4	60.0
	38	6	6.0	2.9	2.6	2	3.2	68.0
G.20. *TEMPERATE SOUTH AMERICA*								
Argentina	26	9	3.7	1.8	1.6	39	1.7	66.5
Chile	22	8	3.0	1.5	1.3	24	1.4	70.5
	28	9	3.8	1.9	1.6	10	1.9	64.0
G.21. *CARIBBEAN*								
Cuba	36	11	4.9	2.4	2.0	26	2.5	60.0
Dominican Republic	34	6	4.5	2.2	2.0	8	2.8	68.5
Puerto Rico	48	12	7.2	3.5	2.8	4	3.7	57.0
Trinidad & Tobago	25	6	3.4	1.7	1.5	3	1.9	72.0
	28	7	3.8	1.9	1.7	1	2.2	68.0

the applied trends are quite conservative.[4] Having established that the relatively high probability of our mortality trends resembles future developments, we can be more confident about the population growth implications shown by our set of hypothetical projections for Latin America than, for instance, in the case of Africa. However, such a consideration does not exclude a possible reversal of mortality trends caused by natural or human-induced catastrophes.

To give an idea about the order of typical future population growth alternatives for Latin America we have selected three countries: Brazil, Mexico, and the Dominican Republic. The first two, because their populations are big and, at the same time, representative of other populations, and the Dominican Republic because its population is probably the fastest-growing one in the world.

As data of Table 5-19 indicate, the growth potential of Latin American countries is large. With a rapid fertility decline (Projection Three) their populations would double by the end of this century and triple by the middle of the next century. If, however, the fertility decline of the next two to three decades is slow, Latin American populations might reach over 2.5 times their current size by 2000 and 5 to 8 times the current size by 2050.

In terms of crude population density, in most countries of Latin America even a slow fertility decline would not generate situations that by contemporary world-wide comparison would be considered extreme. For example, the population density of Brazil in 2050 would be, 54 inhabitants per square kilometer (compared with 11 in 1970); that of Mexico would be 170 inhabitants per square kilometer (compared with 26 in 1970). The only region where even at present population density is already rather high is the Caribbean: 105 persons per square kilometer. The trends of population density of the Dominican Republic can serve as a good example: the current density is almost 90 persons per square kilometer. If fertility declined only moderately and mortality also continued to decline, the population density of the Dominican Republic in the middle of the next century could be almost 700 persons per square kilometer.

The high rates of population growth of many Latin American countries will not decrease significantly unless fertility declines rapidly. Currently, for instance, in Mexico around 6.5 children are born per woman of the childbearing ages. Only if the TFR declined each decade by 1.2 children would the rate of population growth be below 2% per year by the end of the twentieth century (Table 5-20). That this is a significant decline can be demonstrated by comparing

Table 5-19 Indices of Population Size (1970 = 100), Brazil, Mexico, and Dominican Republic, Projections 3 and 5, Standard Set, 1970-2100

	Brazil		Mexico		Dominican Republic	
	Projection 3 (NRR = 1.0 in 2000-2005)	Projection 5 (NRR = 1.0 in 2040-2045)	Projection 3 (NRR = 1.0 in 2000-2005)	Projection 5 (NRR = 1.0 in 2040-2045)	Projection 3 (NRR = 1.0 in 2000-2005)	Projection 5 (NRR = 1.0 in 2040-2045)
1970	100	100	100	100	100	100
2000	193	223	214	259	225	277
2050	283	489	331	662	358	771
2100	292	586	342	821	371	977

the assumed fertility declines of Projections Three and Five of Mexico with the actual fertility decline of Great Britian a century earlier (Figure 5-5). The fertility decline curve of Great Britain (1866–1935) appears to be more like the assumptions of Projection Five than those of Projection Three.

If the fertility decline in Mexico (and in other Latin American countries) resembles that assumed by Projection Five, the rates of population growth will remain on a very high level throughout this

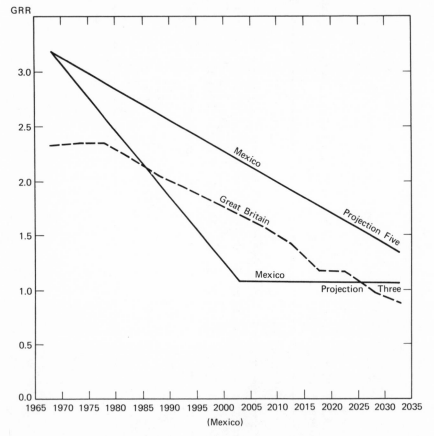

Figure 5–5. Gross reproduction rates, Great Britain, actual, 1865–1935, and Mexico, Projections Three and Five, standard set, 1965–2035.

Table 5-20 Crude Female Vital Rates, Brazil, Mexico, and Dominican Republic, Projections 3 and 5, Standard Set, 1965-2000

	Brazil			Mexico			Dominican Republic		
	Crude Birth Rate	Crude Death Rate	Rate of Natural Increase	Crude Birth Rate	Crude Death Rate	Rate of Natural Increase	Crude Birth Rate	Crude Death Rate	Rate of Natural Increase
				Projection 3					
				(NRR = 1.0 in 2000-2005)					
1965-1970	38	9	2.9	44	8	3.5	48	12	3.7
1975-1980	33	7	2.6	37	7	3.0	41	10	3.2
1985-1990	28	6	2.1	31	6	2.5	33	7	2.7
1995-2000	22	6	1.6	23	5	1.8	24	6	1.9
				Projection 5					
				(NRR = 1.0 in 2040-2045)					
1965-1970	38	9	2.9	44	8	3.5	48	12	3.7
1975-1980	36	7	2.8	40	7	3.4	45	9	3.6
1985-1990	33	6	2.7	38	6	3.2	41	7	3.5
1995-2000	30	6	2.5	35	5	2.9	38	6	3.2

century; they will still be in the neighborhood of 3% per year even
around the year 2000.

NOTES

1. *Taiwan Demographic Monthly,* Republic of China, Vol. 5, No. 11
   (November, 1970), p. 6.
2. Taek Il Kim, John A. Ross, and George C. Worth, *The Korean National
   Family Planning Program* (New York: The Population Council, 1972).
3. Cf. Eduardo E. Arriaga, *New Life Tables for Latin American Populations in
   the 19th and 20th Century,* Population Monograph Series, No. 3, University
   of California, Berkeley, 1968, pp. 2–3.
4. See, for instance, CELADE, *Boletín Demográfico,* Vol. 2, No. 4, (July 1969),
   pp. 20–21.

6 Modifications of Alternatives of Future Population Growth

It is hoped that the most important trends of the main demographic features of populations on their assumed paths to a stationary state have been sufficiently demonstrated in the preceding chapters. However, certain refinements are needed, as well as answers to questions about what might happen in circumstances differing from those assumed thus far. To put it differently, a framework of assumptions mirroring certain fundamental relationships was constructed for the basic analysis. In the present chapter modifications of particular assumptions as well as additional assumptions are tested while other assumptions are maintained the way they were originally designed. The justification for any variation to be introduced is the belief, usually based on historical experience, that it could materialize in specific populations. To this end several variations of the original "model" were constructed in order to elaborate on the following questions:

1. What would be the population growth consequences of fertility settling at a level corresponding to a net reproduction rate (NRR) of not 1.0 but 0.9, in other words, below replacement levels?

2. What would be the population growth consequences of fertility declining not linearly but logarithmically? This variation implies a gross reproduction rate (GRR) and total fertility rate (TFR) that decline at a constant pace until they reach the level at which the NRR is equal to 1.0; in other words, the fertility decline of the near future is faster and that of the more remote future is slower than in the standard set. The ultimate end point is an NRR of 1.0.

3. What would be the population growth consequences of a temporary fertility increase?

4. What would be the population growth consequences of present fertility remaining constant for different periods of time?

5. What would be the population growth consequences of upward or downward shifts in the average ages of childbearing, which would be an expression of changing age patterns of fertility?

6. What would be the population growth consequences of mortality declining at slower rates than has been assumed for the standard set? Because thus far a single assumed trend of mortality decline has been applied to each population, it was considered useful to explore an assumption of slower mortality decline, leaving the assumptions of fertility decline of the standard set, that is, a linear decline of fertility to an NRR of 1.0.

7. What kind of fertility (and crude birth rate) trends would be required to cause the population growth rate to decline linearly to zero at specific times in the future and remain there?

In all these modifications alternative future possibilities are set out as in the rest of this study. For example, when the population growth consequences of a decline of the NRR of 0.9 are explored, five projections have been computed differing from each other by the point of time when the NRR of 0.9 is reached (1970–75, 1980–85, 2000–05, 2020–25, 2040–45).

1. FERTILITY DECLINING TO AN NRR OF 0.9

In this century certain populations have had fertility below the replacement level for some nontrivial period of time (most recently Japan and Hungary in the 1960s, several European countries and the United States during the 1930s and some even in the 1920s). When this has happened the NRR has often fluctuated around 0.9, which is the reason for selecting this value for our calculations. What would happen if such a situation became the prevailing and lasting reproductive pattern?

It goes without saying that the demographically more developed and less developed countries have to be viewed separately. In many *more developed countries* the possibility of achieving such a situation soon is real; as a matter of fact, in some this is currently the case. In Hungary where such a situation prevailed for most of the 1960s, if the NRR of 0.9 were maintained indefinitely the size of the total population around the year 2020 would be the same as it is now. Before then, over the next 20 to 30 years, the population would at first increase by about 3%; thereafter it would decline so that around the year 2050 the total population of Hungary would be about 10% smaller than it is now. At that time the annual rate of population change would be about –0.4% per year (Table 6-1).

In a country like the Netherlands, where the current fertility and the population growth rates are still fairly high, future population growth would be somewhat different, although the general pattern would be similar to that of Hungary. If an NRR of 0.9 were achieved within a few years in the Netherlands, the total population would continue to grow for about four decades to a size roughly 20% larger than it is now and then would start to decline (Figure 6-1 and Table 6-2). If, however, the fertility decline over the coming two to four or

Table 6-1   Basic Demographic Measures, Hungary, Projection 1, Linear Fertility Decline to NRR of 0.9, 1965-2050

	Total Population			Crude Birth Rate	Crude Death Rate	Rate of Natural Increase
	Absolute Size	Index (1970 = 100)				
1970	10.6	100	1965-1970	14	11	0.30
1980	10.9	102	1975-1980	14	12	0.21
1990	11.0	103	1985-1990	12	12	0.05
2000	10.9	102	1995-2000	12	13	-0.07
2020	10.6	99	2015-2020	11	13	-0.22
2040	9.9	93	2035-2040	11	14	-0.33
2050	9.6	90	2045-2050	11	15	-0.38

more decades were fairly slow, total population growth—at least
during the rest of this century and the first half of the next
century—would not differ significantly from the case in which an NRR
of 1.0 was attained. In other words, only if an NRR of 0.9 is reached
"soon" can the effects be meaningful within the lifespan of the current
generation. To summarize, even with a fertility level slightly below
replacement it does not seem likely that any population in the world
will decrease in size during the remainder of the twentieth century.

For the *less developed countries* the interpretation of the
projections is more complex, mainly because it can hardly be expected
that a 0.9 NRR will be achieved within 10 to 15 years in countries
where high fertility has only begun to decline. For most of the less
developed countries it is probably appropriate to consider Projections
One and Two of this variation as unattainable alternatives. If one used
Projection Three as an example of a "realistic" alternative, say, in
Iran, one discovers that in terms of total population growth there is

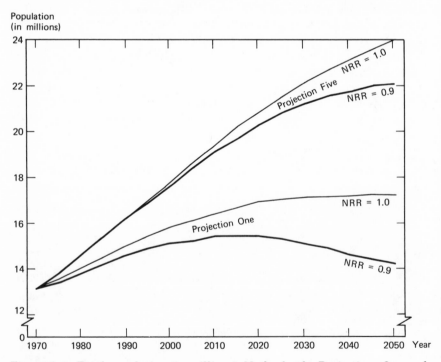

Figure 6–1. Total population (in millions), Netherlands, Projections One and
Five, linear decline of fertility to NRR of 1.0 and 0.9, 1970–2050.

practically no difference for the year 2000 between an NRR of 0.9 and one of 1.0. Gradually during the twenty-first century the gap between the two possibilities widens (Figure 6-2).

Table 6-2   Selected Demographic Measures, Netherlands, Projections 1 and 5, Linear Fertility Decline to NRR of 1.0 and 0.9, 1965-2040

	Total Population and Index (1970 = 100)			Female Rates of Population Growth	
	Fertility Decline to			Fertility Decline to	
	1.0	0.9		1.0	0.9
	Projection 1 *(NRR = 1.0 or 0.9 in 1970-1975)*				
1970	13.1 100	13.1 100	1965-1970	1.1	1.1
1980	14.0 107	13.8 106	1975-1980	0.7	0.6
1990	15.0 115	14.6 111	1985-1990	0.7	0.5
2000	15.8 121	15.1 115	1995-2000	0.5	0.3
2020	16.9 129	15.4 118	2015-2020	0.2	-0.1
2040	17.1 131	14.6 112	2035-2040	0.0	-0.4
	Projection 5 *(NRR = 1.0 or 0.9 in 2040-2045)*				
1970	13.1 100	13.1 100	1965-1970	1.1	1.1
1980	14.6 112	14.6 112	1975-1980	1.1	1.1
1990	16.2 124	16.2 124	1985-1990	1.0	1.0
2000	17.8 136	17.6 135	1995-2000	0.9	0.9
2020	20.9 160	20.3 155	2015-2020	0.7	0.6
2040	23.1 117	21.7 166	2035-2040	0.4	0.2

It seems, therefore, that although the effort to achieve an NRR of 0.9 instead of 1.0 could make a substantial difference in total population growth, this difference will not appear in this century,

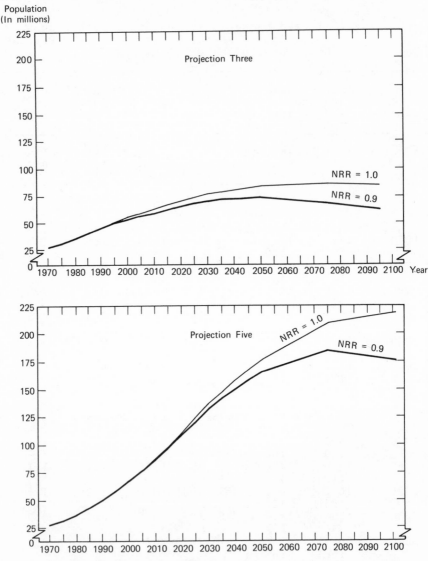

Figure 6–2. Total population (in millions), Iran, Projections Three and Five, linear decline of fertility to NRR of 1.0 (standard set) and linear decline of fertility to NRR of 0.9 (modification 2), 1970–2100.

because for most of the world the probability of achieving an NRR of 0.9 before the end of the twentieth century is not large. For instance, the result of achieving an NRR of 0.9 rather than 1.0 by the beginning of the twenty-first century is a population of 5.8 billion inhabitants rather than one of 5.9 billion. In the year 2050 there would be 7.1 versus 8.2 billion persons. However, in 2100 there would be 6.2 versus 8.4 billion persons, because during the second half of the twenty-first century the world population would be decreasing if an NRR of 0.9 were maintained throughout that century.

2. A LOGARITHMIC FERTILITY DECLINE

Logarithmic fertility decline implies that the trend of fertility decline would first be fast and later would slow down. Such a situation might occur in countries where the implementation of a family planning program would have a significant impact.

Let us take the population of Morocco as an example (Figure 6-3).

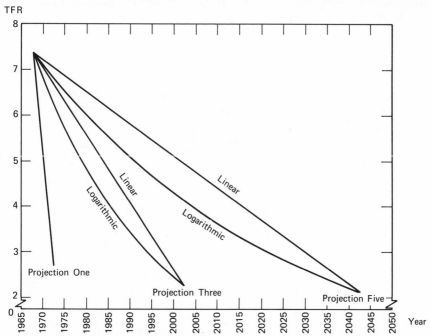

Figure 6-3. Total fertility rate assumptions, Morocco, Projections One, Three, and Five, linear (standard set) and logarithmic decline, 1965–2050.

It is obvious that for Projection One the type of fertility decline does not make any difference because the assumed fertility decline is identical for linear and logarithmic types of decline (whether such a situation can materialize is irrelevant in the present context). For any of the other alternative projections the type of fertility decline does make a difference, even if fertility of replacement levels is ultimately reached at the same point in time. In summary:

1. The difference between linear and logarithmic declines in terms of total population size is greater in the long run. No matter when an NRR of 1.0 is achieved, population growth is slower with a logarithmic fertility decline than with a linear one (Table 6-3).

2. The difference in total population size is significant especially when it takes a long time to achieve an NRR of 1.0. If in general it can be assumed that fertility decline will be a long-term process, ultimate population size will be substantially smaller with a logarithmic rather than a linear path of fertility decline.

These findings represent a different formulation of the argument that the type of current short-term fertility developments are an extremely important factor for long-term population growth.

Table 6-3   Total Population (in millions) and Indices of Population Size (1970 = 100), Morocco, Projections 1, 3, and 5, Linear and Logarithmic Fertility Decline to NRR of 1.0, 1970-2100

	Period in Which NRR of 1.0 Is Reached					
	1970-1975 Projection 1		2000-2005 Projection 3		2040-2045 Projection 5	
	Linear	Log.	Linear	Log.	Linear	Log.
1970	15.8	15.8	15.8	15.8	15.8	15.8
	100	100	100	100	100	100
2000	22.3	22.3	33.4	30.5	41.4	38.0
	141	141	211	193	262	240
2050	27.6	27.6	51.9	45.2	116.1	87.9
	175	175	328	286	735	556
2100	28.2	28.2	53.6	46.6	145.8	103.9
	178	178	339	295	923	658

3. A TEMPORARY 15% INCREASE IN FERTILITY
FOLLOWED BY A LINEAR FERTILITY DECLINE TO AN NRR OF 1.0

The circumstances that inspired this modification were real or anticipated developments in both more developed and some less developed countries.

The smaller or larger baby booms of the more advanced countries are fresh in the memory of most people—many of us participated on either the "cause" or the "consequence" side. In some less developed countries (e.g., Kenya[1]) there seems to be evidence and in several others[2] the assumption of a temporary increase in fertility. For the sake of simplicity we decided to apply a uniform procedure for all populations—a 15% increase of current fertility[3] over a period of 10 years followed by a linear fertility decline to an NRR of 1.0 at different points in time in the future.[4]

There is no reason to believe that such a fertility increase might occur on a worldwide basis, but let us illustrate the population growth consequences on the total world population. If a worldwide temporary fertility increase were to take place during the 1970s and fertility were thereafter to decline, future population growth would be considerably different than without such a fertility increase (Table 6-4). Other things being equal, in the year 2000 the world population would be 1 billion inhabitants larger than according to the standard set assumptions. The long-term consequences of such a baby boom could be far ranging. If the fertility decline following the baby boom were fairly moderate (Projection Five) the world would have 18 instead of 13 billion inhabitants only 80 years hence.

For individual countries the population growth consequences could be of even larger magnitude than described above. As already mentioned, it is believed that the population of Kenya is experienceng a fertility increase compatible with our assumptions. The differences between population growth alternatives of the standard set and the baby boom modification for Kenya are presented in Table 6-5. Even if we assume a rapid fertility decline after the assumed fertility increase (Projection 3), the difference of the total population number in the year 2000 would be almost 5 million inhabitants—25.3 instead of 20.7 million. The long-term consequences of a temporary fertility increase combined with a subsequent moderate fertility decline (Projection Five) are almost unbelievable: in the year 2050 there would be almost 110 million inhabitants in Kenya as a result of a 1970 temporary increase compared with 60 million if such a fertility trend were avoided.

Table 6-4   Total Population (in billions) and Indices of Population Size (1970 = 100), World Population, Projections 3 and 5, Standard Set and Temporary Fertility Increase in the 1970-1985 Period, 1970-2100

| | Period in Which NRR of 1.0 Is Reached | | | |
| | 2000-2005 *Projection 3* | | 2040-2045 *Projection 5* | |
	Standard Set	Temporary Fertility Increase	Standard Set	Temporary Fertility Increase
1970	3.6	3.6	3.6	3.6
	100	100	100	100
2000	5.9	6.9	6.7	7.7
	162	189	183	212
2050	8.2	10.3	13.0	18.1
	224	283	357	497
2100	8.4	10.6	15.1	21.9
	230	292	414	601

A fertility increase in Hungary, for instance, could naturally make a difference in the future growth of its population. The 15% increase employed in our assumptions would, however, bring fertility only slightly above replacement level; thus the difference would not be very significant. If the 1965–70 average fertility were maintained, the total population of Hungary would be about 11.1 million inhabitants around the year 2000; a 15% baby boom might yield a population between 11.6 and 11.8 million in the year 2000. In the long run, the differences between fertility remaining constant or the baby boom modification could be significant, for instance, 10.5 million as opposed to 13.0 million (in the year 2050), respectively.

One is again reminded of the meaningful impact of current fertility trends on long-term population growth. If in any population a fertility increase should occur (whether desired or possibly as a side effect of welfare or other policies), it should be realized that in a demographic situation of declining mortality and large cohorts of

Table 6-5   Total Population (in millions) and Indices of Population Size (1970 = 100), Kenya, Projections 3 and 5, Standard Set and Temporary Fertility Increase in the 1970-1985 Period, 1970-2100

| | Period in Which NRR of 1.0 Is Reached | | | |
| | 2000-2005 Projection 3 | | 2040-2045 Projection 5 | |
	Standard Set	Temporary Fertility Increase	Standard Set	Temporary Fertility Increase
1970	10.9	10.9	10.9	10.9
	100	100	100	100
2000	20.7	25.3	24.8	36.3
	190	231	227	332
2050	30.3	40.0	59.7	107.0
	277	366	546	979
2100	31.1	41.2	71.9	135.7
	284	377	658	1241

childbearing ages such a fertility decline will produce long-lasting effects.

4. CONSTANT FERTILITY FOLLOWED BY FERTILITY DECLINE TO AN NRR OF 1.0

In many less developed countries fertility has basically remained at its traditional levels even though mortality has started to decline. It is the purpose of this modification to point out the population growth consequences of a possible continuation of such trends. As in all the other sets of projections—"standard" or "modified"—the particular assumptions are applied to illustrate the population growth consequences of a theoretical alternative, in this particular case, of maintained, current, constant fertility. It is naturally an open question for any population whether such a situation will materialize and if so, for how long.

Projections One through Five of this modification differ from each other by length of time over which current fertility is held constant (0, 10, 30, 50, 70 years in Projections One through Five, respectively). Once fertility does start to decline, it is assumed that it declines instantly to an NRR level of 1.0. For example, in Projection Three the GRR remains at its 1965–70 level throughout the remainder of the twentieth century and then drops sharply to a level corresponding to an NRR of 1.0. Such a sharp drop in fertility following constant fertility is very unlikely to occur in reality. Therefore, the computed population growth consequences outline the low ("optimistic") limit of what would happen if current fertility were to persist for any extended period of time.

Both the short-run and the long-run population growth consequences of this modification are well known and have been pointed out quite frequently. The total world population could number around 7.5 billion at the turn of the century, and if fertility were to remain constant up to 2040–45, world population in the middle of the next century would be around 25 billion (Table 6-6 and Figure 6-4). Even if fertility thereafter sharply declined, by the end of the twenty-first

Table 6-6   Total Population (in billions) and Indices of Population Size (1970 = 100), World Population, Projections 1, 3, and 5, Standard Set and Constant Fertility Modification, 1970-2100

	Period in Which NRR of 1.0 Is Reached					
	1970-1975 Projection 1		2000-2005 Projection 3		2040-2045 Projection 5	
	Standard Set	Constant Fertility	Standard Set	Constant Fertility	Standard Set	Constant Fertility
1970	3.6	3.6	3.6	3.6	3.6	3.6
	100	100	100	100	100	100
2000	4.7	4.7	5.9	7.4	6.7	7.4
	130	130	162	203	183	203
2050	5.6	5.6	8.2	11.6	13.0	24.9
	153	153	224	318	357	684
2100	5.7	5.7	8.4	12.1	15.1	36.7
	156	156	230	333	414	1006

century world population would be in the order of 40–45 billion inhabitants.

The population-growth consequences of sustained current fertility for individual countries could be extremely difficult to cope with. In

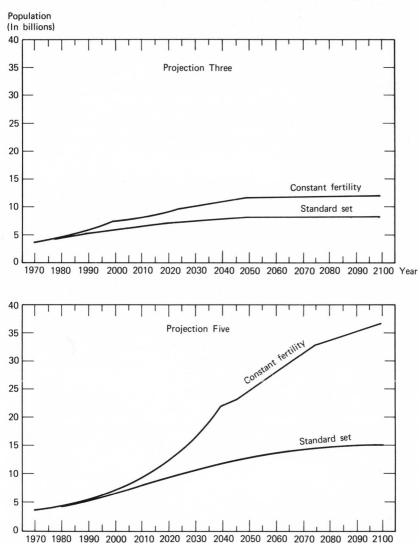

Figure 6–4. Total population (in billions), world population, Projections Three and Five, fertility decline to NRR of 1.0 (standard set) and constant fertility (modification 5), 1970–2100.

Kenya, for instance, if fertility remained constant throughout the remainder of this century (Projection Three), its population could theoretically increase from its current 11 million to almost 30 almost 30 million by the year 2000 and to at least 50 million by the year 2050. If fertility were to remain constant even during the first half of the next century (Projection Five) Kenya could have 150 million inhabitants by 2050 and almost 250 million by 2100 (Table 6-7).

5. CHANGES OF FERTILITY PATTERNS BY AGE

Age patterns of fertility can differ from one population to another. If in a particular population women commence their actual childbearing performance soon they are likely to have a relatively large number of children because:

1. They are exposed to the probability of conceiving for a longer period of their lives.

Table 6-7   Total Population (in millions) and Indices of Population Size (1970 = 100), Kenya, Projections 3 and 5, Standard Set and Constant Fertility Modification, 1970-2100

	Period in Which NRR of 1.0 Is Reached			
	2000-2005 Projection 3		2040-2045 Projection 5	
	Standard Set	Constant Fertility	Standard Set	Constant Fertility
1970	10.9	10.9	10.9	10.9
	100	100	100	100
2000	20.7	28.9	24.8	28.9
	190	265	227	265
2050	30.3	48.5	59.7	150.6
	277	443	546	1377
2100	31.1	50.6	71.9	238.3
	284	463	658	2180

2. At younger ages fewer women have died, and therefore more women are likely to bear children.

3. Because most populations of less developed countries in the past two decades have experienced high fertility and a meaningful mortality decline, they are young populations; each lower age group is considerably larger than the next higher one (the age group 15–19 is larger than the 20–24 group, etc.; e.g., in India in 1970 the former was estimated to have 27 million women and the latter 23 million). It can naturally make a difference, therefore, at which ages child births occur.

Furthermore, the process of shifting the ages of childbearing in time also has an effect on the total number of births over the period in question: other things being equal, an upward shift will cause a decline in the number of births, and a downward shift will have an opposite effect. One can imagine, say, an upward shift of 1 year in the average age of childbearing as if for a whole year no children were born; in reality the shift is spread out in time and is less conspicuous. Moreover, a certain number of women die during the "childless" year.

This modification has an additional meaning. The examples that are presented illustrate the obvious population growth consequences of changes of age patterns of fertility. Since such changes do occur concurrently with trends of fertility decrease or increase, they should be thought of as a part of the overall process of population growth. In a trend of fertility decline, an upward shift of the mean age of childbearing will reinforce deceleration of population growth, and, to the contrary, a downward shift will retard the deceleration of population growth.

It was considered useful to analyze the effects of changes in fertility patterns separately because a process of fertility decline can be accompanied by a downward, an upward, or no shift in childbearing ages. Yet had the changes in age patterns of fertility been included in the basic part of the analysis, they would have obscured the main exposition.

The reader will recall that in the preceding analysis age patterns of fertility were held constant throughout the projected period. If the GRR for a subsequent period was assumed to have declined by 10%, each age-specific fertility rate would decline by this percentage, but the age pattern of fertility would remain unchanged. In the present variation, in addition to trends of fertility levels, changes in the age patterns of fertility are assumed. Different age patterns of fertility can be approximated by giving the mean age of the fertility schedule. The mean age of the fertility schedule of 27 as opposed to 29, for instance, signifies that more children were born to relatively young women; that is, the age-specific fertility rates with a mean age of 27 are relatively high for the young age groups and relatively low for the older age groups. The model distributions of the age-specific maternity rates applied in this variation are the same as those used by Coale and Demeny in the *Regional Model Life Tables and Stable Populations* and are given in Table 6-8.

Let us illustrate the possible impact of a change in fertility patterns on future population growth. For example, in a country like Kenya with currently high fertility and mortality levels, the impact of a change in age fertility patterns would be quite significant. For the standard set of projections the mean age of childbearing is assumed to be 29 years. If the mean age of childbearing were to decline to an average age of 27 within a decade and then remain at this level, and, at the same time, overall fertility were rapidly to decline to an NRR of 1.0 by the year 2000 (Projection Three), the population of Kenya in 2050 could be 33.5 million as compared with 30.3 million without any change in the mean age of childbearing (Table 6-9). On the other hand, an assumed increase in the mean age of childbearing from 29 to 31

Table 6-8   Fertility Schedules (annual female births per woman in specified age group) with Mean Age (m) Equal to 27, 29, 31, and 33 Years

	Annual Female Births per Woman			
	$m = 27$	$m = 29$	$m = 31$	$m = 33$
15-19	.029	.018	.008	.002
20-24	.055	.052	.032	.019
25-29	.054	.056	.054	.047
30-34	.037	.044	.050	.056
35-39	.020	.028	.034	.046
40-44	.004	.010	.018	.025
45-49	.001	.002	.004	.005
GRR	1.000	1.000	1.000	1.000

Source: Ansley J. Coale and Paul Demeny. *Regional Model Life Tables and Stable Populations*. Princeton: Princeton University Press, 1966, p. 30.

years with overall fertility decreasing as above would result in a population of 29.1 million instead of 30.3 million in 2050. If the overall trends of fertility decline were somewhat slower (Projection Four) and an NRR of 1.0 were not reached until 2020–25 the downward shift would generate a population of 49 million in 2050 compared with 43 million generated without changes of the age patterns of fertility. In most demographically more developed countries there was a tendency of the mean age of childbearing to drop during periods of fertility decline.[5] Such a development in Kenya could cancel some of the consequences of a possible fertility decline.

To summarize, changes in the age patterns of fertility could be a significant factor influencing population growth trends in the less developed countries. Several facets of life underlie changing age patterns of fertility: changes in marriage patterns—especially changes in the age of marriage (which can be in either direction)—and the

Table 6-9   Total Population (in millions) and Indices of Population Size (1970 = 100), Kenya, Projections 3 and 4, Standard Set and Modifications of Varying Mean Age of Fertility, 1970-2050

	Rise in Mean Age of Fertility from 29 to 31	Standard Set (mean age of fertility = 29)	Decline in Mean Age of Fertility from 29 to 27
Projection 3 (NRR = 1.0 in 2000-2005)			
1970	10.9	10.9	10.9
	100	100	100
2000	20.2	20.7	21.9
	185	190	200
2050	29.1	30.3	33.5
	266	277	306
Projection 4 (NRR = 1.0 in 2020-2025)			
1970	10.9	10.9	10.9
	100	100	100
2000	22.7	23.4	24.9
	208	214	228
2050	40.7	43.2	49.3
	372	395	451

gradual adoption of family planning in societies that previously practiced a minimum of family limitation, which has often in the initial stages caused a larger decline of fertility in the older age groups than in the younger age groups and consequently a decline in the mean age of childbearing.

In demographically more developed countries we are confronted with a different dimension of this interaction of fertility trends and changes of age patterns of fertility. The level of overall fertility is not likely to undergo changes of an order comparable to what may occur in the less developed countries. At first glance it seems as if changes of the age patterns of fertility have only trivial effects. Even if one takes a country like Trinidad and Tobago, which is still amidst the "demographic transition" (our estimates for 1965–70: GRR = 1.9, female e_0^0 = 68), the population growth consequences of quite an increase in the mean age of childbearing, namely from 26 to 29 years, seem to be negligible (Table 6-10).

Table 6-10   Total Population (in millions) and Indices of Population Size (1970 = 100), Trinidad & Tobago, Projections 3 and 5, Standard Set and Modifications of Varying Mean Age of Fertility, 1970-2050

	Rise in Mean Age of Childbearing from 26 to 29	Standard Set (mean age = 26)
Projection 3 (NRR = 1.0 in 2000-2005)		
1970	1.09	1.09
	100	100
2000	1.87	1.88
	172	173
2050	2.55	2.59
	235	239
Projection 5 (NRR = 1.0 in 2040-2045)		
1970	1.09	1.09
	100	100
2000	2.03	2.05
	187	188
2050	3.50	3.61
	322	333

The point of the matter is that changes in age patterns of fertility can be meaningful even in more developed countries. The measures of fertility that have been used throughout this analysis do have some deficiencies. They were good enough for most of the calculations, but some subtleties cannot be captured by this procedure. This study has used so-called period or cross-section measures, which refer to all women at a specific point or period in time. For instance, fertility data about the 1965–70 period refer to the cross section of women in that period. In order to calculate the real consequences of changes in the age patterns of fertility, one would have to utilize so-called cohort measures. These measures refer to women of, say, a certain birth cohort (i.e., women born in 1935–40) and their fertility experience throughout their lifetime.

Because cohort calculations for most countries are practically impossible to carry out for lack of necessary data, a substitute calculation based on findings of previous research[6] has been designed. This calculation gives approximate results for the situation when a population approaches and then stabilizes at the fertility level of replacement, but at the same time a roughly 2-year increase in the mean age of childbearing occurs. In terms of period NRR trends this process is expressed by a temporary (approximately 15 years) decline of the NRR below 1.0 and followed by a stabilization of fertility at the replacement level. As illustrated in Table 6-11, the rise in the mean age of childbearing can cause quite significant differences in future population size, both in the remainder of this century as well as in the long run.

From the vantage point of population policy, fertility patterns by age are certainly a factor to keep in mind, whether they are induced by postponement of marriage or by any other means. On the other hand, our computations do show only the general outline of the matter—the broad significance of this factor both in less developed countries and in the more developed countries. Considerably more research along these lines is necessary. Even according to our rough computations, it would seem that fertility patterns should certainly not be neglected. The difference in the size of the world population in the short and in the long run can be significantly influenced by age patterns of fertility, other things being equal (Table 6-12). Simply as a result of alternative trends of age fertility patterns (with a world NRR of 1.0 reached by the year 2000) the world population in the middle of the next century could, for instance, number 7.8 rather than 8.6 billion inhabitants.

Table 6-11   Total Population (in millions) and Indices of Population Size (1970 = 100), Japan and Netherlands, Projection 2, Standard Set and Substitute Calculation of Rise in Mean Age of Cohort Fertility, 1970-2050

	Rise in Mean Age of Cohort Fertility	Standard Set
Japan		
1970	105.8	105.8
	100	100
2000	126.9	130.7
	120	123
2050	128.9	138.3
	122	131
Netherlands		
1970	13.1	13.1
	100	100
2000	15.8	16.3
	121	125
2050	17.0	18.1
	130	139

6. LINEAR FERTILITY DECLINE TO AN NRR OF 1.0 WITH A "SLOW" DECLINE OF MORTALITY

Throughout the entire study a single path of mortality change has been assumed for each population unit. Its general feature is that respective current rates of mortality decline are assumed to continue during the next two decades or so, then the rate of mortality decline would gradually slow down. The fact that this pattern—in very broad limits—is historically justified, is, of course, no gurantee that mortality will continue to go along similar paths. It is the purpose of this section to illustrate the magnitude of population growth consequences of possible variations in the path of mortality change.

To visualize the consequences of an abnormal worldwide

Table 6-12   Total Population (in billions) and Indices of
Population Size (1970 = 100), World Total,
Projection 3, Standard Set and Modifications
of Varying Mean Age of Fertility, 1970-2050

	Rise in Mean Age of Fertility from 29 to 31	Standard Set (mean age of fertility = 29)	Decline in Mean Age of Fertility from 29 to 27
1970	3.6	3.6	3.6
	100	100	100
2000	5.8	5.9	6.1
	158	162	167
2050	7.8	8.2	8.6
	214	224	236

catastrophe is not too difficult. A possible third world war in which
nuclear weapons would be used could signify the end of life on earth
altogether. On the other hand, wars, famines, and epidemics of the
kind experienced during the past century or so probably did not alter
the magnitude of world population growth substantially.[7] Let it be
repeated that past trends are no guarantee for the future, and there
may be a period ahead of us in which in some countries or regions of
the world populations will experience increased mortality rates as a
result of human-induced and, of course, undesired disasters, for
example, imbalance of the ecosystem or unmanageable population
density.

Thus far, however, there does not seem to be any evidence that
current trends of mortality decline will suddenly cease and mortality
conditions remain constant. Therefore, to illustrate the population
growth consequences of a "reasonable" variation of our standard
mortality assumption, it was assumed that, whatever the present level
of mortality, it would decline at a linear rate from now to the point in
time when it reaches its "original" stabilized level of the female e_0^0 of
values between 71.0 and 77.5.

First of all it is obvious that the described calculations are
meaningless in countries where mortality is already low, because in
any event mortality cannot (with present medical technology) decline
much further. It is, however, almost surprising that even in countries
where mortality is still very high a difference in the path of mortality

decline of the type described above does not have major population growth consequences. For instance, in Iran (fertility declining to an NRR level of 1.0 by 2000–05) the total population would increase by 96% with a "slow" mortality decline instead of 101% with a "standard" mortality decline; by the year 2050 the country's population growth indices would be 196% instead of 207%, respectively (Table 6-13). Even in a country like Kenya, where the estimated female $e_0{}^0$ for the 1965–70 period was only 45 years, both the short-run and long-run population growth consequences of somewhat slower paths of mortality decline are rather insignificant (Table 6-14).

7. DEMOGRAPHIC CONDITIONS NEEDED TO GENERATE AN ABSOLUTE DISCONTINUATION OF POPULATION GROWTH

Thus far throughout the study the population growth consequences of different paths of fertility change have been explored. The main assumption in almost all projections is a specific type of fertility

Table 6-13   Total Population (in millions) and Indices of Population Size (1970 = 100), Iran, Projection 3, Standard Set and "Slow" Mortality Decline Modification, 1965-2050

| | Assumed Mortality Trends (e_0^0) | | Population at End of Period (NRR = 1.0 in 2000-2005) | |
| | | | Mortality Decline Being | |
	Standard	"Slow"	Standard	"Slow"
1965-1970	52.0	52.0	27.9	27.9
			100	100
1995-2000	65.5	61.0	56.2	54.7
			201	196
2020-2025	72.0	68.5	75.3	72.2
			269	258
2045-2050	74.5	74.5	85.9	82.8
			307	296

change—this is the dominant independent variable, and most other demographic features of the respective population unit are dependent variables. Among these the evolution of the population growth rates is a function of assumed fertility behavior.

This section illustrates demographic consequences of certain types of population growth rate developments. What would demographic behavior have to be like in order to achieve a specific rate of population growth by a certain date?

There are innumerable ways of investigating these relationships. Because, however, a zero population growth rate is so often discussed in various connections, let this be the guideline. Again, there are five alternative projections. They differ from each other by speed of decline of the population growth rate. In each projection the point of departure is the estimated 1970 population and the average population growth rate of the 1965–70 period. In Projection One it is assumed that the respective population units will stop growing immediately. In Projection Two the population growth rate drops linearly from its 1965–70 level to zero by 1980–85, in Projection Three by 2000–05, and

Table 6-14   Total Population (in millions) and Indices of Population Size (1970 = 100), Kenya, Projection 3, Standard Set and "Slow" Mortality Decline Modification, 1965-2050

	Assumed Mortality Trends (e_0^0)		Population at End of Period (NRR = 1.0 in 2000-2005) Mortality Decline Being	
	Standard	"Slow"	Standard	"Slow"
1965-1970	45.0	45.0	10.9	10.9
			100	100
1995-2000	59.0	57.0	20.7	20.5
			190	187
2020-2025	67.5	64.5	26.8	26.1
			245	239
2045-2050	72.0	72.0	30.3	29.5
			277	270

so on. The mortality assumptions are the same as in all other sets of projections.

An immediate cessation of population growth may occur in some more developed countries, but in most countries of the world such a development seems quite unlikely. In many *more developed countries*, if it were considered desirable to generate an immediate cessation of population growth, fertility would immediately have to drop considerably below replacement levels (Table 6-15). Even, for instance, in Belgium where the population growth rate at the end of the 1960s was only 0.3% per year, total fertility would have to decline to 1.7 in the 1980s.

In the *demographically less developed countries* it is inconceivable that their population growth might cease during the next few years. What kind of demographic trends would have to be engendered in order to bring about a cessation of population growth by the end of the

Table 6-15   Selected Demographic Measures, Netherlands and Belgium, Projection 1, Linear Decline to Zero Rate of Population Growth, 1965-2000

	Female Rate of Population Growth	Total Fertility Rate	Net Reproduction Rate	Female Crude Birth Rate
Netherlands				
1965-1970	1.1	2.8	1.3	19
1970-1975	0.0	1.2	0.6	8
1975-1980	0.0	1.1	0.5	9
1980-1985	0.0	1.2	0.6	10
1985 1990	0.0	1.2	0.6	10
1990-1995	0.0	1.4	0.7	11
1995-2000	0.0	1.7	0.8	11
Belgium				
1965-1970	0.3	2.4	1.1	15
1970-1975	0.0	2.0	0.9	13
1975-1980	0.0	1.9	0.9	13
1980-1985	0.0	1.8	0.8	13
1985-1990	0.0	1.7	0.8	12
1990-1995	0.0	1.8	0.9	12
1995-2000	0.0	1.9	0.9	12

twentieth century and to maintain a zero population growth rate throughout the twenty-first century?[8] In most less developed countries fertility would have to decline very rapidly throughout the remainder of this century, and by the beginning of the twenty-first century an almost 1-child family would have to be the prevailing pattern. In India, for example, the average number of children per woman would have to be around 1.2 for about 20 years starting in the second half of the 1990s (Table 6-16). Because such a "baby-recession" would produce small cohorts of potential mothers in the 2030s and the 2040s, fertility could start to increase in the 2030s—a zero population growth would be maintained even with a 3-child family pattern during years when "baby-recession" children would enter the childbearing ages. To put it differently, an attempt to generate a nongrowing population in the less developed regions fairly "soon" implies an extremely rapid fertility decline that would have to go way below the replacement level. As a matter of fact, for a nontrivial period of time the average family size could be only slightly higher than 1 child.

The age structure evolution would also be very unbalanced. If a zero population growth rate could at all be achieved by the year 2000, say, in India, by the 2020s the persons eligible for university study and entering the labor force would be so few that the young labor force age groups would decline very rapidly (Table 6-17).

Table 6-16   Selected Demographic Measures, India, Projection 3, Linear Decline to Zero Rate of Population Growth, 1965-2050

	Female Rate of Population Growth	Total Fertility Rate	Net Reproduction Rate	Female Crude Birth Rate
1965-1970	2.4	5.5	2.0	40
1975-1980	1.7	3.9	1.5	30
1985-1990	1.0	2.4	1.0	21
1995-2000	0.4	1.4	0.6	13
2005-2010	0.0	1.1	0.5	10
2015-2020	0.0	1.6	0.7	11
2025-2030	0.0	2.5	1.2	13
2035-2040	0.0	3.2	1.5	16
2045-2050	0.0	3.0	1.4	16

Table 6-17 Female Population of Selected Age Groups (in millions) and Annual Growth Rates of Age Groups (in %), India, Projection 3, Zero Population Growth Modification, 1965-2025

ABSOLUTE NUMBER

	1965	1970	1975	1980	1985	1990	1995	2000	2005	2010	2015	2020	2025
0-4	39.3	43.1	42.4	40.4	37.0	33.0	27.9	22.3	16.6	17.6	18.8	20.6	22.6
5-9	32.3	37.1	41.1	40.6	39.0	35.9	32.2	27.3	22.0	16.4	17.4	18.7	20.4
10-14	27.3	31.6	36.4	40.5	40.1	38.5	35.6	31.9	27.1	21.8	16.3	17.3	18.6
15-19	23.3	26.8	31.1	35.8	40.0	39.6	38.2	35.3	31.7	27.0	21.7	16.2	17.3
20-24	20.4	22.7	26.1	30.4	35.2	39.3	39.1	37.7	34.9	31.4	26.7	21.6	16.1
TOTAL	237.0	267.1	295.9	322.4	345.3	363.6	376.4	383.0	383.0	383.0	383.0	383.0	383.0

ANNUAL GROWTH RATE

	1965-70	1970-75	1975-80	1980-85	1985-90	1990-95	1995-2000	2000-05	2005-10	2010-15	2015-20	2020-25
0-4	1.9	-0.4	-1.0	-1.7	-2.3	-3.3	-4.3	-5.8	1.2	1.4	1.8	1.9
5-9	2.8	2.1	-0.2	-0.8	-1.6	-2.2	-3.2	-4.3	-5.7	1.2	1.4	1.8
10-14	3.0	2.9	2.2	-0.2	-0.8	-1.6	-2.2	-3.2	-4.3	-5.7	1.2	1.4
15-19	2.8	3.0	2.9	2.2	-0.2	-0.8	-1.6	-2.1	-3.2	-4.2	-5.7	1.3
20-24	2.1	2.9	3.1	3.0	2.2	-0.1	-0.7	-1.5	-2.1	-3.1	-4.2	-5.7
TOTAL	2.4	2.1	1.7	1.4	1.0	0.7	0.4	0.0	0.0	0.0	0.0	0.0

8. A SUMMARY

Within the framework of investigating paths to stationary populations, the purpose of this chapter is to illustrate the population growth consequences of certain modifications of the standard set of assumptions. The modifications are constructed to demonstrate features of future population growth that would result as a consequence of possible real developments and—as in the last variation—to demonstrate the demographic developments that would have to be generated to achieve a certain type of population growth.

1. Whether an NRR of 1.0 or 0.9 is ultimately reached in a less developed country does not make a meaningful difference in terms of population growth throughout the remainder of this century. As a matter of fact, even if an NRR of 0.9 were attained and maintained, many of the populations of the more developed countries would still grow throughout the coming three to four decades, although more slowly than with an NRR of 1.0.

2. In a less developed country fertility decline that was fast in the near future and that decelerated later would have a significantly larger impact on future population growth than a linear decline of fertility. Such a logarithmic decline in a more developed country would have almost no effect whatsoever because it would represent only a minor deviation from a linear fertility decline.

3. A temporary fertility increase of the "baby boom" type of the 1950s in a more developed country would certainly engender a significantly faster population growth than a linear decline of fertility in both the short run and the long run. Such a fertility increase is anticipated even in a number of less developed countries. Should it occur, these populations would grow very rapidly and, for example, by 2050 they could be twice as big as with a moderate fertility decline (i.e., 10 times their current size).

4. The population growth consequences of sustained constant fertility would also be extremely difficult to cope with. In the short run such a development would be less meaningful than the temporary fertility increase: in the long run, however, population numbers of enormous quantities could develop, for example, a world population of 25 billion inhabitants in the year 2050.

5. Changes in the age patterns of fertility are no doubt a subtlety compared with most of the other possible trends. Often, however, they do occur concurrently with other trends, and they can either decelerate or accelerate the overlying trends. In the absence of other trends, for

example, if, the level of fertility would be almost constant, a shift in the age patterns of fertility can have visible effects.

6. Provided that mortality declines, populations will grow at an almost equal pace irrespective of whether the rate of future mortality decline is moderately fast or moderately slow.

7. If a cessation of population growth is considered desirable in the more developed countries within the next few years and in the less developed countries not later than in the beginning of the next century, in most countries incredibly rapid fertility declines would be needed. Furthermore, when zero population growth is attained, fertility will have to be far below replacement levels and remain there for about two to three decades.

NOTES

1. According to a press release by the Minister for Finance and Economic Planning on the 1969 Kenya Population Census the TFR was estimated at 7.6. In reference to a previous TFR estimate of 6.8 (1962) it is stated: "While it is possible that the latter may have been underestimated, there is nevertheless some evidence that fertility has risen during the intercensal period."

2. The conjecture that fertility might increase in some countries of Middle Africa has been expressed by Etienne Van de Walle in "Future growth of population and changes in population composition: Tropical Africa," *World Population Conference, 1965*, Vol. II (New York: United Nations, 1967), p. 45.

3. For example, in the United States the GRR in 1950 was 24% higher than in 1945; in Kenya in 1969 the GRR was estimated to be 12% higher than in 1962.

4. The NRR of 1.0 in Projections Three through Five is reached in the same years as in the standard set (2000–05, 2020–25, 2040–45). In Projections One and Two a 10 year time lag was unavoidable because of the nature of the modification so that Projections One and Two of this modification and of the standard set are not strictly comparable.

5. The few available data for the developing countries seem to indicate such a trend. In the 1950s and 1960s the mean age of childbearing was declining in Taiwan (1950—30.6; 1960—29.8; 1969—27.7), South Korea (1960—30.8; 1970—29.8), and Puerto Rico (1950—28.4; 1960—27.9; 1970—27.3), and was unchanged in Hong Kong (1961 and 1968—29.4), and in Costa Rica (1960 and 1968—29.2).

6. Tomas Frejka, "Reflections on the Demographic Conditions Needed to

Establish a U.S. Stationary Population Growth," *Population Studies,* Vol. 22, No. 3 (November 1968), p. 396.

7. It can be calculated schematically that all the national and regional disasters on record since 1850, terrible as they have been, have delayed the growth in world population by no more than about ten years. Had there been no war, famine or epidemic since 1850 the world's population might have totalled more than 2,000 million in 1920 instead of in 1930, and more than 3,500 million in 1960 instead of in 1970." *A Concise Summary of the World Population Situation in 1970* (New York, United Nations, 1971), p. 4.

8. Cf. J. Bourgeois-Pichat and S. A. Taleb, "Un taux d'accroissement nul pour les pays en voie de développement en l'an 2000. Rêve ou réalite?" *Population,* Vol. 25, No. 5, September-October 1970, p. 957.

7

Population Growth Alternatives of the United States

1. THE ISSUE

The future growth and a possible cessation of growth of the United States populations[1] has certainly become an issue of American public life. Discussions and debates are a permanent part of the scene, not only in professional academic journals but also in the daily newspapers, radio, television, and popular journals. The general public[2] as well as the intellectual and political elite are increasingly concerned with the growth (and distribution) of actual numbers of the United States population and even more so with the effects of this population growth on the future physical and mental health and wealth of United States society. Opinions about the economic, ecological, sociological, and so on determinants and consequences of United States population growth vary tremendously.[3]

In the context of the present study it is not the determinants and consequences of population growth that are being explored, but rather the demographic principles, patterns, prospects, and current and future interaction of demographic characteristics of population. Compared with many other nations, the American public of the early 1970s probably is well informed about the possible population growth alternatives that can be expected to materialize. The wealth of literature available on this subject[4] leaves no need to elaborate on those aspects of future United States population growth that have been widely discussed. For the sake of completeness, the main points of what is fairly well understood are summarized before discussing some "new" aspects of possible future United States population growth.[5]

Important aspects of possible future United States population growth that are fairly well known include:

1. Provided the United States population will within 2 to 3 years adopt and then maintain indefinitely a net reproduction rate (NRR) of 1.0, and provided the age patterns of fertility will not change, compared with 1970, it will grow by about 20% to the year 2000, and before the middle of the next century it will stop growing at a number roughly 35% larger than it is now. To put it differently, if the 2-child family soon becomes the accepted average family norm (this enables a wide choice from childless to 10+-child families, but 2 children would have to be the average), the United States will have about 250 million inhabitants in the year 2000 and 280 million in the year 2050.

2. If the current trend of fertility decline slows and an NRR of 1.0 is not reached until at some more-or-less remote point in the future, (and age patterns of fertility remain constant), United States population growth will be faster than described in item 1. How much faster depends on when the NRR of 1.0 is achieved. If, for instance, the NRR of 1.0 is reached at the turn of the century, the United States population in the year 2000 could be 265 million inhabitants, and by the year 2050 it could be over 310 million. In other words, a moderate fertility decline as opposed to a sharp fertility decline—even though United States fertility is by world standards quite low already—can signify nontrivial differences in population size around the turn of the century and even larger differences in the long run.

3. To achieve a zero population growth within a few years seems very unlikely because it would require an almost 1-child family to be the norm. For about 20 years or so, the total fertility rate (TFR) would have to be in the order of 1.1 to 1.2 children.

2. MODIFIED POPULATION GROWTH ALTERNATIVES OF THE UNITED STATES

Prior research has outlined the population growth implications of several assumed fertility trends *en route* to a United States stationary population, the highlights of which are summarized above. It is the intention of this section to investigate the influence on future United States population growth of some variations in fertility trends that have not been discussed so far.

2–1. Fertility Declining to an NRR of 0.9

If fertility dropped immediately to an average of fewer than 2 children per family, a rate somewhat below that of the 1930s, and remained there, the United States population would nevertheless continue to grow for at least another 50 years. Only in the second quarter of the twenty-first century would its population start to decline. Its growth would naturally be smaller with a sustained 0.9 NRR than with a sustained 1.0 NRR. Assuming a 0.9 NRR, the United States population would reach its peak around the year 2020 and would be about 20% larger than it is now, that is, about 247 million. With a sustained 1.0 NRR the comparable number would be 273 million inhabitants. After 2020 it would start to decline, at first at a rate of about –0.3% per year and ultimately –0.4 annually. By the year 2050, for instance, it would decline by 20 million persons and be in the order of 227 million inhabitants.

As a natural consequence of a sustained 0.9 NRR there would also be a specific type of age structure. In the year 2030, for example, the 0–14 age group would comprise about 17% of the total population, and the 65+ age group would contain 21% of the population, compared with 19 and 18% in the respective age groups as a result of a sustained 1.0 NRR. The median age of the female population in 2050 would be 42 years with a sustained 0.9 NRR or 39 years with a sustained 1.0 NRR compared with the 1970 median age of 29 years.

2–2. An Increase in the Mean Age of Childbearing

Because the average age of childbearing in the United States is now fairly low, there is a possibility that women might decide to have children somewhat later than is the current pattern.

For the standard set it is estimated that the average age of childbearing in the United States in the period 1965–70 was 26.5

years. If we keep all other assumptions of the standard set (including the fact that fertility declines to the 1.0 NRR level) but modify the age patterns of fertility so that the mean age of childbearing rises to 29 years of age within 10 to 15 years, the population growth consequences in the United States would be almost negligible for all practical purposes. Such a calculation, however, would be misleading. The crucial point is that changes of the average age of childbearing *per se* influence the value of the NRR (see Section 6-5). The level and trends of the NRR of a certain year are the result not only of fertility levels of age cohorts of women but also of changes in the age pattern of childbearing. When the age of childbearing is rising, other things being equal, the period NRR declines, because births are stretched out over time (the same amount of births occurs in a longer period of time; for example, 20 million births take place during 6 instead of 5 years) and therefore all period measures related to fertility are affected. If the level of fertility were to decline to the replacement level and the age of childbearing concurrently to rise, the period NRR would decline temporarily below the 1.0 level. In the present worldwide study the detailed calculations have not been pursued because in almost all countries sufficient data are not at hand. A substitute calculation was designed; namely, it is assumed that at the time when both fertility approaches the replacement level and the mean age of childbearing rises, the period NRR declines temporarily (15 years) to 0.9 and then rises to 1.0. The results of this calculation illustrate the order of effect that a rise in the childbearing age might have on future population growth of the United States.

If in the United States during the next 10 to 15 years fertility were to stabilize at the replacement level and the mean age of childbearing were to rise, the United States population in the year 2000 would be less than 244 million. By comparison a permanent 1.0 NRR would yield a population of 250 million in the year 2000, a difference of 6 million persons. In the long run the significance of this process becomes more pronounced; for instance, in the year 2050 the total United States population would be less than 265 million inhabitants, compared with almost 280 million without the 15-year "dent" of a 0.9 NRR.

2–3. A Temporary 15% Increase in Fertility Followed by a Linear Fertility Decline to an NRR of 1.0

A repetition of the baby boom of the 1950s in the United States does not seem very likely. Yet no matter how improbable the baby boom may seem, there is always a chance that fertility trends might change quite unexpectedly. Therefore a moderate (compared with the 1950s) baby boom of the 1970s has been simulated. The gross reproduction rate (GRR) is assumed to increase from the average 1965–70 estimate of 1.25 to 1.44 throughout the 1970s (in 1959 the GRR was about 1.8) and then to decline to the replacement level.

If a replacement level of fertility is reached immediately after the simulated baby boom, that is, in the early 1980s, the total United States population in the year 2000 would be around 270 million inhabitants; by the middle of the twenty-first century it would be almost 320 million compared with 250 and 280 million, respectively, if instead of a baby boom there had been a sustained 1.0 NRR starting in the early 1970s. The female crude birth rate during the 1970s would be in the order of 21 to 22 per thousand population compared with the 1965–70 average of 17 per thousand population.

2–4. Constant Fertility Followed by Fertility Decline to an NRR of 1.0

It would be quite surprising to experience a break in the fertility decline of the 1960s and for United States average fertility behavior to stabilize at the level of the late 1960s for any extended period of time. However, it seems more likely to occur than the previous assumption of a baby boom; therefore this modification of fertility trends has also been explored. To show the effects of fertility of the late 1960s remaining constant for different periods of time, it is further assumed that when fertility finally starts to decline it drops quickly to an NRR of 1.0 and remains at this level. Although in reality such sudden changes of fertility trends are unlikely, it enables a clear illustration of the population growth consequences of constant current fertility for specified periods of time.

By world standards average United States fertility of the late 1960s was certainly not very high (even by developed standards it was slightly below average). Yet if United States fertility of the late 1960s remains constant even for only a few decades, the resulting total population growth could be quite significant. For instance, current fertility remaining constant either to the year 1980 or to the year 2000 would result in a United States population of 260 million or 280 million, respectively, for the year 2000 and 300 million or almost 350 million, respectively, for the year 2050. If its fertility behavior of the late 1960s became the prevailing pattern for the next 80 years the population in the year 2000 would be 280 million and in the middle of the next century around 420 million inhabitants.

3. A REVIEW

It is clearly impossible to predict the actual future population growth of the United States. It is, however, possible to illustrate the population growth consequences of various demographic developments that are directly related to various patterns of fertility behavior. As is mentioned above, some important general aspects of future United States population growth are widely realized. In most of the considerations about possible future fertility trends, emphasis is concentrated on exploring the demographic consequences of reaching and then maintaining an NRR of 1.0, which ultimately leads to a nongrowing, stationary population. The one exception is the investigation of a possible immediate cessation of population growth, which (at least in the United States) would require extremely abrupt changes of fertility behavior, namely, an instant adoption of a 1-child-family size norm for about 20 years. In other words, the implications of reaching an NRR of 1.0 and the implications of a zero population growth, that is, the implications of adopting an average 2-child—or 1-child—family, have been explored in quite some detail. Almost no attention has been paid to the possibility of fertility behavior being between these two "extremes" and the demographic consequences of such a development.

It might very well happen that in the years to come a type of fertility behavior may develop that will be characterized by an NRR below unity (Table 7-1). As is demonstrated in Section 7 2-1, a sustained 0.9 NRR beginning in the early 1970s would signify only a 20% growth of the United States population (as compared with 35% with an NRR of 1.0) and around the year 2020 population growth would not only cease, but in fact a slow population decrease would commence. The 1970 population of 206 million would not be reached until over 100 years from now.

An NRR of 0.9 implies a TFR of almost 1.9; that is, it still enables quite a choice of individual family size as long as the average is close to 1.9 children per family.

Whether an NRR even lower than 0.9 is possible for any meaningful period of time is difficult to say. The fact that it has not occured in modern history on a nationwide basis does not prove that it cannot occur in the future.

Provided average fertility settled at the replacement level and at the same time the average age of childbearing rose, an NRR of 0.9 would be the reproductive pattern for a limited period, and after 10 to 15 years the NRR would settle at 1.0. Such a development would naturally have a smaller effect than an indefinitely sustained NRR of

Table 7-1 Total Population (in millions) and Indices of Population Size (1970 = 100), United States, Standard Set and Selected Modifications, 1970-2100

	Standard Set Projection 1 (NRR = 1.0 in 1970-1975)		Fertility below Replacement Projection 1 (NRR = 0.9 in 1970-1975)		Substitute Calculation for Rise in Cohort Mean Age of Childbearing Projection 1 (NRR = 0.9 in 1970-1975 and 1.0 in 1985-1990)		Changed Age Patterns of Fertility Projection 1 (rise in childbearing age from 26.5 to 29.0 NRR = 1.0 in 1970-1975)		"Baby Boom" Projection 1 (15% increase of fertility NRR = 1.0 in 1980-1985)		Constant Current Fertility Projection 3 (constant fertility to 2000 NRR = 1.0 in 2000-2005)	
1970	205.7	100	205.7	100	205.7	100	205.7	100	205.7	100	205.7	100
1980	220.7	107	217.4	106	217.4	106	219.7	107	234.3	114	228.1	111
1990	237.5	115	230.3	112	232.2	113	235.8	115	251.5	122	253.6	123
2000	250.4	122	238.3	116	243.6	118	249.2	121	269.9	131	278.8	136
2020	272.6	133	246.8	120	261.6	127	269.9	131	302.2	147	317.8	155
2050	279.2	136	227.0	110	264.2	128	275.8	134	317.8	155	347.6	169
2100	279.8	136	186.7	91	264.2	128	276.2	134	319.9	156	353.3	172

0.9, but nevertheless it is evident that changes solely in the ages of childbearing could have a nontrivial effect on future population size, especially in the long run. In the middle of the next century United States population could number less than 265 million inhabitants instead of almost 280 million because of such changes in the age patterns of fertility.

The above modifications of United States fertility trends signify a slower population growth than that generated by a sustained 1.0 NRR. On the other hand, although not expected, other fertility trends might develop that would generate a population growth that would be faster than that brought about by a 1.0 NRR.

A baby boom of a much smaller magnitude than the previous one (late 1940s and 1950s) could signify 300 instead of 270 million Americans 50 years from now. The long-term population growth consequences of the current (average 1965–70) NRR remaining constant indefinitely would be substantial. If this NRR remained constant until the end of this century and then decreased to an NRR of 1.0, by 2050, the United States would have 350 instead of 280 million inhabitants with a sustained 1.0 NRR; if the 1965–70 NRR remained constant indefinitely the 400 million mark would be reached in 2040–70 years from now.

NOTES

1. The population growth alternatives of the United States are discussed in a separate chapter, among other reasons because the author performed the initial research in this field on the United States population.
2. Cf. John F. Kantner, "American Attitudes on Population Policy: Recent Trends", *Studies in Family Planning*, Vol. 1, No. 30, May 1968, pp. 1–7; "Survey Finds Population Growth Is Viewed as a Potential Problem," *New York Times*, April 16, 1971.
3. See, for example, Ansley J. Coale, "Man and His Environment," *Science*, Vol. 170, 1970, pp. 132–136, and P. R. Ehrlich and J. P. Holdren, "Impact of Population Growth," *Science*, Vol. 171, 1971, pp. 1212–1217.
4. To take only some of the most recent widely distributed publications and articles: *Population Growth and the American Future*, An Interim Report Prepared by the Commission on Population Growth and the American Future, Washington, D.C., March 1971; "The Future Population of the United States," *Population Bulletin* (Population Reference Bureau), Vol. 27, No. 1, February 1971; L. A. Mayer, "U.S. Population Growth: Would Slower Be Better?," *Fortune*, June 1970, p. 80; L. A. Mayer, "New Questions About the U.S. Population," *Fortune*, February 1971, p. 80.

5. Just to make sure it will not be overlooked, let it be pointed out that all calculations for the United States population were carried out on the basis of the same guidelines as for all other population units as described in Chapters 2 and 6. Statements referring to the future size and composition of the United States population, therefore, do not include any migration assumptions, or better to say, they include a "no-migration" assumption. Clearly, migratory movements will not cease from now on, but since the prime objective of this study is to illustrate alternative population growth consequences of differing fertility behavior, consequences of possible immigration and emigration have to be studied separately. Coale has done so in "Alternative Paths to a Stationary Population," paper prepared for the Commission on Population Growth and the American Future, unpublished manuscript (May 1971), pp. 9–10.

8 A Crude Evaluation of Proclaimed Population Growth Objectives

When a country becomes sufficiently concerned about the nature of its population growth that it seeks means to alter demographic trends, objectives are often formulated. These are usually placed within the framework of a more-or-less comprehensive population policy.

Governments adopting pronatalist population policies attempt to institute measures directed toward increasing the speed of population growth; however, their objectives have usually been very general and vague.[1] On the other hand, governments favoring antinatalist policies have at times formulated their objectives quite concretely (Table 8-1); the government of Taiwan, for example, wants to achieve a crude birth rate of 25.1 per thousand population by 1975; that of the Dominican Republic, a crude birth rate of 28 by 1977, and so on. Moreover, influential people occasionally express views about the direction or pace of population change desirable for the world or its subdivisions. It is possible to examine some of these proclaimed objectives in the light of the analysis developed in this book. By comparing any particular, defined objective with the data computed for the respective population one can visualize the kind of demographic developments that would have to be generated to attain the proclaimed objective.

First, two qualifications have to be mentioned:

1. The alternative projections presented here are designed to provide a fairly general idea of the kind of population growth trends

Table 8-1   Specified Target of Official Population Control Policy of Different Countries

| | Year of Program Start | Target (as of 1970) | |
		Item	Level (year)
ASIA			
China (Mainland)	1962	Family size	Small
India	1952	CBR[a]	40-45 (1969) to 32 (1975)
Indonesia	1968	CBR	Decrease (level unspecified)
Iran	1967	NI[b]	3% (1967) to 2% (year unspecified)
Republic of Korea	1961	NI	Decrease to 2% (December 1971)
Malaysia	1966	NI	Decrease to 2% (1985)
Nepal	1966	NI	Decrease to 2% (year unspecified)
Pakistan	1970	CBR	41 to 43 (1970) to 33.2 (1975)
Philippines	1970	NI	Control
Singapore	1965	CBR	32 (1964) to 20 (1970)
Taiwan	1964	CBR	25.1 (1975)
Thailand	1970	NI	3.3% (1970) to 2.4% (1980)
Turkey	1965	Family size	Desired number[c]
AFRICA			
Ghana	1969	NI	Decrease to achieve desired family size
Kenya	1966	NI	Control (level unspecified)
Mauritius	1965	CBR	30 (1965) to 20 (1975)
Morocco	1965	CBR	50 (1965) to 45 (1972) to 35 (1985)
Tunisia	1964	CBR	45 (1969) to 34 (1975)
U.A.R.	1965	CBR	Reduce 1 point per year for 10 years beginning in 1969
LATIN AMERICA			
Barbados	1967	NI	Control
Dominican Republic	1967	CBR	48 (1967) to 28 (1977)
Jamaica	1966	CBR	Decrease to 25 (1976)
Puerto Rico	1970	NI	Control
Trinidad & Tobago	1967	CBR	38 (1967) to 19 (1977)

[a]CBR = crude birth rate or births per thousand population.
[b]NI = natural increase. In percent, this yields births minus deaths per hundred population.
[c]In a national survey of married women conducted in 1968 (sample size = 3290), desired number of children was found to be an average of 3.79, a figure 27% lower than the 5.2 children being produced according to the age-specific fertility rates found in the 1966 Turkish demographic survey.

Source: Dorothy Nortman. *Current Status of Family Planning in Relation to Targets.* Paper presented at IPPF South-East Asia and Oceania Regional Conference, March 1971.

that would, sooner or later, lead to a stationary population. Therefore, they cover 5-year periods and not single years; thus most demographic measures are 5-year averages. In most cases therefore our evaluation indicates only the likelihood of achieving a certain goal, especially when the targets are formulated for specific years. More refined procedures might render more accurate answers.

2. In almost all the projections only a single alternative of future mortality trends is assumed, because, as mentioned a number of times, the main thrust of the study is to illustrate population growth consequences of particular changes in fertility behavior. However, since mortality trends other than those assumed might occur, rates of population growth could be decreased by high mortality. This applies mainly to those objectives formulated in terms of rates of natural increase. Because most objectives are formulated as crude birth rates to be achieved, this qualification is not a very serious one.

1. COMMENTS ON STATEMENTS REFERRING TO GROWTH PROBABILITIES OR OBJECTIVES OF THE WORLD POPULATION

The conviction that the earth can support a population a number of times larger than its present size and that the current rate of population growth is not a major cause of social and economic problems is still held by some people,[2] although possibly less so than a decade or two ago. At the same time there are people who are convinced that "if everyone is to have a good and healthy life, population should be stabilized at about 500 million". . ."the world's population would have to be reduced to one-seventh of its present size."[3]

The mainstream of the international community *inter alia* through the various agencies of the United Nations,[4] is increasingly concerned about the current speed of world population growth and is developing more and more activities geared toward the slowing down of population growth rates. Population is considered to be one of the most important problems, for the well-being of many nations and the world as a whole could fall into serious danger if the rate of population growth is not reduced. At the same time it is understood that the population problem is merely one of many fields of concern and needed action. If a reduction of population growth rates is achieved without progress in other fields of social and economic development, the welfare of nations would certainly not be guaranteed.

Several views have been voiced on the acuteness of the population problem, on measures to be applied toward alleviating it, and on quantitative features of future world population growth. It is the latter that can be commented on within the context of this study.

Consider some examples of statements that have been made in the recent past:

1. Robert McNamara: "Today the average birth rate for developing countries is 40 to 45 per 1000 population. To get this rate down to the 17 to 20 per 1000 that is common in contemporary Europe would require a reduction in the developing world of some 50 million births a year". . ."Indeed, even with family planning, no such promising results are feasible in less than two or three decades."[5]

2. Bernard Berelson: In the less developed countries "any non-trivial reduction in birth rates within a decade or any non-trivial expediting of the reduction over 2–3 decades could be truly historic contributions to human welfare (and unprecedented in affecting demographic performance), even though not full 'solutions' to the population problem, and they would be leading in the right direction. Achievement of the birth rate 25–30 / growth rate 1% target in a decade or two would be both socially and demographically significant, would be a real breakthrough leading to 'solution'. . ." ". . . it would appear that the developed world can and will move toward replacement level fertility within the next few decades and may, for example, reach a growth rate below 0.5 percent, which itself may be considered a successful outcome pointing to 'solution'."[6]

3. Donald Bogue: "I would suspect that the world population will continue to grow but at a diminishing rate, so that at the 21st century, there will be roughly five-and-a-quarter billion people. And at that moment, the population will be growing at a very slow rate, if at all. It is my guess that by the end of this century, the population problem will be a matter of history; that at that time the world's growth rate will be zero, or so nearly zero that it will not be regarded as a problem, except in perhaps a few sporadic areas of the world."[7]

4. William H. Draper, Jr.: "The coordinated world population program now getting under way could well set a zero growth rate as the world target, and then measure progress with each recurring census. Zero growth for the world in 30 years? This goal would be reached if the present world rate of 2% is brought down by 1/20 of 1% a year for 20 years, and then by 1/10 of 1% a year for the following ten years. Several countries have recently experienced this rate of decline. So it can be done, if men and women everywhere will use their God-given intellect and their power of will."[8]

5. The Carolina Population Center, The University of North Carolina: "The situation poses a crucial challenge to the American government, to undertake a 10-year, global population program effort with (three) goals: (1) A one-third

decrease in the world population growth rate by 1980, covering the first one-third segment of a curve leading to zero population growth by the year 2000; (2) Reduction of birth rates in half of the high-fertility populations to a threshold birth rate of 30 per thousand by 1980;". . ."Also, birth rates in the United States and industrial countries should fall by as much as one-half to bring them close to a zero growth rate. On the other hand, some countries in Africa and in Latin America would be expected still to have fairly high growth rates by 1980, but would be ready for steeper declines during the following decade."[9]

Since certain ideas come up several times in only slightly modified versions, it might be useful to select, group, and organize the above statements to enable a discussion by topics:

I. Ideas on future world population growth:
   1. The growth rate should be reduced by one-third by 1980.
   2. A zero population growth rate will be (should be, can be) attained by the beginning of the twenty-first century.
   3. World population will number around 5.25 billion inhabitants around the year 2000.

II. Ideas on population growth of the less developed countries:
   1. The crude birth rate should be reduced to 30 by 1980 in half of the less developed countries.
   2. The achievement of a crude birth rate of 25 to 30 and a growth rate of 1% in a decade or two would be socially and demographically significant.
   3. It is not feasible to reduce the crude birth rate to 17 to 20 in less than two to three decades.

III. Ideas on population growth of the more developed countries:
   1. Attainment of replacement level fertility within the next few decades.
   2. Attainment of a growth rate below 0.5% within the next few decades.
   3. The birth rate in the United States and the industrial countries should fall by as much as one half to bring them close to a zero growth rate by 1980.

The following discussion assesses which of the ideas seem to be "realistic" and thus attainable and demonstrates why it does not seem likely that situations depicted by the other ideas will materialize.

In general, the ideas about future growth of *the world population* seem to be rather "unrealistic." In order to achieve a world population of 5.25 billion by the beginning of the twenty-first century, a very rapid worldwide fertility decline would have to occur and a world net reproduction rate (NRR) of 1.0 would have to be attained during the 1980s (Table 8-2). A meaningful fertility decline in South Asia, Africa, and Latin America during the 1970s is implied. Since one cannot expect fertility in the more developed countries to decline markedly below replacement levels, one would have to expect the demographic situation in the majority of the less developed countries to approach the current demographic situation of the more developed countries within 10 to 15 years.

What would be even more difficult to bring about (ruling out major

Table 8-2   Selected Basic Demographic Measures, World Population, Projections 2 and 3, Standard Set, 1965-2005

	Total Fertility Rate	Net Repro- duction Rate	Total Population at End of Period (in billions)	Female Rate of Growth
		Projection 2		
		(NRR = 1.0 in 1980-1985)		
1965-1970	4.7	1.9	3.6	2.0
1970-1975	3.9	1.6	4.0	1.6
1975-1980	3.1	1.3	4.2	1.3
1980-1985	2.3	1.0	4.4	0.9
1985-1990	2.3	1.0	4.6	1.0
1990-1995	2.3	1.0	4.9	1.0
1995-2000	2.3	1.0	5.1	1.0
2000-2005	2.2	1.0	5.3	0.8
		Projection 3		
		(NRR = 1.0 in 2000-2005)		
1965-1970	4.7	1.9	3.6	2.0
1970-1975	4.4	1.8	4.0	1.9
1975-1980	4.0	1.7	4.4	1.8
1980-1985	3.7	1.6	4.8	1.7
1985-1990	3.3	1.4	5.2	1.6
1990-1995	2.9	1.3	5.6	1.5
1995-2000	2.6	1.2	5.9	1.2
2000-2005	2.2	1.0	6.2	1.0

catastrophes and overall deterioration of mortality conditions) is a zero
rate of population growth at the turn of the century. Fertility behavior
around the world would have to resemble that of Japan and Hungary
by 1990, and by the year 2000 each woman (even for instance in India,
Nigeria, and Brazil) on the average could bear only slightly more than
1 child (Table 8-3). Such low levels of fertility are not known to have

Table 8-3 Selected Demographic Measures, World Population,
           Projections 3 and 4, Linear Decline of Growth
           Rate to Zero, 1965-2025

	Total Fertility Rate	Net Repro- duction Rate	Total Population at End of Period (in billions)	Female Rate of Growth
Projection 3 (growth rate = 0 in 2000-2005)				
1965-1970	4.7	1.9	3.6	2.0
1970-1975	4.1	1.7	4.0	1.7
1975-1980	3.4	1.4	4.3	1.4
1980-1985	2.7	1.2	4.5	1.1
1985-1990	2.1	0.9	4.7	0.9
1990-1995	1.7	0.7	4.8	0.6
1995-2000	1.3	0.6	4.9	0.3
2000-2005	1.1	0.5	4.9	0.0
2005-2010	1.2	0.5	4.9	0.0
2010-2015	1.3	0.6	4.9	0.0
2015-2020	1.6	0.7	4.9	0.0
2020-2025	2.0	0.9	4.9	0.0
Projection 4 (growth rate = 0 in 2020-2025)				
1965-1970	4.7	1.9	3.6	2.0
1970-1975	4.2	1.7	4.0	1.8
1975-1980	3.7	1.5	4.3	1.6
1980-1985	3.2	1.4	4.6	1.5
1985-1990	2.8	1.2	4.9	1.3
1990-1995	2.4	1.1	5.2	1.1
1995-2000	2.1	0.9	5.5	0.9
2000-2005	1.9	0.9	5.7	0.7
2005-2010	1.8	0.8	5.8	0.5
2010-2015	1.6	0.7	5.9	0.4
2015-2020	1.5	0.7	6.0	0.2
2020-2025	1.4	0.7	6.0	0.0

occurred in any country, not even during the 1930s in Europe. To achieve a zero population growth rate, however, they would have to be the world average situation.

A reduction of the world growth rate by one-third by 1980, although most improbable, is still the easiest of the goals concerning population growth of the world. Such a reduced growth rate would be generated by a fertility decline somewhat slower than that of Projection Two (Table 8-2). Even if such a reduction were achieved this is by no means the "first one-third segment of a curve leading to zero population growth by the year 2000." Because of the young age structure of the world population, fertility would have to decline significantly below the replacement level if a zero population growth rate were to be achieved by the year 2000.

The ideas concerning population growth features of the *less developed countries* are far more realistic. All the statements referring to the crude birth rate imply a fertility decline that would bring about an NRR of 1.0 in the less developed countries by the turn of the century (Table 8-4). It does seem, however, that it would be most difficult to achieve a population growth rate of 1% in a decade or two. The data of the hypothetical projections indicate that a 1% growth rate would emerge at the time when an NRR came close to 1.0. Because this is unlikely to occur in the less developed countries before the end of the century, even a 1% growth rate cannot be expected earlier. It is interesting to note that the 1% growth rate would persist for about two decades after fertility stabilized at the replacement level. To put it differently, the 1% growth rate as a whole is an ambitious goal; moreover it will take some time to get below it.

The attainment of replacement-level fertility in the *more developed countries* within the next few decades is the situation to which demographic trends of the last 10 to 15 years are converging. There is no evident reason why this should not materialize. At the same time our computations indicate that the population growth rate of the more developed countries will settle around 0.5% for two to three decades if fertility were to stabilize at the replacement level (Table 8-5).

It is true that if the crude birth rate in the more developed countries fell by as much as one half within 10 to 15 years, the population growth rate of these countries would be around zero. At the same time, however, fertility would have to drop far below the replacement level. For two decades the total fertility rate (TFR) would

Table 8-4   Selected Demographic Measures, Less Developed
Countries, Projections 2 and 3, Standard Set,
1965-2015

	Crude Birth Rate	Total Fertility Rate	Net Repro duction Rate	Female Rate of Growth
Projection 2 *(NRR = 1.0 in 1980-1985)*				
1965-1970	41	5.7	2.1	2.6
1970-1975	33	4.7	1.8	2.1
1975-1980	27	3.6	1.4	1.5
1980-1985	20	2.5	1.0	1.0
1985-1990	21	2.5	1.0	1.1
1990-1995	22	2.4	1.0	1.2
1995-2000	21	2.4	1.0	1.1
2000-2005	19	2.3	1.0	1.0
2005-2010	17	2.3	1.0	0.8
2010-2015	16	2.3	1.0	0.7
Projection 3 *(NRR = 1.0 in 2000-2005)*				
1965-1970	41	5.7	2.1	2.6
1970-1975	37	5.3	2.0	2.4
1975-1980	34	4.8	1.8	2.3
1980-1985	32	4.3	1.7	2.1
1985-1990	29	3.8	1.5	1.9
1990-1995	26	3.3	1.4	1.7
1995-2000	23	2.8	1.2	1.4
2000-2005	20	2.3	1.0	1.1
2005-2010	19	2.3	1.0	1.1
2010-2015	19	2.3	1.0	1.0

have to be about 1.4, implying very small families; significant
numbers of women would have to remain childless or have only 1 child.
Theoretically there is no reason why this could not happen.
Nevertheless, it is important to realize that modern history does not
have a precedent. The NRR of 0.6 or 0.7 would have to persist for two
decades (Table 8-6).

Table 8-5   Selected Basic Demographic Measures, More
             Developed Countries, Projections 1 and 2,
             Standard Set, 1965-2000

	Crude Birth Rate	Total Fertility Rate	Net Reproduction Rate	Female Rate of Growth
	Projection 1			
	(NRR = 1.0 in 1970-1975)			
1965-1970	18	2.7	1.3	0.9
1970-1975	15	2.1	1.0	0.5
1975-1980	16	2.1	1.0	0.5
1980-1985	16	2.1	1.0	0.6
1985-1990	16	2.1	1.0	0.6
1990-1995	15	2.1	1.0	0.5
1995-2000	14	2.1	1.0	0.4
	Projection 2			
	(NRR = 1.0 in 1980-1985)			
1965-1970	18	2.7	1.3	0.9
1970-1975	17	2.5	1.2	0.8
1975-1980	17	2.3	1.1	0.7
1980-1985	16	2.1	1.0	0.6
1985-1990	15	2.1	1.0	0.6
1990-1995	15	2.1	1.0	0.5
1995-2000	15	2.1	1.0	0.5

2. THE FEASIBILITY OF ATTAINING PROCLAIMED
OBJECTIVES OF POPULATION GROWTH
OF INDIVIDUAL COUNTRIES

It is a matter of course that objectives of population growth, vaguely
formulated, cannot be quantitatively evaluated. Further, it is not
possible to evaluate objectives formulated by governments of countries
for which data that would enable the calculation of projections are not
available.

   It is, however, not implied that a country which has spelled out an
objective that seems to be almost impossible to achieve necessarily has

Table 8-6   Selected Demographic Measures, More Developed
Countries, Projections 1 and 2, Linear Decline
of Growth Rate to Zero, 1965-2000

	Crude Birth Rate	Total Fertility Rate	Net Repro- duction Rate	Female Rate of Growth
Projection 1 (growth rate = 0 in 1970-1975)				
1965-1970	18	2.7	1.3	0.9
1970-1975	10	1.4	0.7	0.0
1975-1980	10	1.4	0.6	0.0
1980-1985	11	1.4	0.6	0.0
1985-1990	11	1.4	0.7	0.0
1990-1995	11	1.6	0.8	0.0
1995-2000	12	1.9	0.9	0.0
Projection 2 (growth rate = 0 in 1980-1985)				
1965-1970	18	2.7	1.3	0.9
1970-1975	16	2.2	1.0	0.6
1975-1980	13	1.8	0.8	0.3
1980-1985	10	1.4	0.6	0.0
1985-1990	10	1.3	0.6	0.0
1990-1995	11	1.4	0.7	0.0
1995-2000	11	1.6	0.8	0.0

a family planning program worse than that of a country which has
managed to formulate an attainable population growth objective. The
former might have found it wise to set hard goals. On the other hand
goals may have been set but the necessary calculations were not made.

In the light of the alternative projections of this study, it seems
possible to make a crude evaluation of population growth goals of 11
countries (Table 8-7). In half of these countries the likelihood of their
goals being materialized is low, often actually zero. In three countries
it seems most probable that their population growth goals will be
achieved, and in three other countries it is doubtful but not impossible
that their goals will be achieved.

Let us start with those countries where the realization of goals
seems attainable, proceed to the doubtful ones, and then take up the
most improbable ones.

The population growth goals of *Singapore* and the *Republic of*

Table 8-7   Formal Likelihood of Achieving Proclaimed
            Population Growth Objectives, Selected Coun-
            tries (see Table 8-1)

	Likelihood of Achieving Objective		
	Strong	Medium	Weak
ASIA			
India			X
Republic of Korea	X		
Singapore	X		
Taiwan	X		
Thailand		X	
AFRICA			
Mauritius			X
Morocco		X	
Tunisia			X
U.A.R.		X	
LATIN AMERICA			
Dominican Republic			X
Trinidad & Tobago			X

Korea were formulated several years ago and referred to 1970 and 1971, respectively. Thus reality is used to judge their validity. In both cases the goals have been nearly, if not exactly, met. Furthermore, the projections of this book show that in both countries, even with a further decrease in fertility, the crude birth and death rates and the growth rates will probably follow their current trends for the coming 5 to 10 years.

The population growth objective of *Taiwan* of a crude birth rate of 25.1 for 1975 is ambitious; nevertheless the probability of attaining it is quite high. Even if the fertility decline of the last 10 years or so slowed down slightly, the proclaimed goal of a crude birth rate of 25.1 per thousand population for 1975 could still be achieved. Only a slight slowing of the fertility decline is permissible, however, because large numbers of women will soon be entering the prime childbearing ages, and the achievement of the proclaimed goal necessitates a further significant decline of the fertility level (Table 8-8).

To reduce the annual rate of population growth in *Thailand* to 2.5% by the end of 1976 is an ambitious goal.[10] Currently the population growth rate is around 3.0% per year, and the goal implies a fertility decline similar to that underlying Projection Three, that is, an achievement of an NRR of 1.0 by the end of the century (Table 8-8). However, conjectures about future fertility development are extremely difficult to make because all organized actions to influence fertility behavior are of a very recent date and their effectiveness is yet to be proven.

Morocco's proclaimed goals of a crude birth rate of 45 per thousand population by 1972 and 35 by 1985 appear very ambitious. To attain these objectives would require a fertility decline similar to the one assumed in Projection Three of the standard set (Table 8-8). However, because fertility is currently extremely high in Morocco (crude birth rate = 51, TFR = 7. 4), to materialize the assumptions of Projection Three requires a substantial fertility decline, the achievement of which appears to be most uncertain.

The goal of reducing the *United Arab Republic's* crude birth rate by 1 point per year for 10 years beginning in 1969 may be ambitious but is nevertheless reasonable. Such an evolution roughly implies the assumptions of Projection Three of the standard set (Table 8-8). Because by North African standards fertility in the United Arab Republic is low (TFR = 6.1), the rate of fertility decline required to achieve this goal is considerably less than that for Morocco, for instance.

Now let us turn to the countries where, judged by current standards, almost inconceivable developments would have to occur to generate the proclaimed goals.

If the crude birth rate of *India* is to reach a level of about 32 per thousand population by the year 1975 (in the late 1960s it was about 40 per thousand population), changes in average fertility behavior would have to be extremely rapid (Table 8-8). Within 10 years a decline of fertility would be needed that required about 40 years in Germany at the turn of the nineteenth and twentieth centuries. In terms of our projections, future population growth would have to proceed roughly along the lines of Projection Two (NRR = 1.0 in 1980–85), and this does not seem to be a realistic assumption for India.

For a developing country, fertility is already very low in

Table 8-8 Comparison of Proclaimed Targets of Population Policy and Selected Data of Projections

	Target	Projection 1 (NRR = 1.0 in 1970-1975)		Projection 2 (NRR = 1.0 in 1980-1985)		Projection 3 (NRR = 1.0 in 2000-2005)	
		TFR[a]	CBR[b]	TFR	CBR	TFR	CBR
INDIA	CBR 32 in 1975						
1965-1970				5.6	40.4	5.6	40.4
1970-1975				4.5	33.5	5.1	37.2
1975-1980				3.5	27.3	4.6	34.5
TAIWAN	CBR 25.1 in 1975						
1965-1970				4.4	30.3	4.4	30.3
1970-1975				3.6	26.9	4.1	29.9
1975-1980				2.9	24.1	3.7	30.2
MAURITIUS	CBR 20 in 1975						
1965-1970		4.6	30.5	4.6	30.5		
1970-1975		2.3	17.4	3.8	28.1		
1975-1980		2.3	19.7	3.0	24.7		
MOROCCO	CBR 45 in 1972 and 35 in 1985						
1965-1970				7.4	50.8	7.4	50.8
1970-1975				5.8	39.5	6.7	45.1
1975-1980				4.1	29.6	5.9	40.4
1980-1985				2.5	19.8	5.2	36.8
TUNISIA	CBR 34 in 1975						
1965-1970				6.8	44.2	6.8	44.2
1970-1975				5.3	35.4	6.1	40.2
1975-1980				3.9	27.4	5.5	37.0
UNITED ARAB REPUBLIC	Reduce 1 point per year for 10 years, beginning in 1969						
1965-1970				6.1	43.4	6.1	43.4
1970-1975				4.9	35.0	5.6	39.3
1975-1980				3.7	27.4	5.0	35.8
DOMINICAN REPUBLIC	CBR 28 in 1977						
1965-1970		7.2	48.3	7.2	48.3		
1970-1975		2.5	18.1	5.6	38.6		
1975-1980		2.5	20.2	4.0	29.4		

Table 8-8 (continued)

	Target	Projection 1 (NRR = 1.0 in 1970-1975)		Projection 2 (NRR = 1.0 in 1980-1985)		Projection 3 (NRR = 1.0 in 2000-2005)	
		TFR	CBR	TFR	CBR	TFR	CBR
TRINIDAD & TOBAGO	CBR 19 in 1977						
1965-1970		3.8	28.4	3.8	28.4		
1970-1975		2.3	18.2	3.3	26.1		
1975-1980		2.2	19.8	2.8	23.4		
THAILAND	RNI[c] 2.5 in 1976			TFR	RNI	TFR	RNI
1965-1970				6.2	3.0	6.2	3.0
1970-1975				4.9	2.4	5.6	2.8
1975-1980				3.6	1.8	5.0	2.7

[a]Total fertility rate.
[b]Crude birth rate.
[c]Rate of natural increase.

Mauritius. Nevertheless it does seem most unlikely for this population to reach a crude birth rate of 20 per thousand population by 1975. Fertility would have to decline at an extremely rapid rate during the early 1970s and the 2-to3-child family would have to be almost universal. It would seem more likely that the crude birth rate might be in the order of 25 to 26 per thousand population by 1975. With the given age structure of Mauritius a crude birth rate of 20 per thousand population can be achieved only with a gross reproduction rate (GRR) close to 1.0 by 1975 (Table 8-8). Provided the respective governmental institutions of Mauritius consider this an attainable fertility level, their proclaimed goal is reasonable. If not, they might consider reformulating their objective to, say, a crude birth rate of 25 per thousand, which even so implies a significant lasting fertility decline.

From a purely technical viewpoint it would seem that *Tunisia's* proclaimed objective of a crude birth rate of 34 by 1975 will be extremely difficult to achieve, for in the late 1960s the crude birth rate was 44. A rate of 34 would require the actual fertility decline to fall between the assumptions of Projection Two and Projection Three of the standard set, probably closer to Projection Two than to Projection Three (Table 8-8). For example, the speed of fertility decline would have to be faster than it was in Taiwan between 1959 and 1969, where the TFR dropped from 6.0 in 1959 to 5.1 in 1964 and 4.1 in 1969.

In the *Dominican Republic* the crude birth rate of 48 in the late 1960s is supposed to decline to 28 per thousand population by 1977. In order to achieve such a goal, the TFR, for example, would have to decline from 7.2 to about 4.0 within 10 years (Table 8-8). This is a much faster decline than the fertility trend in Taiwan between 1959 and 1969. It seems most unlikely that such a rapid fertility decline could occur, and thus their objectives seem unrealistic.

To achieve a crude birth rate of 19 per thousand population by 1977 in *Trinidad* and *Tobago*, where in the late 1960s the crude birth rate was 28, seems almost impossible. Fertility would have to decline to a replacement level almost instantly, and to expect such a development appears to be wishful thinking.

The reason why several proclaimed goals of population growth are unattainable is difficult to pinpoint without profound investigation. One explanation could be that these goals were occasionally defined merely on the basis of speculation and wishful thinking. Logically, population growth goals should be proclaimed as a result of thorough computations and projections, which would take into account both "inadvertent" trends and factors that might accelerate or decelerate these trends. This is a most complex task, but at least the proclaimed population growth objectives would be within the limits of the logic of population growth.

NOTES

1. For example, the French Minister of Labor and Population, Joseph Fontanet, said at a news conference in April 1970: "We are an underpopulated nation." In a newspaper report on the respective news conference: "The French Government is thinking of making adjustments in its social benefit system that would encourage families with two children to have one or two more." *New York Times* April 13, 1970.

2. Cf. Colin Clark, *Population Growth and Land Use* (New York: Macmillan Co., 1968). On the basis of elaborate calculations Clark states: "Each person's land requirements for American type food consumption are some 2000 sq.m., or one-fifth of a hectare (half an acre), or 2250 sq.m. including requirement of forest land. If we take world resources of agricultural land at 10.7 billion hectares of standard land equivalent, this could feed, at maximum standards, 47 billion people." And, further: "For people living at Japanese standards of food consumption and Asian standards of timber requirements only 680 sq.m./person is required, and the world's potential agricultural and forest land could supply the needs of 157 billion people." (Page 153.)

3. See Richard A. Watson and Philip M. Smith, "The Limit: 500 Million," *1970 Focus,* Midwest Publishing Company, Vol. 8, No. 52, pp. 25–27.

4. In the late 1960s the U.N. Fund for Population Activities was founded, and the establishment of a world population institute is under serious consideration. See "The Feasibility of Establishing a World Population Institute," report of a U.N. UNESCO WHO mission, ST/SOA/SER.R/12, New York, 1971.

5. Robert S. McNamara, "Global Strategy to Control Population," *Population Review,* Vol. 13, Nos. 1 and 2, January–December 1969.

6. Bernard Berelson, "Notes on Population Efforts: 20 Propositions," July 1970, pp. 6 and 8, unpublished manuscript.

7. Transcript of a CBS program, *The 21st Century,* "Standing Room Only," CBS Television Network, Sunday, May 7, 1967, 6:00–6:30 P.M., EDT, pp. 1–2.

8. William H. Draper, Jr., "Is Zero Population Growth the Answer?" an address at a testimonial dinner in Washington, D.C., December 2, 1969, published by Population Crisis Committee, p. 5.

9. The Carolina Population Center, The University of North Carolina at Chapel Hill, "Cracking the World Population Problem: A U.S. Goal for the '70's," December 1969, pp. 2 and 10.

10. This is the formulation applied in the National Family Planning Project of the Ministry of Public Health. It is a specification of the more general data given in Table 8-1. *Family Planning in Thailand 1965-70,* Bangkok, 1971, p. 23.

9 Some Implications for Other Types of Projections

1. LONG-TERM IMPLICATIONS OF NATIONAL AND INTERNATIONAL PROJECTIONS

Various thoughts may underlie population projections of a national statistical office or an international agency. Generally, however, population projections have in common the desire to convey a plausible picture of future population growth. In contrast, the principal intentions underlying the projections of the present study are to illustrate trends of demographic measures that would have to be generated if populations were, sooner or later, to achieve the stationary state. Because of these differences, the former projections apply to relatively shorter periods of up to 30 years, whereas the latter range over much longer time spans.

Despite the differences in intent, one can compare the population projections of both types for the same unit, thereby acquiring an admittedly very crude but meaningful idea of the long-term population growth implications of the "statistical office" projections.

For example, let us take the medium projection of the United Nations for the world population, which was prepared in 1968. According to this projection the world would have about 6.5 billion inhabitants in the year 2000. By examining the fertility and mortality trends that were applied in the projection and by comparing them with past experience and by taking into account whatever knowledge and opinion one has about economic and social development, as well as about population policy and family planning programs, one can judge the degree of plausibility of the projection. This procedure, however, does not provide much information about long-term implications of world population growth, if it were to proceed according to this projection. How would world population continue to grow after it reaches 6.5 billion inhabitants in the year 2000? Very crude information of this type comes by comparing the United Nations projection with projections illustrating the attainment of a stationary state at some point in the future.

A comparison of the United Nations medium projection with the projections of the standard set of the world population shows that the former is in between Projections Four and Five (Table 9-1). Although this observation does provide a new view, great caution is necessary in the interpretation of the data. One can speculate that if the world population were to develop according to the United Nations medium projection, it is not likely to cease growing after the year 2000 and settle around 6.5 billion. Quite significant growth during the first half of the twenty-first century may be expected. In fact, a leveling off of the world population in the order of 10 billion inhabitants seems more consistent with the growth trend than a leveling off around, for instance, 8 billion.

The same crude procedure can be applied to national population projections. An example is supplied in Table 9-2. The population of Costa Rica according to the national projection computed in 1967 grows roughly as indicated by Projection Five of the standard set. Therefore, one can come to the superficial conclusion that further growth similar to that indicated by Projection Five is implied in the demographic trends assumed by the 1967 Costa Rican projections.

Lest our use of the comparison be mistakenly interpreted, we shall reiterate that the described procedure cannot provide more than a general idea of the long-term population growth trends implied in a particular projection.

Table 9-1 Total Population (in billions) and Indices of Population Growth (1970 = 100), World Total, United Nations Medium Projection and Projections 3, 4, and 5, Standard Set, 1970-2100

| | U.N. Medium Projection | | Period in Which NRR of 1.0 Is Reached | | | | | |
| | | | 2000-2005 Projection 3 | | 2020-2025 Projection 4 | | 2040-2045 Projection 5 | |
	In Billions	In %	In Billions	In %	In Billions	In %	In Billions	In %
1970	3.6	100	3.6	100	3.6	100	3.6	100
1980	4.5	123	4.4	120	4.4	122	4.5	122
1990	5.4	150	5.2	142	5.4	148	5.5	150
2000	6.5	179	5.9	162	6.4	176	6.7	183
2050	--	--	8.2	224	10.5	287	13.0	357
2100	--	--	8.4	230	11.2	306	15.1	414

Source: United Nations Population Division. *World Population Prospects, 1965-2000, as Assessed in 1968.* ESA/P/WP.37, 17 December 1970, p. 14.

Table 9-2 Total Population (in millions) and Indices of Population Size (1970 = 100), Costa Rica, National Projection and Projections 4 and 5, Standard Set, 1970-2050

| | National Projection | | Period in Which NRR of 1.0 Is Reached | | | |
| | | | 2020-2025 Projection 4 | | 2040-2045 Projection 5 | |
	In Millions	In %	In Millions	In %	In Millions	In %
1970	1.77	100	1.74	100	1.74	100
1975	2.10	119	2.03	117	2.04	117
1980	2.49	141	2.39	137	2.40	138
1985	2.96	167	2.79	160	2.83	163
1990	3.49	197	3.23	186	3.31	190
2000	--	--	4.18	240	4.41	253
2020	--	--	6.09	350	7.12	409
2050	--	--	8.07	464	10.84	623

Source: Ricardo Jiménez Jiménez et al. "Proyección de la Población de Costa Rica por Sexo y Grupos de Edad, 1965-1990." *Revista de Estudios y Estadísticas,* no. 8 (October 1967), p. 4.

2. DEMOGRAPHIC TRENDS IMPLIED BY THE STABILIZED WORLD MODELS OF *THE LIMITS TO GROWTH*[1]

A team of scientists under the direction of Dennis Meadows constructed a systems analysis world model "specifically to investigate five major trends of global concern—accelerating industrialization, rapid population growth, widespread malnutrition, depletion of non-renewable resources, and a deteriorating environment. These trends are all interconnected in many ways, and their development is measured in decades or centuries. . ." (page 21). Although they recognize imperfections and simplifications of the model, they nevertheless consider it to be a reasonable approximation of trends and interrelations in the real world.

The conclusions of the research project reported in *The Limits to Growth* are:

1. If the present growth trends in world population, industrialization, pollution, food production, and resource depletion continue unchanged, the limits to growth on this planet will be reached sometime within the next one hundred years. The most probable result will be a rather sudden and uncontrollable decline in both population and industrial capacity.

2. It is possible to alter these growth trends and to establish a condition of ecological and economic stability that is sustainable far into the future. The state of global equilibrium could be designed so that the basic material needs of each person on earth are satisfied and each person has an equal opportunity to realize his individual human potential.

3. If the world's people decide to strive for this second outcome rather than the first, the sooner they begin working to attain it, the greater will be their chance of success. (pages 23–24)

The type of calculations that led to the formulation of conclusion 1 above are illustrated in Figure 9-1, which is reproduced directly from the book, *The Limits to Growth*. The authors claim that, "the basic behavior mode of the world system is exponential growth of population and capital, followed by collapse" (page 142) even after having tested several additional assumptions (especially accelerated technological progress).

The authors then investigate and illustrate conditions under which their model—and presumably the real world—could continue to exist without experiencing a state of collapse; that is, they attempt to define the conditions of "the state of global equilibrium." According to Meadows et al., equilibrium could be brought about only by implementing policies that would significantly alter existing trends:

both population and capital growth would have to be substantially curbed, possibly even stopped within a few decades; technological changes of considerable importance would have to be developed (resource consumption per unit of industrial output would have to be

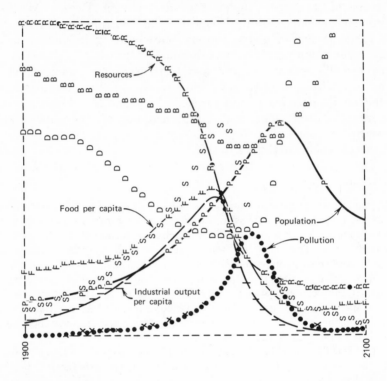

Figure 9–1. World model standard run.

The "standard" world model run assumes no major change in the physical, economic, or social relationships that have historically governed the development of the world system. All variables plotted here follow historical values from 1900–1970. Food, industrial output, and population grow exponentially until the rapidly diminishing resource base forces a slowdown in industrial growth. Because of natural delays in the system, both population and pollution continue to increase fo some time after the peak of industrialization. Population growth is finally halted by a rise in the death rate due to decreased food and medical services.

Source: Donella H. Meadows et al., *The Limits to Growth*, New York: Universe Books and Potomac Associates, Inc., 1972, p. 124. Reprinted by permission.

reduced to a fraction of its 1970 value before the end of the century, pollution generation per unit of output would have to be considerably reduced); meaningful value changes would have to take place (a considerable shift in consumption from factory-produced material goods toward services; high priority would be placed on the production of sufficient food for all people).

Let us look in greater detail at the proposed demographic trends that constitute an indispensible component of the development conditions that would enable the world system to approach a state of equilibrium as conceived in the *The Limits to Growth.*

The most general demographic requirement is that the world's population would sooner or later have to cease growing. In an example designated by Meadows et al. as the "stabilized world model I" that indicates "a set of mutually consistent goals that are attaina-ble . . . under the most optimistic assumptions," (p. 166) world population is assumed to cease growing by 1975. This goal of an immediate cessation of population growth is considered unrealistic by the authors; therefore in the "stabilized world model II," "an average desired family size of two children" is assumed to be universally adopted by 1975. The authors realize that even this goal would require a sudden change of fertility trends, and because they recognize that stability should be approached gradually, a further set of assumptions is applied. Or, rather, the stabilizing policies that in the world model II were assumed to be implemented by 1975 are assumed to be implemented in the year 2000.

As even the titles imply, the stabilized world models I and II do lead in the direction of an equilibrium and not a collapse. If, however, the stabilizing policies—including the universal adoption of a 2-child family—are assumed to materialize at the end of this century, then "the equilibrium state is no longer sustainable" (p. 169). The collapse occurs later and in a smoother fashion than illustrated in Figure 9-1. Consequently, if one were forced to formulate concisely the demo-graphic conditions that would avoid a collapse of the world system in accordance with the other stabilizing policies, as defined in the *The Limits to Growth,* this would be the answer: ideally a cessation of population growth immediately; at the other extreme, that is, the maximum the world system seems to be able to tolerate is the universal adoption of the 2-child family before the end of the century. Let us illustrate some demographic trends implied by these conditions.

To bring about a cessation of world population growth during the

Table 9-3   Selected Demographic Measures, World Popula-
             tion, Projections 1 and 2, Linear Decline of
             Growth Rate to Zero, 1965-2005

	Female Rate of Growth	Total Fer- tility Rate	Net Repro- duction Rate
Projection 1 (growth rate = 0 in 1970-1975)			
1965-1970	2.0	4.7	1.9
1970-1975	0.0	1.4	0.6
1975-1980	0.0	1.2	0.5
1980-1985	0.0	1.1	0.5
1985-1990	0.0	1.0	0.5
1990-1995	0.0	1.1	0.5
1995-2000	0.0	1.4	0.6
2000-2005	0.0	1.8	0.8
Projection 2 (growth rate = 0 in 1980-1985)			
1965-1970	2.0	4.7	1.9
1970-1975	1.3	3.5	1.4
1975-1980	0.7	2.2	0.9
1980-1985	0.0	1.1	0.5
1985-1990	0.0	1.0	0.4
1990-1995	0.0	1.0	0.4
1995-2000	0.0	1.1	0.5
2000-2005	0.0	1.3	0.6

1970s or early 1980s would require universal fertility levels that have
never before been experienced on a national basis. The average global
TFR would have to decline rapidly to a value close to 1.0 and remain at
that level for about two decades (Table 9-3). The magnitude of the
changes that would have to be generated becomes even more evident if
one realizes that the average TFR in the less developed countries is
currently in the neighborhood of 6.0. To achieve the goal of immediate
nongrowth, women all over the world during the coming decades would
have to be persuaded (or coerced) not to have more than 1 child, or
exceptionally 2 children.

As noted above, the authors of *The Limits to Growth* consider such
a development unrealistic. They do, however, come to the conclusion
that the viability of the world system requires the adoption of an
average 2-child family before the end of the current century. Since
Projection Three of our standard set assumes that fertility would

Table 9-4 Selected Demographic Measures, World Population, Projections 2 and 3, Standard Set, 1965-2045

	Total Fertility Rate	Net Reproduction Rate	Total Population at End of Period (in billions)	Female Rate of Growth
		Projection 2 (NRR = 1.0 in 1980-1985)		
1965-1970	4.7	1.9	3.6	2.0
1970-1975	3.9	1.6	4.0	1.6
1975-1980	3.1	1.3	4.2	1.3
1980-1985	2.4	1.0	4.4	0.9
1985-1990	2.3	1.0	4.6	1.0
1990-1995	2.3	1.0	4.9	1.0
1995-2000	2.3	1.0	5.1	1.0
2000-2005	2.2	1.0	5.3	0.8
2020-2025	2.2	1.0	6.0	0.5
2040-2045	2.1	1.0	6.3	0.1
		Projection 3 (NRR = 1.0 in 2000-2005)		
1965-1970	4.7	1.9	3.6	2.0
1970-1975	4.4	1.8	4.0	1.9
1975-1980	4.0	1.7	4.4	1.8
1980-1985	3.7	1.6	4.8	1.7
1985-1990	3.3	1.4	5.2	1.6
1990-1995	2.9	1.3	5.6	1.5
1995-2000	2.6	1.2	5.9	1.2
2000-2005	2.2	1.0	6.2	1.0
2020-2025	2.2	1.0	7.4	0.7
2040-2045	2.1	1.0	8.1	0.3

decline roughly to that level by the year 2000, trends of fertility decline illustrated by Projection Three have to be considered as an example of what should not happen (Table 9-4). Even the prohibitively slow trends of fertility decline of Projection Three would require the transformation of fertility behavior in the less developed countries of the world from traditional to modern patterns within 30 years. This is roughly the rate of fertility decline that occurred in Taiwan in the late 1950s and during the 1960s (see Figure 1-6)—the total fertility rate declined from 6.5 in 1956 to 4.1 in 1969.

A path of population stabilization that would satisfy the requirement of reaching the state of global equilbrium would be the trends illustrated by Projection Two of the standard set (Table 9-4). Such a development would require the transition of fertility patterns to occur within a period of about 15 years, that is, a rate of fertility decline almost twice that experienced in Taiwan during recent years. The rate of fertility decline outlined in Projection Two would lead to a leveling off of the total world population in the order of 6.5 billion inhabitants around the middle of the twenty-first century.

In sum, the population growth requirements flowing from this analysis are very demanding. It is in this vein that they are conceived by the Meadows team—namely, that profound changes in several fundamental facets of economic and social life, including fertility behavior, are essential in order to avoid a collapse of the world system.

NOTES

1. Meadows, Donella H. et al. *The Limits to Growth*, New York, Universe Books, 1972.

EPILOGUE

It is hoped that by investigating demographic trends that would ultimately lead to stationary populations, this study has helped to clarify some aspects of future population growth that—within broad limits—can and cannot be expected to occur at least during the next 50 years or so. Practically all countries with currently low fertility are not likely to experience a reduction of their population even if fertility should be somewhat below replacement. Countries with currently high fertility can expect quite substantial population growth even if they manage to decrease their fertility rather rapidly.

In the demographically less developed countries, the starting date of fertility decline, the speed of fertility decline, and consequently the point in time when fertility levels approximating replacement are reached are crucial moments for the nature of their future long-term population growth. At least in those countries where there is a general consensus that, other things being equal, the slowing down of population growth would favor social and economic progress, it is worthwhile to make efforts to this end as soon as possible. "The sooner the better" counts here more than in other fields. The population growth potential of most less developed countries is very high—many of them *could* reach four times or more their present size within 50 years from now, provided mortality continues to decline as expected. To put it differently, the eventual size of the population in the developing countries is closely related to the nature of their demographic transition: will it be a matter of one generation or of two or more generations?

Several demographically more developed countries have expressed their fear of lack of population growth. In terms of total population numbers, this fear does not seem to be justified—a 20 to 30% increase of their population can be expected even if they maintain fertility of replacement from now on. Thus far, only in exceptional cases can nations expect a stagnation of their total number; however, even for them a decrease of numbers seems most unlikely throughout the remainder of the twentieth century.

It would be unwise to expect the population of almost any country in the world to stop growing during the twentieth century. In order to achieve a nongrowing population, even in most of the more developed countries fertility would have to decline significantly below the replacement level. In the less developed countries such a situation seems inconceivable during the coming 50 years provided, of course, mortality conditions do not deteriorate and there are no major natural or human-induced disasters. The achievement of stationary nongrowing populations (provided this is considered desirable) is a matter of several decades in the more developed countries and of many decades in the less developed countries.

Throughout the study we have investigated the population growth consequences of specific types of fertility behavior without analyzing the factors that can or do affect fertility behavior. This is a boundless area of research endeavor of increasing interest to demographers and social scientists in general—and rightly so. As we have seen, the future of population numbers, which undoubtedly affects human well-being and possibly even human survival, depends very much on how rapidly current fertility behavior will be changed.

The history of the past few decades has many examples of how complex a task it is to engender fertility trends of a desired direction. Frequently, in countries in which a decrease of population growth rates is considered desirable, it turns out to be extremely difficult to achieve such a trend. On the other hand, many countries that wish to accelerate their population growth are experiencing at least sustained low fertility if not indeed a fertility decline. As a matter of fact, in several countries, although specific actions have been undertaken to induce higher fertility, these measures are undermined by the antinatalist side effects of actual developments. These countries probably do not realize that the enhancement of living standards and improvements in the quality of life would be even more difficult to attain than they are now if population growth rates were higher than they are.

In the light of growing yet constantly questionable and unsatisfactory knowledge about—

1. The difficulties that growing world population is causing in maintaining a viable ecological balance of our planet;

2. The fact that the functioning of a late-twentieth-century society and economy has a tendency to be capital—and not labor-intensive;

3. The fact that a slower population growth, other things being equal, seems to make a modern society more manageable than a fast-growing population; problems of nutrition, housing, education, health, sanitation, transportation, recreation, and so on are probably easier to tackle in a country with slow rather than fast population growth;

4. The fact that in a modern society, again other things being equal, smaller families are better off than larger families and children from smaller families can get (but do not necessarily have to get) a better start in life;

5. The built-in inertia of population growth—

in the light of these observations, it seems that slow-growing populations should be content that they are growing slowly and fast-growing populations should develop major efforts to decelerate their rate of population growth.

The methods applied and the projections presented in this study are intended to aid in evaluating the current demographic situations of nations. They are supposed to illustrate the possible population growth prospects of nations, and they are meant to be instrumental in assessing realistic goals of population change, wherever and whenever this is considered desirable.

List of Sources

The sources are grouped by major areas. Two books are used continuously:

Coale, Ansley J. and Paul Demeny. *Regional Model Life Tables and Stable Populations.* Princeton: Princeton University Press, 1966.

United Nations, Population Division. *World Population Prospects, 1965–2000, as Assessed in 1968.* (ESA/P/WP.37), 17 December 1970.

A. East Asia

Barnett, K. M. A., Ed. *Hong Kong By-Census: Population Projection 1966–1981.* Hong Kong Government Press, 1968.

———. *Hong Kong By-Census: Hong Kong Life Tables 1963–1978.* Hong Kong Government Press, 1968.

Ministry of Health and Welfare, Tokyo, Japan. *Standardized Vital Rates by Prefectures: 1965.* Institute of Population Problems Research Series No. 180. Tokyo: December 1, 1967.

————. *The 21st Abridged Life Tables (April 1, 1967–March 31, 1968).* Institute of Population Problems Research Series No. 191. Tokyo: May 20, 1969.

Population Index. Office of Population Research, Princeton University. Vol. 35, No. 2, April–June 1969.

Republic of Korea, Economic Planning Board. *1966 Population Census Report of Korea.* Whole Country, 12–1.

Republic of Korea, Ministry of Health and Social Affairs. *The Findings of the National Survey on Family Planning 1967.* Seoul: Planned Parenthood of Korea, December 1968.

Taiwan Provincial Government Department of Civil Affairs. *The Monthly Bulletin of Population Registration Statistics of Taiwan.* Vol. 3, No. 10, October 1968.

————. *The Monthly Bulletin of Population Registration Statistics of Taiwan.* Vol. 4, No. 2, February 1969.

————. *The Monthly Bulletin of Population Registration Statistics of Taiwan.* Vol. 4, No. 4, April 1969.

————. 1965 Taiwan Demographic Fact Book. October 1966.

United Nations, Statistical Office. *1967 United Nations Demographic Yearbook.* New York.

Data on mortality for Korea based on correspondence between Dr. Lee Jay Cho of the East-West Population Institute, Honolulu, and Dr. John Ross of The Population Council, New York.

B. South Asia

Amani, M. "Overview of the Demographic Situation of Iran." Paper, University of Teheran, May 1970.

Aromin, Basilio B. "Considerations for a Philippine Population Policy." *The Philippine Statistician.* Vol. 12, No. 4, December 1963.

Balasubramanian, K., L. B. Kahawatte, and R. N. Sharma. "Mortality Level in Ceylon 1953–63 and Life Table for 1963." Mimeographed. Bombay, India: Demographic Training and Research Centre Programme 1968–1969, June 1969.

Bean, Lee L., Masihur Rahman Khan, and A. Razzaque Rukanuddin. *Population Projections for Pakistan: 1960–2000.* Economics of Development Monograph No. 17. Karachi: Pakistan Institute of Development Economics, January 1968.

Central Bureau of Statistics. *Statistical Abstract of Israel 1966.* No. 17. Jerusalem: Government Press, August 1966.

————. *Statistical Abstract of Israel 1969.* No. 20. Jerusalem: Government Press, September 1969.

Department of Census and Statistics. *Statistical Abstract of Ceylon 1967–1968.* Colombo: Department of Government Printing, 1970.

Immerwahr, G. E., and U. P. Sinha. "Mortality Rates for India 1951–81 for Use of Computer Simulation Model (COMPSIN)." Under preparation.

Lorimer, Frank W. "Analysis and Projections of the Population of the Philippines," First Conference on Population. Manila: 22–24 November 1965.

National Census of Population and Housing, November 1966: Total Country-Settled Population. Translated by Djamchid Momeni. Plan Organization, Iranian Statistical Centre, Vol. 168, March 1968.

National Sample Survey. "Fertility and Mortality Rates in Rural India." Report No. 89, 10th round. Mimeographed.

Office of Statistical Coordination and Standards, National Economic Council. *The Population and Other Demographic facts of the Philippines.* Oscas Monograph No. 4. Manila: September 1963.

Office of the Prime Minister of Thailand. National Statistical Office. *The Survey of Population Change 1964–67.* E-SuR-No. 3–69.

Perangkaan, Jabatan. *Estimates of Fertility for West Malaysia (1957–1967).* Research Paper No. 3. Kuala Lumpur: June 1969.

————. Estimates of Population for West Malaysia (1967). Research Paper No. 1. Kuala Lumpur: March 1969.

————. *Life Tables for West Malaysia 1966.* Research Paper No. 2. Kuala Lumpur: June 1969.

Registrar General, India. *Sample Registration Bulletin.* Provisional Statistics No. 28. Gandhinagar: Government Central Press, April 1969.

Report of the Population Growth Estimation Experiment: Description and Some Results for 1962 and 1963. Karachi: Pakistan Institute of Development Economics, Special Publication, Vol. 22, December 1968.

Republic of Turkey, Ministry of Health and Social Welfare. *Vital Statistics From the Turkish Demographic Survey 1966–67.* Ankara: Hacettepe Press; and State Institute of Statistics Printing Division, 1970.

Shorter, Frederic C., and Samira Berksaw. "The Turkish Population: Its Fertility, Mortality, Growth and International Migration." Paper, November 1966.

State of Singapore. *Population Projections of Singapore.* Singapore: April 1961.

United Nations, Statistical Office. *1969 United Nations Demographic Yearbook.* New York.

Wright, Nicholas. "The Relationship of Demographic Factors and Marital Fertility to the Recent Fertility Decline." *Studies in Family Planning.* No. 59, November 1970.

C. Europe

Bacci, Massimo Livi. "Modernization and Tradition in Italian Fertility." *Demography*. Vol. 4, No. 2, 1967.

Central Bureau of Statistics. "Bevolking, Huwelijk, Echtscheiding, Geboorte, Sterfte, Binnen Enbaitenlandse Migratie, 1946–1965." (Population, Marriages, Divorces, Births, Deaths, Internal and External Migration, 1946–1965 inclusive.) Gravenhage, Netherlands: 1966.

Központi Statisztikai Hivatal. *Demográfiai Évkonyv 1965*. Budapest: Magyarország Népesedése, 1966.

National Statistical Service of Greece. *Monthly Statistical Bulletin*. Vol. 12, No. 2, February 1967.

Population Index. Office of Population Research, Princeton University. Vol. 35, No. 2, April–June 1969.

Republikës Popullore Te Shqipërise. *Vjetari Statistikor*. Albania, 1967–1968.

Srb, Vladimir. *Demografická Příručka*. Praha: Nakladatelství Svoboda, 1967.

Staatliche Zentralverwaltung fur statistik. *Bevölkerungsstatistisches Jahrbuch der Deutschen Demokratischen Republik 1967*. East Berlin: 1967.

Statistisches Bundesamt. *Statistisches Jahrbuch für die Bundesrepublik Deutschland 1969*. Wiesbaden: W. Kohlhammer GMBH/Stuttgart and Mainz.

Statistisches Landesamt. *Statistisches Jahrbuch Berlin 1968*. Berlin: Kulturbuch.

United Nations, Statistical Office. *1965 United Nations Demographic Yearbook*. New York.

———. *1966 United Nations Demographic Yearbook*. New York.

———. *1967 United Nations Demographic Yearbook*. New York.

———. *1969 United Nations Demographic Yearbook*. New York.

U.S. Department of Commerce, Bureau of the Census. "Projections of the Population of the Communist Countries of Eastern Europe by Age and Sex: 1969 to 1990." *International Population Reports*. Series P-91, No. 18. December 1969.

Widen, Lars. "Methodology in Population Projections: A Method Study Applied to Conditions in Sweden." Report No. 9. Gothenburg, Sweden: University of Gothenburg, 1969.

D. U.S.S.R.

Unpublished data from the United Nations Population Division and the two books mentioned at the beginning of the list.

E. Africa

Cairo Demographic Centre. "Demographic Measures for Arab Countries of North Africa and South-West Asia." April 1969.

The Economic Bulletin of Ghana. Vol. 11, No. 3.

Gaisie, S. K. *Dynamics of Population Growth in Ghana.* Ghana Population Studies No. 1. Accra: University of Ghana, 1968.

————. "Estimation of Vital Rates for Ghana." *Population Studies.* Vol. 23, No. 1 (March 1969).

Honore, L. "Demographic and Population Characteristics in Mauritius." Paper presented at the Seminar on Population Growth and Economic Development, 14–22 December 1969 at the University College Nairobi.

Jones, H. M. *Report on the 1966 Swaziland Population Census.* Mbabane: Swaziland Printing and Publishing Company, 1968.

Lapham, Robert J. "Fertility Determinants in the SAIS Plain of Central Morocco"; University of Michigan, 1970.

1969 Population Census of Tanzania. Vol. 6, (forthcoming).

Olusanya, P. O. "Nigeria: Population Growth and its Components and the Nature and Direction of Population Change." *Population Growth and Socioeconomic Change in West Africa.* Ed. John C. Caldwell. (forthcoming).

Page, Hillary J. and Ansley J. Coale. "Estimates of Fertility and Child Mortality in Africa South of the Sahara." Paper presented at the Seminar on Population Growth and Economic Development, 14–22 December 1969 at University College Nairobi.

Roussel, Louis M. *Population: Etudes Regionales 1962–1965.* Abidjan: Ministere du Plan, July 1967.

Som, Ranjan K. "Age Patterns of Fertility in African Countries." United Nations Economic Commission for Africa, unpublished paper.

United Nations, Statistical Office. *1966 United Nations Demographic Yearbook.* New York.

————. *1969 United Nations Demographic Yearbook.* New York.

Vallin, Jacques and Robert Lapham. "Place du Planning Familial dans l'Evolution Recente de la Natalite en Tunisie." *Revue Tunisienne de Sciences Sociales.* Vol. 6, Nos. 17–18 (June–September 1969).

Zachariah, K.C. *The Demographic Measures of Arab Countries: A Comparative Analysis.*

Data for Liberia was based on results from a May 1969–April 1970 survey and was given to us by John Rumford.

F. Northern America

Dominion Bureau of Statistics. *1969 Canada Yearbook.* Ottawa, 1970.

Population Index. Office of Population Research, Princeton University. Vol. 35, No. 2, April–June 1969.

United Nations, Statistical Office. *1965 United Nations Demographic Yearbook.* New York.

————. *1969 United Nations Demographic Yearbook.* New York.

U.S. Department of Commerce, Bureau of the Census. *Current Population Reports.* Series P-25, No. 385, February 14, 1968.

————. *Statistical Abstract of the United States 1969.* 90th Annual Edition.

G. Latin America

Alens Z., Alex A. "República del Salvador Proyección de la población por sexo y grupos de edad 1961–1981." CELADE E/CN.CELADE/C.25,B.64.2/2.1. Santiago, Chile: 1964.

Arriaga, Eduardo E., and Kingsley Davis. "The Pattern of Mortality Change in Latin America." *International Population and Urban Research.* Population Reprint Series, No. 32. August 1969.

Bazan-Gutierrez, Carlos A., and Krishna Roy. "Comparative Estimates of Vital Rates Based on Census Information of 1876, 1940, and 1961." Lima, Peru: National Directorate of Statistics and Census, 1969.

Benítez Zenteno, Raul. *Análisis Demográfico de México.* México, D.F.: Instituto de Investigaciones Sociales, Universidad Nacional, 1961.

Cámel V., Fayad. "Natalidad y fecundidad en Venezuela." Presented at III Congreso Venezolano de Salud Publica. Ponencia No. 1: Poblacion. 20–26 March 1966, Caracas.

Camisa, Zulma C. "Argentina: Proyección de la población por sexo y edad, 1960–1980." CELADE Series C, No. 62.

CELADE. "América Latina, nivel de la mortalidad: Tasas brutas anuales de mortalidad en la población estacionaria y en la población real, por países, período 1965–1970." *Boletín demográfico,* Año 2, No. 4, Santiago, Chile: July 1969.

Department of Health, Division of Demographic Registry and Vital Statistics, Puerto Rico. *Informe annual de estadísticas vitales 1967.*

Government of Trinidad & Tobago, Central Statistical Office. *Population and Vital Statistics 1967 Report.*

Jiménez Jiménez, Ricardo, et al. "Proyección de la población de Costa Rica por sexo y grupos de edad: 1965–1990." *Revista de estudios y estadísticas.* Serie Demográfica No. 5 No. 8, October 1967.

Ministério do Planejamento e Coordenecao Económica. *Demografia.* Escritorio de Pesquisa Económica Aplicada. August 1966.

Pérez S., Enrique. *Proyecciones de la población colombiana 1965–1958.* Monografía no. 28. Bogotá, Colombia: Centro de Estudios sobre Desarrollo Económico, October 1968.

Population Index. Office of Population Research, Princeton University, Vol. 35, No. 2, April–June 1969.

República de Costa Rica, Dirección General de Estadística y Censos. *Estadística vital 1967.* No. 34.

República de Honduras, Direccion General de Estadística y Censos. *Anuario estadístico 1964.* Tegucigalpa: October 1965.

Salazar H., Julia. "Metodología y datos básicos utilizados en la proyección de la poblacion del Perú por sexo y grupos quinquenales de edad, período 1960–1980." *Boletín de análisis demográfico.* No. 3. Lima, Perú: 1965.

―――. "La posible situación demográfica del Perú en el año 2000." *Boletín de análisis demográfico.* No. 8, Lima, Peru: 1968.

United Nations Bulletin. No. 7. New York.

United Nations, Statistical Office. *1965 United Nations Demographic Yearbook.* New York.

―――. *1966 United Nations Demographic Yearbook.* New York.

―――. *1969 United Nations Demographic Yearbook.* New York.

U.S. Department of Commerce, Bureau of the Census. "Population of Chile: Estimates and Projections 1961–1991." *Demographic Reports for Foreign Countries.* Publication Series P. 96, No. 1. December 1969.

―――. "Projections of the Population of Cuba, by Age and Sex: 1968 to 1990." *International Population Reports.* Washington, D.C. March 1970.

H. Oceania

Official Yearbook of the Commonwealth of Australia. No. 53. Canberra, Australia: Commonwealth Bureau of the Census. 1967.

APPENDIX 1 Technical Notes on the Methodology

The basic procedures utilized throughout the study are those of population projections. The *information* needed for our apparatus is as follows:

1. The female population of 1965 divided by 5-years age groups up to 70+.

2. An estimate of average 1965–70 mortality conditions, especially the female expectation of life at birth.

3. An estimate of average 1965–70 fertility, especially age-specific fertility rates by 5-year age groups, which imply knowledge about the value of the GRR and, together with item 3, about the NRR.

4. An estimate of the mean age of childbearing, which can be computed from the data from item 3.

5. Assumptions about paths of mortality and fertility changes

(these are sufficiently described in Chapter 2, Sections 2 and 3).

The *apparatus* itself is built mainly on the following equations:

$$F_x(a) = F_{x-1}(a-1) \cdot p_x(a-1) \tag{1}$$

where $F_x(a)$ = female population of a 5-year[1] age group a at the end of the 5-year period x.

$F_{x-1}(a-1)$ = female population of the preceding (younger) 5-year age group $a-1$ at the end of period $x-1$;

and $p_x(a-1)$ = survival rate of age groups $a-1$ in period x.

$$F_x(0\text{--}4) = B_x \cdot p_x(a_o) \tag{2}$$

where $F(0\text{--}4)$ = female population of age group 0–4 years at the end of period x;

B_x = total number of female births in period x;

$p_x(a_o)$ = female survival rate of all females born in period x $(5 L_0 / {}^{5l}0)$.

$$B_x = 5 \Sigma \bar{F}_x(a) \cdot m_{65\text{--}70}(a) \cdot K_x \tag{3}$$

where B_x = total number of female births in period x;

$\bar{F}_x(a)$ = average number of females in age group a in period x;

$m_{65\text{--}70}(a)$ = maternity frequency[2] of age group a in period 1965–70;

K_x = the fertility coefficient in period x.

$$K_x = GRR_x / GRR_{65\text{--}70} \tag{4}$$

where K_x = the fertility coefficient of period x;

GRR_x = the gross reproduction rate of period x;

$GRR_{65\text{-}70}$ = the gross reproduction rate of the 1965–70 period.

$$GRR_x = NRR_x / p_x(\bar{a}) \tag{5}$$

where GRR_x = the gross reproduction rate of period x;

NRR_x = the net reproduction rate of period x;

$p_x(\bar{a})$ = survival rate from age 0 to average age of childbearing in period x.

A note of clarification should be introduced at this point. Equation

(5) seems to indicate that the NRR_x is the independent variable. This is true only to a certain degree. The assumptions of fertility change were so calculated that the terminal value of the NRR (1.0, 0.9, or any other) would be reached as desired, *but* the linear (or any other) type of fertility decline was performed on the true fertility indicator, that is, the GRR (see Chapter 2, Section 2).

$$TFR_x = GRR_x \cdot \delta \tag{6}$$

where TFR_x = total fertility rate in period x;
δ = total births/female births, the sex ratio at birth, which was assigned the value 2.05.

$$b_x = (B_x/5)/[(\Sigma F_x(a) + \Sigma F_{x-1}(a))/2] \cdot 1000 \tag{7}$$

where b_x = crude birth rate (female) of period x;
B_x = total number of female births in period x;
$\Sigma F_x(a)$ = total female population at the end of period x;
$\Sigma F_{x-1}(a)$ = total female population at the end of period $x - 1$ (or beginning of period x).

$$r_x = \left[e^{\,[\log_e (\Sigma F_x(a)/\Sigma F_{x-1}(a))/5]} - 1.0 \right] \times 100 \tag{8}$$

where r_x = average annual female rate of population growth in period x;
e = the base of natural logarithms;
$\Sigma F_x(a)$ = total female population at the end of period x;
$\Sigma F_{x-1}(a)$ = total female population at the end of period $x - 1$ (or beginning of period x).

$$d_x = b_x - 10\, r_x \tag{9}$$

where d_x = crude death rate (female) of period x;
b_x = crude birth rate (female) of period x;
r_x = average annual female rate of population growth of period x.

In Chapter 6 a slight adjustment of the set of equations was necessary:

1. For the variation in which it is assumed that age patterns of fertility change over time, Equation (3) is adjusted. $m_{65-70}(a)$ is replaced by $m_x(a)$, that is, the age-specific maternity rate may vary over time.

2. For the variation in which the annual rate of population growth is considered the independent variable, the interrelations of the equations are identical; however, the chain of the computations is adjusted as required in order to meet the modified dominant assumption.

3. In all other variations the equations are absolutely identical with the standard set, but the paths of fertility or mortality change differ from the paths of the standard set.

Table A-1 to A-4 illustrate the computations outlined by the Equations (1) to (9) on the example of Projection One of Turkey for the periods 1965–70 and 1970–75.

The computer program naturally follows the steps indicated by the equations. It is available upon request from the Population Council in New York.

NOTES

1. Throughout the project *5-year age groups* and *5-year periods* are applied.
2. Maternity frequency = daughters per year per woman = age-specific fertility taking into account only daughters, not all children [See Louis I. Dublin and Alfred J. Lotka, "On The Time Rate of Natural Increase," *Journal of the American Statistical Association, 20, (September 1925) pp. 307ff.*]

Table A-1 Equation (1) and Result of Equation (2), Turkey, Projection 1

(1)	For Period 1965-1970			For Period 1970-1975		
	$F_{x-1}(a-1)$ (2)	$p_x(a-1)$ (3)	$F_x(a)$ (4)=(2)·(3)	$F_{x-1}(a-1)$ (5)	$p_x(a-1)$ (6)	$F_x(a)$ (7)=(5)·(6)
	Female Population 1965	Female Survival Rate 1965-70	Female Population 1970	Female Population 1970	Female Survival Rate 1970-75	Female Population 1975
Age Group						
0-4	2575	0.96402	2566*	2566	0.97067	1414*
5-9	2140	0.98690	2482	2482	0.98902	2491
10-14	1823	0.98611	2112	2112	0.98826	2455
15-19	1481	0.98113	1798	1798	0.98392	2087
20-24	1118	0.97706	1453	1453	0.98034	1769
25-29	1059	0.97384	1092	1092	0.97744	1424
30-34	1037	0.97022	1031	1031	0.97408	1067
35-39	875	0.96587	1006	1006	0.96985	1004
40-44	631	0.95970	845	845	0.96365	976
45-49	500	0.94810	606	606	0.95243	814
50-54	559	0.92949	474	474	0.93465	577
55-59	521	0.89921	520	520	0.90574	443
60-64	417	0.85236	468	468	0.86039	471
65-69	328 }709		355	355 }802		403
70+	381	0.63115	447	447	0.63794	512
TOTAL	15445	- -	17257	17257	- -	17909
FEMALE e^0	- -	56.0	- -	- -	58.5	- -

*Result of equation (2).

215

Table A-2 Equations (2) and (3), Turkey, Projection 1

	For Period 1965-1970			For Period 1970-1975		
Age Group	$\bar{F}_x(a)$ Average Number of Females	$m_{65-70}(a)$ Average Maternity Frequency	$\bar{F}_x(a) \cdot m_{65-70}(a)$ Average Number of Female Births	$\bar{F}_x(a)$ Average Number of Females	$m_{65-70}(a)$ Average Maternity Frequency	$\bar{F}_x(a) \cdot m_{65-70}(a)$ Average Number of Female Births
(1)	(2)	(3)	(4)=(2)·(3)	(5)	(6)	(7)=(5)·(6)
15-19	1639	.0393	64.4	1942	.0393	76.3
20-24	1285	.1310	168.3	1610	.1310	210.9
25-29	1075	.1269	136.4	1258	.1269	159.6
30-34	1034	.1019	105.4	1049	.1019	106.9
35-39	940	.0729	68.5	1005	.0729	73.3
40-44	738	.0293	21.6	910	.0293	26.7
45-49	552	.0161	8.9	709	.0161	11.4
TOTAL	7266	- -	573.6	8487	- -	665.1
GRR $[=5\Sigma m_{65-70}(a)]$		2.5870	- -		2.5870	- -

$$B_x=5\Sigma\bar{F}_x(a) \cdot m_{65-70}(a) \cdot K_x^*$$
$$2867.8=5 \cdot 573.6 \cdot 1.0000$$

$$B_x=5\Sigma\bar{F}_x(a) \cdot m_{65-70}(a) \cdot K_x^* \quad (3)$$
$$1555.4=5 \cdot 665.1 \cdot 0.4677$$

$$F_x(0-4)= B_x \cdot p_x(a_o)$$
$$2566=2867.8 \cdot 0.89470$$

$$F_x(0-4)= B_x \cdot p_x(a_o) \quad (2)$$
$$1414=1555.4 \cdot 0.90882$$

*Result of equation (4).

216

Table A-3 Equations (4), (5), (6), Turkey, Projection 1

For Period 1965-1970	For Period 1970-1975	
$GRR_x = NRR_x / p_x (\bar{a})$	$GRR_x = NRR_x / p_x (\bar{a})$	(5)
$2.5870 = 2.0664 / 0.79876$	$1.2100 = 1.0000 / 0.82647$	
$K_x = GRR_x / GRR_{65-70}$	$K_x = GRR_x / GRR_{65-70}$	(4)
$1.0000 = 2.5870 / 2.5870$	$0.4677 = 1.2100 / 2.5870$	
$TFR_x = GRR_x \cdot \delta$	$TFR_x = GRR_x \cdot \delta$	(6)
$5.30 = 2.5870 \cdot 2.05$	$2.48 = 1.2100 \cdot 2.05$	

Table A-4 Equations (7), (8), (9), Turkey, Projection 1

For Period 1965-1970	**For Period 1970-1975**

$$b_x = (B_x/5) \;/\; [(\Sigma F_x(a) + \Sigma F_{x-1}(a))/2] \cdot 1000 \qquad (7)$$

For Period 1965-1970:
$$35.1 = 573.6 \;/\; [((17257 + 15445)/2] \cdot 1000$$

For Period 1970-1975:
$$b_x = (B_x/5) \;/\; [(\Sigma F_x(a) + \Sigma F_{x-1}(a))/2] \cdot 1000$$
$$17.7 = 311.0 \;/\; [((17909 + 17257)/2] \cdot 1000$$

$$r_x = \left[e^{[\log_e (\Sigma F_x(a)/\Sigma F_{x-1}(a))/5]} - 1.0 \right] \cdot 100 \qquad (8)$$

For Period 1965-1970:
$$2.24 = \left[e^{[\log_e (17257/15445)/5]} - 1.0 \right] \cdot 100$$

For Period 1970-1975:
$$r_x = \left[e^{[\log_e (\Sigma F_x(a)/\Sigma F_{x-1}(a))/5]} - 1.0 \right] \cdot 100$$
$$0.74 = \left[e^{[\log_e (17909/17257)/5]} - 1.0 \right] \cdot 100$$

$$d_x = b_x - 10r_x \qquad (9)$$

For Period 1965-1970:
$$12.7 = 35.1 - 10\,(2.24)$$

For Period 1970-1975:
$$d_x = b_x - 10r_x$$
$$10.3 = 17.7 - 10\,(0.74)$$

APPENDIX 2   Detailed Tables

Standard Sets of Projections
for the World,
the More Developed Regions,
and the Less Developed Regions

TABLE A   TOTAL POPULATION (IN MILLIONS) AND INDICES OF POPULATION SIZE (1970 = 100), 1970-215?
LINEAR DECLINE OF FERTILITY TO NRR LEVEL OF 1.0

WORLD TOTAL

PROJECTIONS 1 - 5

YEAR	PERIOD IN WHICH NET REPRODUCTION RATE OF ONE IS REACHED				
	1970-1975 PROJ 1	1980-1985 PROJ 2	2000-2005 PROJ 3	2020-2025 PROJ 4	2040-2045 PROJ 5
1970	3645.0 100	3645.0 100	3645.0 100	3645.0 100	3645.0 100
1975	3771.9 103	3953.2 108	4007.0 110	4022.2 110	4029.6 111
1980	3932.7 108	4212.8 116	4387.1 120	4436.3 122	4460.3 122
1985	4126.7 113	4403.5 121	4782.5 131	4889.6 134	4941.9 136
1990	4344.8 119	4628.0 127	5182.3 142	5377.5 148	5473.0 150
1995	4560.2 125	4873.1 134	5570.4 153	5893.3 162	6051.8 166
2000	4746.1 130	5115.6 140	5922.4 162	6422.1 176	6669.8 193
2010	5031.4 138	5522.6 152	6523.6 179	7473.2 205	8003.4 220
2020	5270.0 145	5831.8 160	7116.0 195	8425.9 231	9418.1 258
2030	5441.6 149	6077.8 167	7599.2 208	9215.9 253	10813.2 297
2040	5505.8 151	6215.6 171	7942.0 218	9930.5 272	12038.7 330
2050	5591.6 153	6286.2 172	8172.2 224	10473.2 287	13024.6 357
2075	5674.9 156	6399.8 176	8357.3 229	11084.6 304	14660.5 402
2100	5690.7 156	6416.8 176	8388.5 230	11168.8 306	15102.3 414
2125	5689.0 156	6413.2 176	8388.4 230	11171.9 307	15154.3 416
2150	5684.0 156	6407.4 176	8381.9 230	11164.8 306	15147.9 416

TABLE B BASIC DEMOGRAPHIC MEASURES FOR SELECTED TIME PERIODS 1965 - 2150
LINEAR DECLINE OF FERTILITY TO NRR OF 1.0 IN 1970-5

WORLD TOTAL

PROJECTION 1

PERIOD	FEMALE CRUDE BIRTH RATE	FEMALE CRUDE DEATH RATE	TOTAL FERTILITY RATE	GROSS REPRO- DUCTION RATE*	NET REPRO- DUCTION RATE	TOTAL POPULATION AT END OF PERIOD (IN MILLIONS)	FEMALE AVERAGE ANNUAL RATE OF GROWTH (IN PERCENT)	FEMALE EXPECTATION OF LIFE AT BIRTH
1965-1970	33.2	13.3	4.74	2.31	1.86	3645.0	1.99	56.5
1970-1975	17.9	11.0	2.46	1.20	1.00	3771.9	0.69	59.0
1975-1980	18.8	10.4	2.40	1.17	1.00	3932.7	0.84	61.0
1980-1985	19.7	10.0	2.35	1.14	1.00	4126.7	0.97	63.0
1985-1990	20.1	9.8	2.31	1.13	1.00	4344.8	1.04	64.5
1990-1995	19.3	9.6	2.27	1.11	1.00	4560.2	0.97	66.0
1995-2000	17.6	9.6	2.25	1.10	1.00	4746.1	0.80	67.0
2000-2005	16.1	9.7	2.22	1.08	1.00	4899.3	0.64	68.0
2005-2010	15.2	9.9	2.20	1.07	1.00	5031.4	0.53	69.0
2010-2015	15.0	10.1	2.18	1.06	1.00	5154.7	0.49	70.0
2015-2020	15.0	10.6	2.16	1.06	1.00	5270.0	0.44	71.0
2020-2025	14.8	11.1	2.15	1.05	1.00	5368.0	0.37	72.0
2025-2030	14.3	11.6	2.13	1.04	1.00	5441.6	0.27	73.0
2030-2035	13.9	12.3	2.13	1.04	1.00	5486.7	0.17	73.5
2035-2040	13.7	13.0	2.12	1.03	1.00	5505.8	0.07	74.0
2040-2045	13.7	12.3	2.11	1.03	1.00	5545.1	0.14	74.5
2045-2050	13.7	12.0	2.11	1.03	1.00	5591.6	0.17	75.0
2070-2075	13.4	13.1	2.11	1.03	1.00	5674.9	0.02	75.0
2095-2100	13.3	13.4	2.11	1.03	1.00	5690.7	0.00	75.0
2120-2125	13.3	13.3	2.11	1.03	1.00	5689.0	0.00	75.0
2145-2150	13.3	13.3	2.11	1.03	1.00	5684.0	0.00	75.0

* THE INITIAL AGE-SPECIFIC MATERNITY RATES ARE AS FOLLOWS

	15-19	20-24	25-29	30-34	35-39	40-44	45-49
1965-1970	0.0416	0.0971	0.1295	0.1017	0.0647	0.0231	0.0046

221

TABLE C   BASIC DEMOGRAPHIC MEASURES FOR SELECTED TIME PERIODS 1965 - 2150
LINEAR DECLINE OF FERTILITY TO NRR OF 1.0 IN 1980-5

WORLD TOTAL

PERIOD	FEMALE CRUDE BIRTH RATE	FEMALE CRUDE DEATH RATE	TOTAL FERTILITY RATE	GROSS REPRODUCTION RATE*	NET REPRODUCTION RATE	TOTAL POPULATION AT END OF PERIOD (IN MILLIONS)	FEMALE AVERAGE ANNUAL RATE OF GROWTH (IN PERCENT)	FEMALE EXPECTATION OF LIFE AT BIRTH
1965-1970	33.2	13.3	4.74	2.31	1.86	3645.0	1.99	56.5
1970-1975	27.9	11.6	3.94	1.92	1.60	3953.2	1.64	59.0
1975-1980	23.2	10.4	3.14	1.53	1.31	4212.8	1.28	61.0
1980-1985	18.4	9.5	2.35	1.14	1.00	4403.5	0.89	63.0
1985-1990	19.3	9.3	2.31	1.13	1.00	4628.0	1.00	64.5
1990-1995	19.5	9.1	2.27	1.11	1.00	4873.1	1.04	66.0
1995-2000	18.9	9.2	2.25	1.10	1.00	5115.6	0.98	67.0
2000-2005	17.6	9.2	2.22	1.08	1.00	5335.0	0.84	68.0
2005-2010	16.2	9.3	2.20	1.07	1.00	5522.6	0.69	69.0
2010-2015	15.3	9.4	2.18	1.06	1.00	5685.3	0.58	70.0
2015-2020	14.9	9.8	2.16	1.06	1.00	5831.8	0.51	71.0
2020-2025	14.7	10.3	2.15	1.05	1.00	5963.7	0.45	72.0
2025-2030	14.5	10.7	2.13	1.04	1.00	6077.8	0.38	73.0
2030-2035	14.2	11.4	2.13	1.04	1.00	6163.8	0.28	73.5
2035-2040	13.9	12.2	2.12	1.03	1.00	6215.6	0.17	74.0
2040-2045	13.7	12.5	2.11	1.03	1.00	6251.1	0.11	74.5
2045-2050	13.6	12.4	2.11	1.03	1.00	6286.2	0.11	75.0
2070-2075	13.3	13.2	2.11	1.03	1.00	6399.8	0.01	75.0
2095-2100	13.3	13.3	2.11	1.03	1.00	6416.8	0.00	75.0
2120-2125	13.3	13.3	2.11	1.03	1.00	6413.2	0.00	75.0
2145-2150	13.3	13.3	2.11	1.03	1.00	6407.4	0.00	75.0

* THE INITIAL AGE-SPECIFIC MATERNITY RATES ARE AS FOLLOWS

1965-1970	15-19	20-24	25-29	30-34	35-39	40-44	45-49
	0.0416	0.0971	0.1295	0.1017	0.0647	0.0231	0.0046

TABLE D BASIC DEMOGRAPHIC MEASURES FOR SELECTED TIME PERIODS 1965 - 2150
LINEAR DECLINE OF FERTILITY TO NRR OF 1.0 IN 2000-5

WORLD TOTAL

PERIOD	FEMALE CRUDE BIRTH RATE	FEMALE CRUDE DEATH RATE	TOTAL FERTILITY RATE	GROSS REPRODUCTION RATE*	NET REPRODUCTION RATE	TOTAL POPULATION AT END OF PERIOD (IN MILLIONS)	FEMALE AVERAGE ANNUAL RATE OF GROWTH (IN PERCENT)	FEMALE EXPECTATION OF LIFE AT BIRTH
1965-1970	33.2	13.3	4.74	2.31	1.86	3645.0	1.99	56.5
1970-1975	30.8	11.7	4.38	2.14	1.78	4007.0	1.91	59.0
1975-1980	28.9	10.6	4.02	1.96	1.67	4387.1	1.83	61.0
1980-1985	27.0	9.6	3.66	1.79	1.56	4782.5	1.74	63.0
1985-1990	25.1	8.9	3.30	1.61	1.43	5182.3	1.62	64.5
1990-1995	23.0	8.5	2.94	1.44	1.30	5570.5	1.45	66.0
1995-2000	20.6	8.3	2.58	1.26	1.15	5922.5	1.23	67.0
2000-2005	18.0	8.2	2.22	1.08	1.00	6218.6	0.98	68.0
2005-2010	17.8	8.2	2.20	1.07	1.00	6523.6	0.96	69.0
2010-2015	17.4	8.2	2.18	1.06	1.00	6827.6	0.92	70.0
2015-2020	16.7	8.4	2.16	1.06	1.00	7116.0	0.83	71.0
2020-2025	15.9	8.7	2.15	1.05	1.00	7374.6	0.72	72.0
2025-2030	15.0	9.0	2.13	1.04	1.00	7599.2	0.60	73.0
2030-2035	14.5	9.6	2.13	1.04	1.00	7788.1	0.49	73.5
2035-2040	14.2	10.3	2.12	1.03	1.00	7942.0	0.39	74.0
2040-2045	14.0	10.8	2.11	1.03	1.00	8069.3	0.32	74.5
2045-2050	13.9	11.3	2.11	1.03	1.00	8172.2	0.25	75.0
2070-2075	13.4	12.9	2.11	1.03	1.00	8357.3	0.05	75.0
2095-2100	13.3	13.3	2.11	1.03	1.00	8388.5	0.00	75.0
2120-2125	13.3	13.4	2.11	1.03	1.00	8388.4	0.00	75.0
2145-2150	13.3	13.3	2.11	1.03	1.00	8381.9	0.00	75.0

* THE INITIAL AGE-SPECIFIC MATERNITY RATES ARE AS FOLLOWS

	15-19	20-24	25-29	30-34	35-39	40-44	45-49
1965-1970	0.0416	0.0971	0.1295	0.1017	0.0647	0.0231	0.0046

TABLE E BASIC DEMOGRAPHIC MEASURES FOR SELECTED TIME PERIODS 1965 - 2150
LINEAR DECLINE OF FERTILITY TO NRR OF 1.0 IN 2020-5

PROJECTION 4

WORLD TOTAL

PERIOD	FEMALE CRUDE BIRTH RATE	FEMALE CRUDE DEATH RATE	TOTAL FERTILITY RATE	GROSS REPRODUCTION RATE*	NET REPRODUCTION RATE	TOTAL POPULATION AT END OF PERIOD (IN MILLIONS)	FEMALE AVERAGE ANNUAL RATE OF GROWTH (IN PERCENT)	FEMALE EXPECTATION OF LIFE AT BIRTH
1965-1970	33.2	13.3	4.74	2.31	1.86	3645.0	1.99	56.5
1970-1975	31.6	11.7	4.50	2.20	1.83	4022.2	1.99	59.0
1975-1980	30.4	10.6	4.27	2.08	1.78	4436.3	1.98	61.0
1980-1985	29.3	9.6	4.03	1.97	1.72	4889.6	1.96	63.0
1985-1990	28.1	8.9	3.80	1.85	1.65	5377.5	1.92	64.5
1990-1995	26.8	8.3	3.56	1.74	1.57	5893.3	1.85	66.0
1995-2000	25.4	8.0	3.33	1.62	1.48	6422.1	1.73	67.0
2000-2005	23.8	7.8	3.09	1.51	1.39	6953.0	1.60	68.0
2005-2010	22.1	7.6	2.85	1.39	1.30	7473.2	1.45	69.0
2010-2015	20.4	7.4	2.62	1.28	1.20	7970.2	1.30	70.0
2015-2020	18.6	7.4	2.38	1.16	1.10	8425.9	1.12	71.0
2020-2025	16.8	7.5	2.15	1.05	1.00	8821.7	0.92	72.0
2025-2030	16.5	7.7	2.13	1.04	1.00	9215.9	0.88	73.0
2030-2035	16.1	8.1	2.13	1.04	1.00	9591.6	0.80	73.5
2035-2040	15.6	8.6	2.12	1.03	1.00	9930.5	0.70	74.0
2040-2045	14.9	9.1	2.11	1.03	1.00	10224.9	0.59	74.5
2045-2050	14.4	9.5	2.11	1.03	1.00	10473.2	0.48	75.0
2070-2075	13.5	12.5	2.11	1.03	1.00	11084.6	0.10	75.0
2095-2100	13.4	13.2	2.11	1.03	1.00	11168.8	0.02	75.0
2120-2125	13.3	13.3	2.11	1.03	1.00	11171.9	0.00	75.0
2145-2150	13.3	13.4	2.11	1.03	1.00	11164.8	0.00	75.0

* THE INITIAL AGE-SPECIFIC MATERNITY RATES ARE AS FOLLOWS

	15-19	20-24	25-29	30-34	35-39	40-44	45-49
1965-1970	0.0416	0.0971	0.1295	0.1017	0.0647	0.0231	0.0046

TABLE F BASIC DEMOGRAPHIC MEASURES FOR SELECTED TIME PERIODS 1965 - 2150
LINEAR DECLINE OF FERTILITY TO NRR OF 1.0 IN 2040-5

PROJECTION 5

WORLD TOTAL

PERIOD	FEMALE CRUDE BIRTH RATE	FEMALE CRUDE DEATH RATE	TOTAL FERTILITY RATE	GROSS REPRODUCTION RATE*	NET REPRODUCTION RATE	TOTAL POPULATION AT END OF PERIOD (IN MILLIONS)	FEMALE AVERAGE ANNUAL RATE OF GROWTH (IN PERCENT)	FEMALE EXPECTATION OF LIFE AT BIRTH
1965-1970	33.2	13.3	4.74	2.31	1.86	3645.0	1.99	56.5
1970-1975	32.0	11.8	4.56	2.23	1.85	4029.6	2.03	59.0
1975-1980	31.2	10.6	4.39	2.14	1.83	4460.3	2.05	61.0
1980-1985	30.3	9.6	4.21	2.06	1.80	4941.9	2.07	63.0
1985-1990	29.5	8.9	4.04	1.97	1.75	5473.0	2.06	64.5
1990-1995	28.6	8.3	3.86	1.88	1.70	6051.8	2.03	66.0
1995-2000	27.5	7.9	3.69	1.80	1.64	6669.8	1.96	67.0
2000-2005	26.4	7.6	3.51	1.71	1.58	7322.5	1.88	68.0
2005-2010	25.2	7.3	3.34	1.63	1.52	8003.4	1.79	69.0
2010-2015	24.0	7.0	3.16	1.54	1.45	8706.3	1.70	70.0
2015-2020	22.7	6.9	2.99	1.46	1.38	9418.1	1.58	71.0
2020-2025	21.4	6.8	2.81	1.37	1.31	10125.0	1.46	72.0
2025-2030	20.1	6.8	2.64	1.29	1.24	10813.3	1.32	73.0
2030-2035	18.7	7.0	2.46	1.20	1.16	11458.2	1.17	73.5
2035-2040	17.3	7.4	2.29	1.12	1.08	12038.7	0.99	74.0
2040-2045	15.9	7.7	2.11	1.03	1.00	12539.8	0.82	74.5
2045-2050	15.7	8.1	2.11	1.03	1.00	13024.6	0.76	75.0
2070-2075	13.8	11.0	2.11	1.03	1.00	14660.5	0.28	75.0
2095-2100	13.4	13.0	2.11	1.03	1.00	15102.3	0.04	75.0
2120-2125	13.3	13.3	2.11	1.03	1.00	15154.3	0.01	75.0
2145-2150	13.3	13.3	2.11	1.03	1.00	15147.9	0.00	75.0

* THE INITIAL AGE-SPECIFIC MATERNITY RATES ARE AS FOLLOWS

	15-19	20-24	25-29	30-34	35-39	40-44	45-49
1965-1970	0.0416	0.0971	0.1295	0.1017	0.0647	0.0231	0.0046

TABLE G   AVERAGE ANNUAL RATES OF POPULATION GROWTH (IN PERCENT), 1965-2150
LINEAR DECLINE OF FERTILITY TO NRR LEVEL OF 1.0

PROJECTIONS 1 - 5

WORLD TOTAL

PERIOD IN WHICH NET REPRODUCTION RATE OF ONE IS REACHED

PERIOD	1970-1975 PROJ 1	1980-1985 PROJ 2	2000-2005 PROJ 3	2020-2025 PROJ 4	2040-2045 PROJ 5
1965-1970	1.99	1.99	1.99	1.99	1.99
1970-1975	0.69	1.64	1.91	1.99	2.03
1975-1980	0.84	1.28	1.83	1.98	2.05
1980-1985	0.97	0.89	1.74	1.96	2.07
1985-1990	1.04	1.00	1.62	1.92	2.06
1990-1995	0.97	1.04	1.45	1.85	2.03
1995-2000	0.80	0.98	1.23	1.73	1.96
2000-2005	0.64	0.84	0.98	1.60	1.88
2005-2010	0.53	0.69	0.96	1.45	1.79
2010-2015	0.49	0.58	0.92	1.30	1.70
2015-2020	0.44	0.51	0.83	1.12	1.58
2020-2025	0.37	0.45	0.72	0.92	1.46
2025-2030	0.27	0.38	0.60	0.88	1.32
2030-2035	0.17	0.28	0.49	0.80	1.17
2035-2040	0.07	0.17	0.39	0.70	0.99
2040-2045	0.14	0.11	0.32	0.59	0.82
2045-2050	0.17	0.11	0.25	0.48	0.76
2070-2075	0.02	0.01	0.05	0.10	0.23
2095-2100	0.00	0.00	0.00	0.02	0.04
2120-2125	0.00	0.00	0.00	0.00	0.01
2145-2150	0.00	0.00	0.00	0.00	0.00

226

TABLE H   AVERAGE ANNUAL INCREMENTS OF POPULATION (IN THOUSANDS), 1965-2150
LINEAR DECLINE OF FERTILITY TO NRR LEVEL OF 1.0

WORLD TOTAL

PROJECTIONS 1 - 5

PERIOD	PERIOD IN WHICH NET REPRODUCTION RATE OF ONE IS REACHED				
	1970-1975 PROJ 1	1980-1985 PROJ 2	2000-2005 PROJ 3	2020-2025 PROJ 4	2040-2045 PROJ 5
1965-1970	68464	68464	68464	68464	68464
1970-1975	25395	61654	72411	75449	76931
1975-1980	32158	51907	76011	82821	86146
1980-1985	38803	38146	79090	90655	96306
1985-1990	43621	44901	79960	97591	106222
1990-1995	43065	49015	77625	103148	115772
1995-2000	37191	48511	70400	105764	123592
2000-2005	30635	43881	59222	106179	130537
2005-2010	26413	37504	61001	104038	136188
2010-2015	24668	32553	60810	99412	140571
2015-2020	23067	29288	57667	91139	142357
2020-2025	19584	26385	51736	79148	141394
2025-2030	14724	22824	44911	78850	137641
2030-2035	9018	17196	37774	75135	123998
2035-2040	3830	10368	30799	67778	116085
2040-2045	7851	7088	25443	58889	100219
2045-2050	9307	7018	20588	49651	96964
2070-2075	1177	893	4280	10791	41169
2095-2100	-230	49	80	2296	5464
2120-2125	-191	-70	-337	30	925
2145-2150	-169	-190	-293	-438	-79

TABLE I AGE STRUCTURE OF POPULATION IN SELECTED YEARS (IN PERCENTAGES), 1970-2075
LINEAR DECLINE OF FERTILITY TO NRR LEVEL OF 1.0

PROJECTIONS 1 - 5

WORLD TOTAL

YEAR / AGE GROUP	PERIOD IN WHICH NET REPRODUCTION RATE OF ONE IS REACHED				
	1970-1975 PROJ 1	1980-1985 PROJ 2	2000-2005 PROJ 3	2020-2025 PROJ 4	2040-2045 PROJ 5
1970					
0 - 4	14.2	14.2	14.2	14.2	14.2
5 - 9	11.9	11.9	11.9	11.9	11.9
10 - 14	10.9	10.9	10.9	10.9	10.9
15 - 19	9.7	9.7	9.7	9.7	9.7
20 - 29	15.3	15.3	15.3	15.3	15.3
30 - 44	17.8	17.8	17.8	17.8	17.8
45 - 64	14.8	14.8	14.8	14.8	14.8
65+	5.5	5.5	5.5	5.5	5.5
1985					
0 - 4	9.0	8.4	12.1	13.0	13.5
5 - 9	7.9	9.7	11.5	11.9	12.1
10 - 14	7.1	10.6	10.9	11.0	11.0
15 - 19	12.0	11.2	10.3	10.1	10.0
20 - 29	19.4	18.2	16.7	16.3	16.2
30 - 44	20.9	19.5	18.0	17.6	17.4
45 - 64	17.5	16.4	15.1	14.8	14.6
65+	6.3	5.9	5.4	5.3	5.3
2000					
0 - 4	8.2	8.8	9.5	11.6	12.5
5 - 9	8.5	8.5	9.8	11.0	11.6
10 - 14	8.3	7.9	9.8	10.4	10.6
15 - 19	7.6	7.0	9.5	9.6	9.7
20 - 29	12.8	17.1	17.6	17.0	16.7
30 - 44	26.2	24.3	21.0	19.4	18.6
45 - 64	20.6	19.2	16.5	15.3	14.7
65+	7.8	7.2	6.2	5.7	5.5
2015					
0 - 4	7.2	7.3	8.2	9.5	11.1
5 - 9	7.0	7.4	7.9	9.5	10.6
10 - 14	7.1	7.7	7.6	9.4	10.0
15 - 19	7.5	7.8	8.1	9.2	9.4
20 - 29	15.2	14.5	16.7	17.0	16.7
30 - 44	18.2	21.1	22.9	20.9	19.7
45 - 64	27.9	25.3	21.0	18.0	16.5
65+	10.0	9.0	7.5	6.5	5.9

TABLE I (CONTINUED)

PROJECTIONS 1 - 5

WORLD TOTAL

PERIOD IN WHICH NET REPRODUCTION RATE OF ONE IS REACHED

YEAR	1970-1975	1980-1985	2000-2005	2020-2025	2040-2045
2030					
0 - 4	7.0	7.0	7.2	7.9	9.5
5 - 9	7.0	6.9	7.3	7.6	9.4
10 - 14	6.9	6.8	7.4	8.0	9.2
15 - 19	6.7	6.7	7.3	8.2	8.9
20 - 29	13.2	13.9	13.8	16.3	16.5
30 - 44	21.0	20.4	21.9	22.2	20.7
45 - 64	23.8	25.3	24.8	21.5	18.8
65+	14.3	12.8	10.3	8.5	7.2
2045					
0 - 4	6.7	6.7	6.8	7.2	7.7
5 - 9	6.7	6.7	6.8	7.3	7.9
10 - 14	6.7	6.8	6.7	7.2	8.1
15 - 19	6.8	6.8	6.8	7.1	8.1
20 - 29	13.6	13.3	13.8	13.9	15.9
30 - 44	19.3	19.8	19.6	21.7	21.5
45 - 64	25.3	23.9	25.6	24.3	21.4
65+	15.0	16.0	13.9	11.3	9.3
2060					
0 - 4	6.6	6.6	6.6	6.7	7.3
5 - 9	6.6	6.6	6.7	6.7	7.2
10 - 14	6.6	6.6	6.7	6.7	7.1
15 - 19	6.5	6.5	6.6	6.8	6.9
20 - 29	13.0	13.2	13.1	13.6	14.4
30 - 44	19.7	19.5	19.8	19.6	21.5
45 - 64	24.1	24.7	24.2	25.5	23.9
65+	16.7	16.2	16.4	14.2	11.8
2075					
0 - 4	6.6	6.6	6.6	6.6	6.7
5 - 9	6.5	6.6	6.6	6.6	6.8
10 - 14	6.6	6.6	6.6	6.6	6.8
15 - 19	6.6	6.6	6.6	6.6	6.8
20 - 29	13.1	13.0	13.1	13.1	13.5
30 - 44	19.3	19.4	19.3	19.7	19.9
45 - 64	24.5	24.2	24.7	24.3	25.2
65+	16.9	17.1	16.6	16.5	14.2

TABLE A   TOTAL POPULATION (IN MILLIONS) AND INDICES OF POPULATION SIZE (1970 = 100), 1970-2150
LINEAR DECLINE OF FERTILITY TO NRR LEVEL OF 1.0

MORE DEVELOPED REGIONS

PERIOD IN WHICH NET REPRODUCTION RATE OF ONE IS REACHED, PROJECTIONS 1 - 5

YEAR	1970-1975 PROJ 1	1980-1985 PROJ 2	2000-2005 PROJ 3	2020-2025 PROJ 4	2040-2045 PROJ 5
1970	1122.2 / 100	1122.2 / 100	1122.2 / 100	1122.2 / 100	1122.2 / 100
1975	1151.6 / 103	1165.4 / 104	1169.4 / 104	1170.5 / 104	1171.1 / 104
1980	1183.2 / 105	1204.3 / 107	1216.7 / 108	1220.2 / 109	1221.9 / 109
1985	1216.4 / 108	1237.5 / 110	1263.2 / 113	1270.4 / 113	1274.0 / 114
1990	1250.7 / 111	1272.7 / 113	1309.0 / 117	1321.4 / 118	1327.6 / 118
1995	1280.3 / 114	1305.8 / 116	1350.6 / 120	1370.1 / 122	1379.8 / 123
2000	1305.1 / 116	1335.8 / 119	1388.1 / 124	1416.8 / 126	1431.3 / 128
2010	1349.1 / 120	1389.0 / 124	1456.7 / 130	1508.3 / 134	1536.6 / 137
2020	1388.6 / 124	1434.7 / 128	1521.1 / 136	1592.2 / 142	1641.0 / 146
2030	1409.0 / 126	1462.6 / 130	1564.9 / 139	1653.9 / 147	1728.2 / 154
2040	1416.0 / 126	1475.8 / 132	1593.5 / 142	1702.2 / 152	1799.0 / 160
2050	1423.0 / 127	1481.8 / 132	1610.3 / 143	1735.7 / 155	1852.9 / 165
2075	1426.7 / 127	1487.6 / 133	1621.7 / 145	1770.7 / 158	1931.2 / 172
2100	1426.9 / 127	1488.0 / 133	1623.2 / 145	1775.8 / 158	1952.4 / 174
2125	1426.4 / 127	1487.5 / 133	1622.8 / 145	1776.0 / 158	1955.2 / 174
2150	1425.7 / 127	1486.8 / 132	1622.1 / 145	1775.4 / 158	1954.9 / 174

230

TABLE B BASIC DEMOGRAPHIC MEASURES FOR SELECTED TIME PERIODS 1965 - 2150
LINEAR DECLINE OF FERTILITY TO NRR OF 1.0 IN 1970-5

PROJECTION 1

MORE DEVELOPED REGIONS

PERIOD	FEMALE CRUDE BIRTH RATE	FEMALE CRUDE DEATH RATE	TOTAL FERTILITY RATE	GROSS REPRODUCTION RATE*	NET REPRODUCTION RATE	TOTAL POPULATION AT END OF PERIOD (IN MILLIONS)	FEMALE AVERAGE ANNUAL RATE OF GROWTH (IN PERCENT)	FEMALE EXPECTATION OF LIFE AT BIRTH
1965-1970	18.3	9.7	2.66	1.30	1.25	1122.2	0.86	72.5
1970-1975	15.0	9.8	2.13	1.04	1.00	1151.6	0.57	73.0
1975-1980	15.5	10.0	2.12	1.04	1.00	1183.2	0.54	73.5
1980-1985	15.7	10.2	2.12	1.03	1.00	1216.4	0.56	74.0
1985-1990	15.5	10.0	2.11	1.03	1.00	1250.7	0.56	74.5
1990-1995	14.9	10.2	2.10	1.03	1.00	1280.3	0.47	75.0
1995-2000	14.3	10.4	2.10	1.02	1.00	1305.1	0.38	75.5
2000-2005	13.9	10.4	2.09	1.02	1.00	1327.8	0.35	76.0
2005-2010	13.7	10.5	2.09	1.02	1.00	1349.1	0.32	76.5
2010-2015	13.6	10.5	2.08	1.02	1.00	1370.5	0.32	77.0
2015-2020	13.4	10.8	2.08	1.01	1.00	1388.6	0.26	77.5
2020-2025	13.2	11.4	2.08	1.01	1.00	1401.2	0.18	77.5
2025-2030	13.1	12.0	2.08	1.01	1.00	1409.0	0.11	77.5
2030-2035	13.0	12.4	2.08	1.01	1.00	1413.5	0.06	77.5
2035-2040	13.0	12.7	2.08	1.01	1.00	1416.0	0.03	77.5
2040-2045	13.0	12.5	2.08	1.01	1.00	1419.7	0.05	77.5
2045-2050	13.0	12.5	2.08	1.01	1.00	1423.0	0.05	77.5
2070-2075	12.9	12.8	2.08	1.01	1.00	1426.7	0.01	77.5
2095-2100	12.9	12.9	2.08	1.01	1.00	1426.9	0.00	77.5
2120-2125	12.9	12.9	2.08	1.01	1.00	1426.4	0.00	77.5
2145-2150	12.9	12.9	2.08	1.01	1.00	1425.7	0.00	77.5

* THE INITIAL AGE-SPECIFIC MATERNITY RATES ARE AS FOLLOWS

	15-19	20-24	25-29	30-34	35-39	40-44	45-49
1965-1970	0.0377	0.0715	0.0702	0.0481	0.0260	0.0052	0.0013

231

TABLE C   BASIC DEMOGRAPHIC MEASURES FOR SELECTED TIME PERIODS 1965 - 2150
LINEAR DECLINE OF FERTILITY TO NRR OF 1.0 IN 1980-5

PROJECTION 2

MORE DEVELOPED REGIONS

PERIOD	FEMALE CRUDE BIRTH RATE	FEMALE CRUDE DEATH RATE	TOTAL FERTILITY RATE	GROSS REPRO-DUCTION RATE*	NET REPRO-DUCTION RATE	TOTAL POPULATION AT END OF PERIOD (IN MILLIONS)	FEMALE AVERAGE ANNUAL RATE OF GROWTH (IN PERCENT)	FEMALE EXPECTATION OF LIFE AT BIRTH
1965-1970	18.3	9.7	2.66	1.30	1.25	1122.2	0.86	72.5
1970-1975	17.4	9.8	2.48	1.21	1.17	1165.4	0.76	73.0
1975-1980	16.5	9.9	2.30	1.12	1.08	1204.3	0.66	73.5
1980-1985	15.5	10.0	2.12	1.03	1.00	1237.5	0.55	74.0
1985-1990	15.4	9.8	2.11	1.03	1.00	1272.7	0.56	74.5
1990-1995	15.2	10.0	2.10	1.03	1.00	1305.8	0.51	75.0
1995-2000	14.8	10.2	2.10	1.02	1.00	1335.8	0.46	75.5
2000-2005	14.3	10.2	2.09	1.02	1.00	1363.7	0.41	76.0
2005-2010	13.9	10.3	2.09	1.02	1.00	1389.0	0.37	76.5
2010-2015	13.7	10.2	2.08	1.02	1.00	1413.5	0.35	77.0
2015-2020	13.5	10.5	2.08	1.01	1.00	1434.7	0.30	77.5
2020-2025	13.3	11.1	2.08	1.01	1.00	1450.9	0.22	77.5
2025-2030	13.2	11.6	2.08	1.01	1.00	1462.6	0.16	77.5
2030-2035	13.1	12.0	2.08	1.01	1.00	1470.6	0.11	77.5
2035-2040	13.0	12.3	2.08	1.01	1.00	1475.8	0.07	77.5
2040-2045	13.0	12.5	2.08	1.01	1.00	1479.2	0.05	77.5
2045-2050	13.0	12.6	2.08	1.01	1.00	1481.8	0.03	77.5
2070-2075	12.9	12.9	2.08	1.01	1.00	1487.6	0.00	77.5
2095-2100	12.9	12.9	2.08	1.01	1.00	1488.0	0.00	77.5
2120-2125	12.9	12.9	2.08	1.01	1.00	1487.5	0.00	77.5
2145-2150	12.9	12.9	2.08	1.01	1.00	1486.8	0.00	77.5

* THE INITIAL AGE-SPECIFIC MATERNITY RATES ARE AS FOLLOWS

	15-19	20-24	25-29	30-34	35-39	40-44	45-49
1965-1970	0.0377	0.0715	0.0702	0.0481	0.0260	0.0052	0.0013

PROJECTION 3

MORE DEVELOPED REGIONS

PERIOD	FEMALE CRUDE BIRTH RATE	FEMALE CRUDE DEATH RATE	TOTAL FERTILITY RATE	GROSS REPRODUCTION RATE*	NET REPRODUCTION RATE	TOTAL POPULATION AT END OF PERIOD (IN MILLIONS)	FEMALE AVERAGE ANNUAL RATE OF GROWTH (IN PERCENT)	FEMALE EXPECTATION OF LIFE AT BIRTH
1965-1970	18.3	9.7	2.66	1.30	1.25	1122.2	0.86	72.5
1970-1975	18.1	9.8	2.58	1.26	1.21	1169.4	0.83	73.0
1975-1980	17.8	9.9	2.50	1.22	1.18	1216.7	0.80	73.5
1980-1985	17.4	9.9	2.42	1.18	1.14	1263.2	0.75	74.0
1985-1990	16.8	9.6	2.34	1.14	1.11	1309.0	0.72	74.5
1990-1995	16.0	9.8	2.26	1.10	1.07	1350.6	0.63	75.0
1995-2000	15.4	9.9	2.18	1.06	1.04	1388.1	0.55	75.5
2000-2005	14.7	9.8	2.09	1.02	1.00	1422.6	0.49	76.0
2005-2010	14.6	9.8	2.09	1.02	1.00	1456.7	0.48	76.5
2010-2015	14.3	9.7	2.08	1.02	1.00	1490.8	0.46	77.0
2015-2020	14.0	10.0	2.08	1.01	1.00	1521.1	0.40	77.5
2020-2025	13.7	10.5	2.08	1.01	1.00	1545.5	0.32	77.5
2025-2030	13.4	10.9	2.08	1.01	1.00	1564.9	0.25	77.5
2030-2035	13.3	11.3	2.08	1.01	1.00	1580.7	0.20	77.5
2035-2040	13.2	11.6	2.08	1.01	1.00	1593.5	0.16	77.5
2040-2045	13.1	11.9	2.08	1.01	1.00	1603.4	0.12	77.5
2045-2050	13.1	12.2	2.08	1.01	1.00	1610.3	0.09	77.5
2070-2075	12.9	12.8	2.08	1.01	1.00	1621.7	0.02	77.5
2095-2100	12.9	12.9	2.08	1.01	1.00	1623.2	0.00	77.5
2120-2125	12.9	12.9	2.08	1.01	1.00	1622.8	0.00	77.5
2145-2150	12.9	12.9	2.08	1.01	1.00	1622.1	0.00	77.5

* THE INITIAL AGE-SPECIFIC MATERNITY RATES ARE AS FOLLOWS

	15-19	20-24	25-29	30-34	35-39	40-44	45-49
1965-1970	0.0377	0.0715	0.0702	0.0481	0.0260	0.0052	0.0013

TABLE E BASIC DEMOGRAPHIC MEASURES FOR SELECTED TIME PERIODS 1965 - 2150
LINEAR DECLINE OF FERTILITY TO NRR OF 1.0 IN 2020-5

PROJECTION 4

MORE DEVELOPED REGIONS

PERIOD	FEMALE CRUDE BIRTH RATE	FEMALE CRUDE DEATH RATE	TOTAL FERTILITY RATE	GROSS REPRO- DUCTION RATE*	NET REPRO- DUCTION RATE	TOTAL POPULATION AT END OF PERIOD (IN MILLIONS)	FEMALE AVERAGE ANNUAL RATE OF GROWTH (IN PERCENT)	FEMALE EXPECTATION OF LIFE AT BIRTH
1965-1970	18.3	9.7	2.66	1.30	1.25	1122.2	0.86	72.5
1970-1975	18.3	9.8	2.61	1.27	1.23	1170.5	0.85	73.0
1975-1980	18.2	9.9	2.56	1.25	1.21	1220.2	0.83	73.5
1980-1985	17.9	9.8	2.51	1.22	1.18	1270.4	0.81	74.0
1985-1990	17.5	9.5	2.45	1.20	1.16	1321.4	0.79	74.5
1990-1995	16.9	9.7	2.40	1.17	1.14	1370.1	0.73	75.0
1995-2000	16.5	9.7	2.35	1.14	1.12	1416.8	0.67	75.5
2000-2005	16.1	9.6	2.29	1.12	1.09	1463.3	0.65	76.0
2005-2010	15.6	9.6	2.24	1.09	1.07	1508.3	0.61	76.5
2010-2015	15.2	9.4	2.19	1.07	1.05	1552.5	0.58	77.0
2015-2020	14.6	9.6	2.13	1.04	1.03	1592.2	0.51	77.5
2020-2025	14.1	10.0	2.08	1.01	1.00	1624.9	0.41	77.5
2025-2030	14.0	10.4	2.08	1.01	1.00	1653.9	0.35	77.5
2030-2035	13.8	10.7	2.08	1.01	1.00	1679.7	0.31	77.5
2035-2040	13.6	10.9	2.08	1.01	1.00	1702.2	0.27	77.5
2040-2045	13.4	11.2	2.08	1.01	1.00	1720.9	0.22	77.5
2045-2050	13.3	11.5	2.08	1.01	1.00	1735.7	0.17	77.5
2070-2075	13.0	12.6	2.08	1.01	1.00	1770.7	0.04	77.5
2095-2100	12.9	12.8	2.08	1.01	1.00	1775.8	0.01	77.5
2120-2125	12.9	12.9	2.08	1.01	1.00	1776.0	0.00	77.5
2145-2150	12.9	12.9	2.08	1.01	1.00	1775.4	0.00	77.5

* THE INITIAL AGE-SPECIFIC MATERNITY RATES ARE AS FOLLOWS

	15-19	20-24	25-29	30-34	35-39	40-44	45-49
1965-1970	0.0377	0.0715	0.0702	0.0481	0.0260	0.0052	0.0013

TABLE F   BASIC DEMOGRAPHIC MEASURES FOR SELECTED TIME PERIODS 1965 - 2150
LINEAR DECLINE OF FERTILITY TO NRR OF 1.0 IN 2040-5

MORE DEVELOPED REGIONS

PERIOD	FEMALE CRUDE BIRTH RATE	FEMALE CRUDE DEATH RATE	TOTAL FERTILITY RATE	GROSS REPRODUCTION RATE*	NET REPRODUCTION RATE	TOTAL POPULATION AT END OF PERIOD (IN MILLIONS)	FEMALE AVERAGE ANNUAL RATE OF GROWTH (IN PERCENT)	FEMALE EXPECTATION OF LIFE AT BIRTH
1965-1970	18.3	9.7	2.66	1.30	1.25	1122.2	0.86	72.5
1970-1975	18.3	9.8	2.63	1.28	1.23	1171.1	0.86	73.0
1975-1980	18.4	9.9	2.59	1.26	1.22	1221.9	0.85	73.5
1980-1985	18.2	9.8	2.55	1.24	1.20	1274.0	0.84	74.0
1985-1990	17.8	9.5	2.51	1.22	1.19	1327.6	0.83	74.5
1990-1995	17.3	9.6	2.47	1.20	1.17	1379.8	0.77	75.0
1995-2000	17.0	9.7	2.43	1.19	1.16	1431.3	0.73	75.5
2000-2005	16.7	9.5	2.39	1.17	1.14	1483.8	0.72	76.0
2005-2010	16.4	9.4	2.35	1.15	1.13	1536.6	0.70	76.5
2010-2015	16.0	9.2	2.31	1.13	1.11	1590.1	0.69	77.0
2015-2020	15.6	9.3	2.27	1.11	1.09	1641.0	0.63	77.5
2020-2025	15.2	9.7	2.24	1.09	1.08	1686.9	0.55	77.5
2025-2030	14.9	10.0	2.20	1.07	1.06	1728.2	0.48	77.5
2030-2035	14.5	10.2	2.16	1.05	1.04	1765.6	0.43	77.5
2035-2040	14.2	10.4	2.12	1.03	1.02	1799.0	0.38	77.5
2040-2045	13.8	10.7	2.08	1.01	1.00	1827.5	0.32	77.5
2045-2050	13.7	10.9	2.08	1.01	1.00	1852.9	0.28	77.5
2070-2075	13.1	12.1	2.08	1.01	1.00	1931.2	0.10	77.5
2095-2100	12.9	12.8	2.08	1.01	1.00	1952.4	0.02	77.5
2120-2125	12.9	12.9	2.08	1.01	1.00	1955.2	0.00	77.5
2145-2150	12.9	12.9	2.08	1.01	1.00	1954.9	0.00	77.5

* THE INITIAL AGE-SPECIFIC MATERNITY RATES ARE AS FOLLOWS

	15-19	20-24	25-29	30-34	35-39	40-44	45-49
1965-1970	0.0377	0.0715	0.0702	0.0481	0.0260	0.0052	0.0013

TABLE G   AVERAGE ANNUAL RATES OF POPULATION GROWTH (IN PERCENT), 1965-2150
LINEAR DECLINE OF FERTILITY TO NRR LEVEL OF 1.0

PROJECTIONS 1 - 5

MORE DEVELOPED REGIONS

PERIOD	PERIOD IN WHICH NET REPRODUCTION RATE OF ONE IS REACHED				
	1970-1975 PROJ 1	1980-1985 PROJ 2	2000-2005 PROJ 3	2020-2025 PROJ 4	2040-2045 PROJ 5
1965-1970	0.86	0.86	0.86	0.86	0.86
1970-1975	0.52	0.76	0.83	0.85	0.86
1975-1980	0.54	0.66	0.80	0.83	0.85
1980-1985	0.56	0.55	0.75	0.81	0.84
1985-1990	0.56	0.56	0.72	0.79	0.83
1990-1995	0.47	0.51	0.63	0.73	0.77
1995-2000	0.38	0.46	0.55	0.67	0.73
2000-2005	0.35	0.41	0.49	0.65	0.72
2005-2010	0.32	0.37	0.48	0.61	0.70
2010-2015	0.32	0.35	0.46	0.58	0.69
2015-2020	0.26	0.30	0.40	0.51	0.63
2020-2025	0.18	0.22	0.32	0.41	0.55
2025-2030	0.11	0.16	0.25	0.35	0.48
2030-2035	0.06	0.11	0.20	0.31	0.43
2035-2040	0.03	0.07	0.16	0.27	0.38
2040-2045	0.05	0.05	0.12	0.22	0.32
2045-2050	0.05	0.03	0.09	0.17	0.28
2070-2075	0.01	0.00	0.02	0.04	0.10
2095-2100	0.00	0.00	0.00	0.01	0.02
2120-2125	0.00	0.00	0.00	0.00	0.00
2145-2150	0.00	0.00	0.00	0.00	0.00

TABLE H   AVERAGE ANNUAL INCREMENTS OF POPULATION (IN THOUSANDS), 1965-2150
LINEAR DECLINE OF FERTILITY TO NRR LEVEL OF 1.0

PROJECTIONS 1 - 5

MORE DEVELOPED REGIONS

PERIOD	PERIOD IN WHICH NET REPRODUCTION RATE OF ONE IS REACHED				
	1970-1975 PROJ 1	1980-1985 PROJ 2	2000-2005 PROJ 3	2020-2025 PROJ 4	2040-2045 PROJ 5
1965-1970	9423	9423	9423	9423	9423
1970-1975	5883	8650	9445	9667	9777
1975-1980	6316	7780	9465	9938	10174
1980-1985	6647	6639	9293	10035	10408
1985-1990	6849	7044	9166	10209	10732
1990-1995	5929	6610	8316	9724	10433
1995-2000	4955	6007	7490	9347	10289
2000-2005	4546	5574	6911	9292	10514
2005-2010	4254	5053	6824	9017	10553
2010-2015	4281	4907	6819	8838	10710
2015-2020	3622	4242	6058	7934	10171
2020-2025	2518	3241	4882	6546	9175
2025-2030	1558	2327	3875	5793	8257
2030-2035	913	1609	3155	5164	7480
2035-2040	491	1032	2560	4506	6679
2040-2045	746	689	1974	3737	5711
2045-2050	659	516	1387	2955	5073
2070-2075	90	50	256	641	1976
2095-2100	-15	-18	13	113	317
2120-2125	-28	-26	-26	-5	30
2145-2150	-27	-27	-30	-29	-21

237

TABLE I   AGE STRUCTURE OF POPULATION IN SELECTED YEARS (IN PERCENTAGES), 1970-2075
LINEAR DECLINE OF FERTILITY TO NRR LEVEL OF 1.0

PROJECTIONS 1 - 5

MORE DEVELOPED REGIONS

YEAR	PERIOD	IN	WHICH	NET	REPRODUCTION	RATE	OF	ONE	IS	REACHED
AGE GROUP	1970-1975 PROJ 1	1980-1985 PROJ 2	2000-2005 PROJ 3	2020-2025 PROJ 4	2040-2045 PROJ 5
1970					
0 – 4	8.8	8.8	8.8	8.8	8.8
5 – 9	8.6	8.6	8.6	8.6	8.6
10 – 14	8.5	8.5	8.5	8.5	8.5
15 – 19	8.2	8.2	8.2	8.2	8.2
20 – 29	14.0	14.0	14.0	14.0	14.0
30 – 44	19.8	19.8	19.8	19.8	19.8
45 – 64	21.2	21.2	21.2	21.2	21.2
65+	10.8	10.8	10.8	10.8	10.8
1985					
0 – 4	7.6	7.5	8.4	8.6	8.7
5 – 9	7.2	7.7	8.2	8.4	8.4
10 – 14	6.8	7.8	8.0	8.0	8.0
15 – 19	8.0	7.9	7.7	7.7	7.7
20 – 29	15.7	15.4	15.1	15.0	15.0
30 – 44	20.2	19.9	19.5	19.3	19.3
45 – 64	22.6	22.2	21.8	21.6	21.6
65+	11.8	11.6	11.4	11.3	11.3
2000					
0 – 4	7.0	7.2	7.5	8.0	8.2
5 – 9	7.1	7.2	7.5	7.9	8.1
10 – 14	7.2	7.1	7.6	7.8	7.9
15 – 19	7.1	6.9	7.6	7.7	7.7
20 – 29	13.0	14.3	14.7	14.6	14.6
30 – 44	21.8	21.3	20.5	20.1	19.9
45 – 64	23.3	22.8	21.9	21.5	21.3
65+	13.5	13.2	12.7	12.5	12.3
2015					
0 – 4	6.7	6.7	7.0	7.4	7.8
5 – 9	6.6	6.7	7.0	7.4	7.7
10 – 14	6.6	6.7	6.8	7.3	7.5
15 – 19	6.6	6.8	6.9	7.3	7.4
20 – 29	13.6	13.5	14.0	14.3	14.3
30 – 44	19.0	19.9	20.5	20.2	19.9
45 – 64	26.1	25.3	24.0	23.0	22.5
65+	14.9	14.4	13.7	13.1	12.8

MORE DEVELOPED REGIONS

TABLE I (CONTINUED)

PROJECTIONS 1 - 5

PERIOD IN WHICH NET REPRODUCTION RATE OF ONE IS REACHED

YEAR	1970-1975	1980-1985	2000-2005	2020-2025	2040-2045
2030					
0 - 4	6.5	6.5	6.6	6.9	7.3
5 - 9	6.5	6.5	6.6	6.8	7.3
10 - 14	6.5	6.5	6.7	6.9	7.2
15 - 19	6.5	6.5	6.7	6.9	7.2
20 - 29	12.8	12.9	13.1	13.8	14.0
30 - 44	19.5	19.4	19.8	20.1	19.8
45 - 64	24.2	24.7	24.6	23.7	22.9
65+	17.6	16.9	15.8	15.0	14.3
2045					
0 - 4	6.4	6.4	6.5	6.6	6.8
5 - 9	6.4	6.4	6.5	6.6	6.8
10 - 14	6.4	6.4	6.5	6.6	6.9
15 - 19	6.4	6.4	6.4	6.6	6.9
20 - 29	12.9	12.8	12.9	13.1	13.7
30 - 44	19.0	19.1	19.2	19.8	19.9
45 - 64	24.7	24.3	24.8	24.5	23.7
65+	17.8	18.1	17.3	16.2	15.4
2060					
0 - 4	6.4	6.4	6.4	6.5	6.6
5 - 9	6.4	6.4	6.4	6.5	6.6
10 - 14	6.4	6.4	6.4	6.5	6.6
15 - 19	6.4	6.4	6.4	6.5	6.5
20 - 29	12.7	12.7	12.8	12.9	13.2
30 - 44	19.1	19.0	19.1	19.1	19.7
45 - 64	24.2	24.3	24.3	24.6	24.3
65+	18.5	18.3	18.2	17.5	16.5
2075					
0 - 4	6.4	6.4	6.4	6.4	6.5
5 - 9	6.4	6.4	6.4	6.4	6.5
10 - 14	6.4	6.4	6.4	6.4	6.5
15 - 19	6.4	6.4	6.4	6.4	6.5
20 - 29	12.7	12.7	12.8	12.8	12.9
30 - 44	19.0	19.0	19.0	19.1	19.2
45 - 64	24.3	24.3	24.3	24.3	24.6
65+	18.4	18.5	18.3	18.2	17.4

239

TABLE A   TOTAL POPULATION (IN MILLIONS) AND INDICES OF POPULATION SIZE (1970 = 100), 1970-2150

LINEAR DECLINE OF FERTILITY TO NRR LEVEL OF 1.0

PROJECTIONS 1 - 5

LESS DEVELOPED REGIONS

YEAR	PERIOD IN WHICH NET REPRODUCTION RATE OF ONE IS REACHED				
	1970-1975 PROJ 1	1980-1985 PROJ 2	2000-2005 PROJ 3	2020-2025 PROJ 4	2040-2045 PROJ 5
1970	2529.9 / 100	2529.9 / 100	2529.9 / 100	2529.9 / 100	2529.9 / 100
1975	2632.2 / 104	2800.4 / 111	2849.9 / 113	2863.7 / 113	2870.6 / 113
1980	2764.0 / 109	3023.3 / 120	3185.2 / 126	3230.6 / 128	3252.9 / 129
1985	2922.7 / 116	3177.0 / 126	3533.2 / 140	3633.0 / 144	3687.1 / 146
1990	3100.2 / 123	3359.5 / 133	3882.9 / 153	4067.4 / 161	4158.3 / 164
1995	3275.3 / 129	3561.3 / 141	4221.3 / 167	4531.1 / 179	4684.4 / 185
2000	3426.6 / 135	3763.8 / 149	4528.0 / 179	5015.0 / 198	5259.7 / 208
2010	3657.1 / 145	4103.2 / 162	5044.6 / 199	5991.9 / 237	6531.1 / 258
2020	3853.2 / 152	4361.1 / 172	5566.0 / 220	6883.1 / 272	7922.3 / 313
2030	3992.0 / 158	4565.2 / 180	5989.7 / 237	7609.3 / 301	9316.4 / 368
2040	4049.9 / 160	4687.1 / 185	6299.3 / 249	8293.8 / 328	10564.2 / 418
2050	4136.5 / 164	4762.5 / 188	6525.4 / 258	8838.7 / 349	11590.7 / 458
2075	4231.8 / 167	4889.2 / 193	6726.6 / 266	9481.7 / 375	13374.3 / 529
2100	4251.2 / 168	4910.6 / 194	6763.2 / 267	9571.9 / 378	13863.0 / 548
2125	4250.4 / 168	4908.2 / 194	6764.0 / 267	9575.1 / 378	13917.5 / 550
2150	4246.1 / 168	4903.0 / 194	6757.9 / 267	9568.1 / 378	13909.6 / 550

240

TABLE B   BASIC DEMOGRAPHIC MEASURES FOR SELECTED TIME PERIODS 1965 - 2150
LINEAR DECLINE OF FERTILITY TO NRR OF 1.0 IN 1970-5

PROJECTION 1

LESS DEVELOPED REGIONS

PERIOD	FEMALE CRUDE BIRTH RATE	FEMALE CRUDE DEATH RATE	TOTAL FERTILITY RATE	GROSS REPRO- DUCTION RATE*	NET REPRO- DUCTION RATE	TOTAL POPULATION AT END OF PERIOD (IN MILLIONS)	FEMALE AVERAGE ANNUAL RATE OF GROWTH (IN PERCENT)	FEMALE EXPECTATION OF LIFE AT BIRTH
1965-1970	40.8	15.0	5.74	2.80	2.07	2529.9	2.59	51.0
1970-1975	19.7	11.7	2.66	1.30	1.00	2632.2	0.80	53.5
1975-1980	20.8	11.0	2.58	1.26	1.00	2764.0	0.98	55.5
1980-1985	22.0	10.8	2.51	1.23	1.00	2922.7	1.12	57.5
1985-1990	22.5	10.7	2.46	1.20	1.00	3100.2	1.19	59.0
1990-1995	21.5	10.5	2.42	1.18	1.00	3275.3	1.11	60.5
1995-2000	19.3	10.2	2.37	1.16	1.00	3426.6	0.91	62.0
2000-2005	17.3	10.2	2.33	1.14	1.00	3550.1	0.71	63.5
2005-2010	16.2	10.2	2.29	1.12	1.00	3657.1	0.60	65.0
2010-2015	15.9	10.4	2.26	1.10	1.00	3757.5	0.54	66.5
2015-2020	15.8	10.8	2.22	1.08	1.00	3853.2	0.50	68.0
2020-2025	15.5	11.4	2.20	1.07	1.00	3933.5	0.41	69.0
2025-2030	15.0	12.1	2.18	1.06	1.00	3992.0	0.30	70.0
2030-2035	14.5	12.6	2.16	1.06	1.00	4030.3	0.19	71.0
2035-2040	14.2	13.2	2.15	1.05	1.00	4049.9	0.10	72.0
2040-2045	14.1	12.2	2.13	1.04	1.00	4088.9	0.19	73.0
2045-2050	14.0	11.7	2.12	1.03	1.00	4136.5	0.23	74.0
2070-2075	13.6	13.2	2.12	1.03	1.00	4231.8	0.04	74.0
2095-2100	13.5	13.5	2.12	1.03	1.00	4251.2	0.00	74.0
2120-2125	13.5	13.5	2.12	1.03	1.00	4250.4	0.00	74.0
2145-2150	13.5	13.5	2.12	1.03	1.00	4246.1	0.00	74.0

* THE INITIAL AGE-SPECIFIC MATERNITY RATES ARE AS FOLLOWS

15-19	20-24	25-29	30-34	35-39	40-44	45-49
1965-1970						
0.0504	0.1176	0.1568	0.1232	0.0784	0.0280	0.0056

241

TABLE C   BASIC DEMOGRAPHIC MEASURES FOR SELECTED TIME PERIODS 1965 - 2150
LINEAR DECLINE OF FERTILITY TO NRR OF 1.0 IN 1980-5

PROJECTION 2

LESS DEVELOPED REGIONS

PERIOD	FEMALE CRUDE BIRTH RATE	FEMALE CRUDE DEATH RATE	TOTAL FERTILITY RATE	GROSS REPRODUCTION RATE*	NET REPRODUCTION RATE	TOTAL POPULATION AT END OF PERIOD (IN MILLIONS)	FEMALE AVERAGE ANNUAL RATE OF GROWTH (IN PERCENT)	FEMALE EXPECTATION OF LIFE AT BIRTH
1965-1970	40.8	15.0	5.74	2.80	2.07	2529.9	2.58	51.0
1970-1975	33.4	12.9	4.66	2.28	1.75	2800.4	2.05	53.5
1975-1980	26.8	11.4	3.59	1.75	1.39	3023.3	1.54	55.5
1980-1985	20.2	10.2	2.51	1.23	1.00	3177.0	1.00	57.5
1985-1990	21.3	10.1	2.46	1.20	1.00	3359.5	1.12	59.0
1990-1995	21.7	10.0	2.42	1.18	1.00	3561.3	1.17	60.5
1995-2000	20.9	9.8	2.37	1.16	1.00	3763.8	1.11	62.0
2000-2005	19.2	9.7	2.33	1.14	1.00	3946.9	0.95	63.5
2005-2010	17.4	9.6	2.29	1.12	1.00	4103.2	0.78	65.0
2010-2015	16.1	9.6	2.26	1.10	1.00	4238.2	0.65	66.5
2015-2020	15.6	9.9	2.22	1.08	1.00	4361.1	0.57	68.0
2020-2025	15.5	10.5	2.20	1.07	1.00	4471.3	0.50	69.0
2025-2030	15.3	11.1	2.18	1.06	1.00	4565.2	0.42	70.0
2030-2035	14.8	11.6	2.16	1.06	1.00	4639.2	0.32	71.0
2035-2040	14.4	12.3	2.15	1.05	1.00	4687.1	0.21	72.0
2040-2045	14.1	12.5	2.13	1.04	1.00	4723.5	0.16	73.0
2045-2050	13.9	12.2	2.12	1.03	1.00	4762.5	0.16	74.0
2070-2075	13.6	13.3	2.12	1.03	1.00	4889.2	0.03	74.0
2095-2100	13.5	13.5	2.12	1.03	1.00	4910.6	0.00	74.0
2120-2125	13.5	13.5	2.12	1.03	1.00	4908.2	0.00	74.0
2145-2150	13.5	13.5	2.12	1.03	1.00	4903.0	0.00	74.0

* THE INITIAL AGE-SPECIFIC MATERNITY RATES ARE AS FOLLOWS

	15-19	20-24	25-29	30-34	35-39	40-44	45-49
1965-1970	0.0504	0.1176	0.1568	0.1232	0.0784	0.0280	0.0056

242

TABLE D BASIC DEMOGRAPHIC MEASURES FOR SELECTED TIME PERIODS 1965 - 2150
LINEAR DECLINE OF FERTILITY TO NRR OF 1.0 IN 2000-5

LESS DEVELOPED REGIONS

PERIOD	FEMALE CRUDE BIRTH RATE	FEMALE CRUDE DEATH RATE	TOTAL FERTILITY RATE	GROSS REPRO-DUCTION RATE*	NET REPRO-DUCTION RATE	TOTAL POPULATION AT END OF PERIOD (IN MILLIONS)	FEMALE AVERAGE ANNUAL RATE OF GROWTH (IN PERCENT)	FEMALE EXPECTATION OF LIFE AT BIRTH
1965-1970	40.8	15.0	5.74	2.80	2.07	2529.9	2.58	51.0
1970-1975	37.3	13.2	5.25	2.56	1.97	2849.9	2.41	53.5
1975-1980	34.4	11.9	4.77	2.33	1.84	3185.2	2.25	55.5
1980-1985	31.7	10.7	4.28	2.09	1.70	3533.2	2.10	57.5
1985-1990	29.1	10.0	3.79	1.85	1.54	3882.9	1.91	59.0
1990-1995	26.3	9.4	3.31	1.61	1.37	4221.3	1.69	60.5
1995-2000	23.1	8.9	2.82	1.38	1.19	4528.0	1.41	62.0
2000-2005	19.5	8.6	2.33	1.14	1.00	4780.2	1.09	63.5
2005-2010	19.3	8.5	2.29	1.12	1.00	5044.6	1.08	65.0
2010-2015	18.7	8.4	2.26	1.10	1.00	5310.8	1.03	66.5
2015-2020	17.8	8.4	2.22	1.08	1.00	5566.0	0.94	68.0
2020-2025	16.8	8.8	2.20	1.07	1.00	5794.1	0.81	69.0
2025-2030	15.8	9.1	2.18	1.06	1.00	5989.7	0.67	70.0
2030-2035	15.1	9.6	2.16	1.06	1.00	6157.9	0.56	71.0
2035-2040	14.7	10.2	2.15	1.05	1.00	6299.3	0.46	72.0
2040-2045	14.5	10.6	2.13	1.04	1.00	6421.1	0.38	73.0
2045-2050	14.2	11.0	2.12	1.03	1.00	6525.4	0.32	74.0
2070-2075	13.6	12.9	2.12	1.03	1.00	6726.6	0.07	74.0
2095-2100	13.5	13.5	2.12	1.03	1.00	6763.2	0.00	74.0
2120-2125	13.5	13.5	2.12	1.03	1.00	6764.0	0.00	74.0
2145-2150	13.5	13.5	2.12	1.03	1.00	6757.9	0.00	74.0

* THE INITIAL AGE-SPECIFIC MATERNITY RATES ARE AS FOLLOWS

1965-1970	15-19	20-24	25-29	30-34	35-39	40-44	45-49
	0.0504	0.1176	0.1568	0.1232	0.0784	0.0280	0.0056

TABLE E   BASIC DEMOGRAPHIC MEASURES FOR SELECTED TIME PERIODS 1965 - 2150
LINEAR DECLINE OF FERTILITY TO NRR OF 1.0 IN 2020-5

PROJECTION 4

LESS DEVELOPED REGIONS

PERIOD	FEMALE CRUDE BIRTH RATE	FEMALE CRUDE DEATH RATE	TOTAL FERTILITY RATE	GROSS REPRODUCTION RATE*	NET REPRODUCTION RATE	TOTAL POPULATION AT END OF PERIOD (IN MILLIONS)	FEMALE AVERAGE ANNUAL RATE OF GROWTH (IN PERCENT)	FEMALE EXPECTATION OF LIFE AT BIRTH
1965-1970	40.8	15.0	5.74	2.80	2.07	2529.9	2.58	51.0
1970-1975	38.4	13.3	5.42	2.64	2.03	2863.7	2.51	53.5
1975-1980	36.4	12.0	5.10	2.49	1.97	3230.6	2.44	55.5
1980-1985	34.6	10.9	4.78	2.33	1.90	3633.0	2.38	57.5
1985-1990	33.0	10.1	4.45	2.17	1.81	4067.4	2.28	59.0
1990-1995	31.3	9.4	4.13	2.02	1.71	4531.1	2.18	60.5
1995-2000	29.4	8.9	3.81	1.86	1.60	5015.0	2.05	62.0
2000-2005	27.2	8.3	3.49	1.70	1.50	5506.3	1.89	63.5
2005-2010	24.9	7.9	3.17	1.54	1.38	5991.9	1.70	65.0
2010-2015	22.6	7.5	2.85	1.39	1.26	6456.5	1.50	66.5
2015-2020	20.2	7.3	2.52	1.23	1.14	6883.1	1.29	68.0
2020-2025	17.7	7.4	2.20	1.07	1.00	7245.0	1.03	69.0
2025-2030	17.5	7.7	2.18	1.06	1.00	7609.3	0.99	70.0
2030-2035	17.1	7.9	2.16	1.06	1.00	7965.2	0.92	71.0
2035-2040	16.4	8.3	2.15	1.05	1.00	8293.8	0.81	72.0
2040-2045	15.6	8.6	2.13	1.04	1.00	8585.7	0.69	73.0
2045-2050	14.8	9.0	2.12	1.03	1.00	8838.7	0.58	74.0
2070-2075	13.8	12.5	2.12	1.03	1.00	9481.7	0.12	74.0
2095-2100	13.5	13.3	2.12	1.03	1.00	9571.9	0.03	74.0
2120-2125	13.5	13.5	2.12	1.03	1.00	9575.1	0.00	74.0
2145-2150	13.5	13.5	2.12	1.03	1.00	9568.1	0.00	74.0

* THE INITIAL AGE-SPECIFIC MATERNITY RATES ARE AS FOLLOWS

	15-19	20-24	25-29	30-34	35-39	40-44	45-49
1965-1970	0.0504	0.1176	0.1568	0.1232	0.0784	0.0280	0.0056

TABLE F   BASIC DEMOGRAPHIC MEASURES FOR SELECTED TIME PERIODS 1965 - 2150
LINEAR DECLINE OF FERTILITY TO NRR OF 1.0 IN 2040-5

LESS DEVELOPED REGIONS

PERIOD	FEMALE CRUDE BIRTH RATE	FEMALE CRUDE DEATH RATE	TOTAL FERTILITY RATE	GROSS REPRODUCTION RATE*	NET REPRODUCTION RATE	TOTAL POPULATION AT END OF PERIOD (IN MILLIONS)	FEMALE AVERAGE ANNUAL RATE OF GROWTH (IN PERCENT)	FEMALE EXPECTATION OF LIFE AT BIRTH
1965-1970	40.8	15.0	5.74	2.80	2.07	2529.9	2.58	51.0
1970-1975	38.9	13.3	5.50	2.68	2.07	2870.6	2.56	53.5
1975-1980	37.4	12.0	5.26	2.57	2.03	3252.9	2.53	55.5
1980-1985	36.0	10.9	5.02	2.45	2.00	3682.1	2.51	57.5
1985-1990	34.8	10.1	4.78	2.33	1.94	4158.3	2.46	59.0
1990-1995	33.6	9.4	4.54	2.21	1.88	4644.4	2.41	60.5
1995-2000	32.2	8.8	4.30	2.10	1.81	5258.7	2.34	62.0
2000-2005	30.7	8.2	4.06	1.98	1.74	5876.1	2.24	63.5
2005-2010	29.0	7.7	3.82	1.86	1.66	6531.1	2.14	65.0
2010-2015	27.4	7.2	3.58	1.74	1.58	7216.3	2.02	66.5
2015-2020	25.7	6.8	3.34	1.63	1.50	7922.3	1.88	68.0
2020-2025	24.0	6.8	3.09	1.51	1.41	8627.7	1.72	69.0
2025-2030	22.2	6.7	2.85	1.39	1.31	9316.4	1.55	70.0
2030-2035	20.4	6.7	2.61	1.27	1.21	9970.2	1.37	71.0
2035-2040	18.5	6.9	2.37	1.16	1.10	10564.2	1.16	72.0
2040-2045	16.7	7.1	2.13	1.04	1.00	11076.7	0.96	73.0
2045-2050	16.4	7.3	2.12	1.03	1.00	11590.7	0.91	74.0
2070-2075	14.1	10.6	2.12	1.03	1.00	13374.3	0.34	74.0
2095-2100	13.6	13.2	2.12	1.03	1.00	13863.0	0.04	74.0
2120-2125	13.5	13.4	2.12	1.03	1.00	13917.5	0.01	74.0
2145-2150	13.5	13.5	2.12	1.03	1.00	13909.6	0.00	74.0

* THE INITIAL AGE-SPECIFIC MATERNITY RATES ARE AS FOLLOWS

	15-19	20-24	25-29	30-34	35-39	40-44	45-49
1965-1970	0.0504	0.1176	0.1568	0.1232	0.0784	0.0280	0.0056

245

TABLE G   AVERAGE ANNUAL RATES OF POPULATION GROWTH (IN PERCENT), 1965-2150
LINEAR DECLINE OF FERTILITY TO NRR LEVEL OF 1.0

PROJECTIONS 1 - 5

LESS DEVELOPED REGIONS

PERIOD IN WHICH NET REPRODUCTION RATE OF ONE IS REACHED

PERIOD	1970-1975 PROJ 1	1980-1985 PROJ 2	2000-2005 PROJ 3	2020-2025 PROJ 4	2040-2045 PROJ 5
1965-1970	2.58	2.58	2.58	2.58	2.58
1970-1975	0.80	2.05	2.41	2.51	2.56
1975-1980	0.98	1.54	2.25	2.44	2.53
1980-1985	1.12	1.00	2.10	2.38	2.51
1985-1990	1.19	1.12	1.91	2.28	2.46
1990-1995	1.11	1.17	1.69	2.18	2.41
1995-2000	0.91	1.11	1.41	2.05	2.34
2000-2005	0.71	0.95	1.09	1.89	2.24
2005-2010	0.60	0.78	1.08	1.70	2.14
2010-2015	0.54	0.65	1.03	1.50	2.02
2015-2020	0.50	0.57	0.94	1.29	1.88
2020-2025	0.41	0.50	0.81	1.03	1.72
2025-2030	0.30	0.42	0.67	0.99	1.55
2030-2035	0.19	0.32	0.56	0.92	1.37
2035-2040	0.10	0.21	0.46	0.81	1.16
2040-2045	0.19	0.16	0.38	0.69	0.96
2045-2050	0.23	0.16	0.32	0.58	0.91
2070-2075	0.04	0.03	0.07	0.12	0.34
2095-2100	0.00	0.00	0.00	0.03	0.04
2120-2125	0.00	0.00	0.00	0.00	0.01
2145-2150	0.00	0.00	0.00	0.00	0.00

TABLE H   AVERAGE ANNUAL INCREMENTS OF POPULATION (IN THOUSANDS), 1965-2150
LINEAR DECLINE OF FERTILITY TO NRR LEVEL OF 1.0

PROJECTIONS 1 - 5

LESS DEVELOPED REGIONS

PERIOD	PERIOD IN WHICH NET REPRODUCTION RATE OF ONE IS REACHED				
	1970-1975 PROJ 1	1980-1985 PROJ 2	2000-2005 PROJ 3	2020-2025 PROJ 4	2040-2045 PROJ 5
1965-1970	60459	60459	60459	60459	60459
1970-1975	20460	54103	64002	66777	68142
1975-1980	26365	44591	67074	73375	76473
1980-1985	31741	30739	69593	80482	85839
1985-1990	35492	36491	69938	86881	95233
1990-1995	35032	40362	67685	92733	105228
1995-2000	30257	40497	61336	96787	114863
2000-2005	24710	36627	50431	98259	123464
2005-2010	21395	31255	52896	97118	131005
2010-2015	20081	26999	53228	92920	137034
2015-2020	19126	24578	51038	85320	141205
2020-2025	16069	22040	45618	72381	141086
2025-2030	11709	18794	39138	72852	137744
2030-2035	7651	14785	33622	71177	130748
2035-2040	3912	9579	28290	65729	118812
2040-2045	7804	7294	24359	58386	102894
2045-2050	9517	7799	20859	50583	102398
2070-2075	1568	1384	4718	11666	45539
2095-2100	-122	129	154	2469	5817
2120-2125	-149	-41	-297	51	1020
2145-2150	-144	-165	-270	-445	-62

247

TABLE I   AGE STRUCTURE OF POPULATION IN SELECTED YEARS (IN PERCENTAGES), 1970-2075
LINEAR DECLINE OF FERTILITY TC NRR LEVEL CF 1.0

PROJECTIONS 1 - 5

LESS DEVELOPED REGIONS

YEAR AGE GROUP	PERIOD IN WHICH NET REPRODUCTION RATE OF CNE IS REACHED				
	1970-1975 PROJ 1	1980-1985 PROJ 2	2000-2005 PROJ 3	2020-2025 PROJ 4	2040-2045 PROJ 5
1970					
0 - 4	16.6	16.6	16.6	16.6	16.6
5 - 9	13.2	13.2	13.2	13.2	13.2
10 - 14	11.8	11.8	11.8	11.8	11.8
15 - 19	10.3	10.3	10.3	10.3	10.3
20 - 29	15.8	15.8	15.8	15.8	15.8
30 - 44	16.8	16.8	16.8	16.8	16.8
45 - 64	12.0	12.0	12.0	12.0	12.0
65+	3.4	3.4	3.4	3.4	3.4
1985					
0 - 4	9.7	8.9	13.6	14.8	15.3
5 - 9	8.3	10.6	12.7	13.2	13.4
10 - 14	7.3	11.7	11.9	11.9	11.9
15 - 19	13.4	12.3	11.1	10.8	10.6
20 - 29	20.6	18.9	17.0	16.5	16.3
30 - 44	20.9	19.2	17.3	16.8	16.6
45 - 64	15.5	14.2	12.8	12.4	12.3
65+	4.5	4.1	3.7	3.6	3.6
2000					
0 - 4	8.8	9.5	10.3	13.0	14.1
5 - 9	9.0	9.0	10.6	12.1	12.7
10 - 14	8.7	8.2	10.5	11.2	11.4
15 - 19	7.9	7.2	10.1	10.2	10.2
20 - 29	12.8	18.2	18.5	17.5	17.1
30 - 44	27.3	24.8	2C.6	18.6	17.8
45 - 64	19.5	17.7	14.7	13.3	12.7
65+	6.1	5.5	4.6	4.2	4.0
2015					
0 - 4	7.4	7.5	8.7	1C.3	12.4
5 - 9	7.2	7.7	8.3	10.3	11.6
10 - 14	7.4	8.0	7.8	10.2	10.8
15 - 19	7.8	8.1	8.6	9.8	1C.0
20 - 29	15.8	14.8	17.5	17.6	17.1
30 - 44	18.1	21.5	23.4	20.6	19.1
45 - 64	27.8	24.7	19.7	16.2	14.5
65+	8.5	7.6	6.0	5.0	4.4

248

TABLE I (CONTINUED)

LESS DEVELOPED REGIONS

YEAR	PERIOD IN WHICH NET REPRODUCTION RATE OF ONE IS REACHED				
	1970-1975	1980-1985	2000-2005	2020-2025	2040-2045
2030					
0 - 4	7.2	7.3	7.5	8.3	10.3
5 - 9	7.2	7.2	7.6	7.9	10.2
10 - 14	7.1	7.0	7.7	8.4	9.9
15 - 19	6.9	6.9	7.6	8.6	9.4
20 - 29	13.5	14.3	14.1	17.1	17.1
30 - 44	21.5	20.7	22.5	22.5	20.4
45 - 64	23.5	25.2	24.4	20.3	17.1
65+	13.1	11.4	8.7	6.9	5.6
2045					
0 - 4	6.8	6.8	7.0	7.5	7.9
5 - 9	6.8	6.9	6.9	7.5	8.3
10 - 14	6.9	7.0	6.9	7.5	8.6
15 - 19	7.0	7.0	6.9	7.3	8.6
20 - 29	13.9	13.5	14.1	14.3	16.7
30 - 44	19.5	20.1	19.8	22.4	21.9
45 - 64	25.3	23.6	25.7	23.8	20.2
65+	13.9	15.1	12.7	9.8	7.7
2060					
0 - 4	6.7	6.8	6.8	6.9	7.5
5 - 9	6.7	6.7	6.8	6.8	7.5
10 - 14	6.6	6.6	6.8	6.8	7.3
15 - 19	6.6	6.6	6.7	6.9	7.0
20 - 29	13.2	13.4	13.2	13.9	14.9
30 - 44	20.0	19.7	20.0	19.8	22.1
45 - 64	24.0	24.8	24.1	25.8	23.5
65+	16.0	15.4	15.6	13.1	10.3
2075					
0 - 4	6.6	6.6	6.7	6.7	6.8
5 - 9	6.6	6.6	6.6	6.7	6.9
10 - 14	6.6	6.7	6.6	6.7	6.9
15 - 19	6.7	6.7	6.6	6.6	7.0
20 - 29	13.2	13.1	13.3	13.2	13.7
30 - 44	19.4	19.6	19.4	19.9	20.1
45 - 64	24.6	24.2	24.7	24.3	25.4
65+	16.2	16.5	16.0	15.8	13.?

249

Index

Page references in *italics* refer to illustrations.